PENGUIN BOOKS

The Young H. G. Wells

'Tomalin knows how to tell a cracking story' *Daily Mail*

'Sprightly, generous . . . Claire Tomalin's restrained biography of the prolific writer and philanderer's early years lets readers reach their own verdict on his life and deeds' *Guardian*

'Tomalin is the nimblest of narrators' *Time Out*

'This is a fine and very enjoyable biography of an extraordinary man and his times. Wells is still relevant, still matters. It's good that Tomalin reminds us of how remarkable he was' *Scotsman*

'A new biography by Claire Tomalin is always an event . . . the style is as well-researched and engaging as ever' *Irish Times*

'A deft and informative account which brings its subject vividly to life' *TLS*

'With a flair for colour, pace and plot that matches her subject's, Tomalin does not bury Wells under a monumental tombstone. Instead, her dynamic sketch invites readers to discover – or rediscover – why that volcano still spits fire to light up a changing world' Boyd Tonkin, *Arts Desk*

'Tomalin admits that, although she set out to write about the young Wells, she has followed him into his forties because she found him "too interesting to leave". The same can be said of her book' *Sunday Times*

'For a compact overview of this endlessly fascinating man and writer, Tomalin's *The Young H. G. Wells* is hard to beat, being friendly, astute and a pleasure to read' *Washington Post*

By the same author

The Life and Death of Mary Wollstonecraft

Shelley and His World

Katherine Mansfield: A Secret Life

The Invisible Woman: The Story of Nelly Ternan and Charles
Dickens

The Winter Wife

Mrs Jordan's Profession

Jane Austen: A Life

Several Strangers: Writing from Three Decades

Samuel Pepys: The Unequalled Self

Thomas Hardy: The Time-Torn Man

Charles Dickens: A Life

A Life of My Own

Poems of Thomas Hardy (ed.)

Poems of John Keats (ed.)

Poems of John Milton (ed.)

The Young H. G. Wells

Changing the World

CLAIRE TOMALIN

PENGUIN BOOKS

PENGUIN BOOKS

UK | USA | Canada | Ireland | Australia
India | New Zealand | South Africa

Penguin Books is part of the Penguin Random House group of companies
whose addresses can be found at global.penguinrandomhouse.com.

First published by Viking 2021
Published in Penguin Books 2022

001

Copyright © Claire Tomalin, 2021

Illustrations copyright © David Gentleman, 2021

The moral right of the author has been asserted

The Acknowledgements on pp. ix–x and 239 constitute an extension of this copyright page

Typeset by Jouve (UK), Milton Keynes
Printed and bound in Great Britain by Clays Ltd, Elcograf S.p.A.

The authorized representative in the EEA is Penguin Random House Ireland,
Morrison Chambers, 32 Nassau Street, Dublin DO2 YH68

A CIP catalogue record for this book is available from the British Library

ISBN: 978–0–241–97485–8

www.greenpenguin.co.uk

The man who would revolutionize the world must first revolutionize himself

– H. G. Wells to Elizabeth Healey, March 1888

No writer contributed more to the make-up of the average early-twentieth century man and woman. Maybe they are not fully conscious of it; for when ideas are, as the phrase goes, 'in the air', they cease to be attributed to any particular person . . . he was a writer of genius who was obsessed with the problems of his time . . . the first really gifted writer whose imagination in a scientific age was saturated with scientific ideas . . .

Because he was ordinary, he knew where the shoe of contemporary civilization pinched the average chaotic non-entity today, preventing him or her from walking sure-footedly. Yet he felt the value and believed in the reasonableness of hope. He trusted the generous impulses of adolescence . . . and he appealed to the young. No one understood better, too, their ridiculous amorous predicaments (had he not shared them?)

– Desmond MacCarthy, 'Last Words on Wells', 1946

Wells's failings were all redeemed (he is a bit vulgar, you know) by his being so affectionate – really fond of his fellow creatures.

– Constance Garnett, *c.* 1909

Picture H. G. Wells without a brain . . .

– from Cole Porter's song 'A Picture of Me without You',
listing things that are permanently connected, 1935

Contents

List of Illustrations   ix

Preface   1

1. Two Accidents   5
2. 'What else can you do?'   15
3. Uppark   20
4. 'A bright run of luck'   27
5. Blood   41
6. 'For a young man to marry . . .'   50
7. More Blood   58
8. *The Time Machine*   65
9. 'Uncommonly cheerful and hopeful'   76
10. A House by the Sea   88
11. Fabian Friends   104
12. Joining the Club   115
13. Pressure   125
14. America in 1906   138
15. Webb and Wells   147
16. Amberissima   157
17. Heroines   171
18. *Tono-Bungay*   180
19. Friends and Enemies   188
20. 'I warmed both hands before the fire of Life'   194

Contents

Bibliography   215

Books by Wells 1893–1911   217

Notes   221

Acknowledgements   239

Index   241

Illustrations

Photographic credits in italics.

Every effort has been made to contact all copyright holders. The publishers will be pleased to amend in future editions any errors or omissions brought to their attention.

1. Wells as a boy. *Alamy*.
2. Joseph Wells.
3. Sarah Wells.
4. Uppark, West Sussex. *Alamy*.
5. Midhurst, West Sussex. © *Gravelroots*.
6. Wells at the Normal School of Science in Kensington. *Alamy*.
7. Isabel Wells. *Alamy*.
8. Wells with Jane. *The Rare Book and Manuscript Library, University of Illinois at Urbana-Champaign*.
9. Jane at her typewriter. *The Rare Book and Manuscript Library, University of Illinois at Urbana-Champaign*.
10. Wells taking tea. © *National Portrait Gallery, London*.
11. William Henley. *Getty Images*.
12. Wells's 'picshua' of himself and Jane, inscribed 'Waiting for the verdik'. *The Rare Book and Manuscript Library, University of Illinois at Urbana-Champaign*.
13. Arnold Bennett. *Library of Congress Prints and Photographs Division, Washington, D.C.*
14. Bernard Shaw. *Library of Congress Prints and Photographs Division, Washington, D.C.*
15. George Gissing.
16. Henry James. *Getty Images*.

17. Sidney Webb, portrait by Jessie Holliday. © *National Portrait Gallery, London*.

18. Beatrice Webb, portrait by Jessie Holliday. © *National Portrait Gallery, London*.

19. Arthur Balfour. *Library of Congress Prints and Photographs Division, Washington, D.C.*

20. Cover of H. G. Wells, *This Misery of Boots*, 1907. *Heritage Auctions*.

21. Amber Reeves. *Newnham College Archives. Reproduced with the kind permission of the Principal and Fellows, Newnham College, Cambridge*.

22. Wells in his study at Spade House. *Alamy*.

23. Wells, portrait by Elliot & Fry. © *National Portrait Gallery, London*.

Preface

In the summer of 1914 two eleven-year-old boys, Eric and Cyril, friends at boarding school, became obsessed by a story they were both reading – it was called 'The Country of the Blind'. The book belonged to Cyril, but Eric kept borrowing it and having to return it. One night Eric was so desperate to go on reading that he kept himself awake until four in the morning – it was midsummer and the sun was already up – and he crept along the corridor to Cyril's dormitory, pinched it from beside his bed, took it back to his own bed and read on. The story was by H. G. Wells, who was currently their favourite writer.

What Eric liked about Wells was that he interested himself in science, in mysteries and prophecies – the planets and the bottom of the sea, flying and aerial warfare, space travel, Martians, mermaids, angels, creatures on the moon, distant islands where animals were turned into monstrous men. All these fascinating subjects were quite outside the interests of Eric's middle-class family, or the subjects his teachers were grinding into him and Cyril, Greek and Latin and whatever was needed to get him into a public school, preferably Eton: both their backgrounds were conventional in every way. Wells was not conventional or even respectable. Whether or not Eric and Cyril knew that he was a republican, an atheist and a socialist, they were enthralled by his stories, his thrillingly convincing accounts of what he imagined, and his forecasting of the future, technological, social and political.[1]

Both Eric and Cyril won scholarships to Eton and both became distinguished writers, Cyril Connolly as an editor and essayist, Eric under the name he chose for himself, George Orwell. During the Second World War Orwell wrote, and Connolly published in *Horizon*, the highly regarded magazine he edited, an article about Wells's effect on him:

Thinking people who were born about the beginning of this century
are in some sense Wells's own creation . . . I doubt whether anyone
who was writing books between 1900 and 1920, at any rate in the English language, influenced the young so much. The minds of all of us,
and therefore the physical world, would be perceptibly different if
Wells had never existed . . .

Back in the 1900s it was a wonderful experience for a boy to discover
H. G. Wells.

There you were, in a world of pedants, clergymen and golfers, with
your future employers exhorting you to 'get on or get out', your parents systematically warping your sexual life, and your dull-witted
schoolmasters sniggering over their Latin tags; and here was the wonderful man who could tell you about the inhabitants of the planets
and the bottom of the sea, and who *knew* that the future was not
going to be what respectable people imagined . . . Up to 1914 Wells
was in the main a true prophet.[2]

Yet already in that essay Orwell went on to say that the singleness
of mind that made Wells seem an inspired prophet to the Edward-
ian age made him a shallow, inadequate thinker in 1941 – because
Wells could not understand the forces of nationalism and religious
bigotry: 'Wells is too sane to understand the modern world.' He
might have added that Wells believed world government, an effective United Nations, was what we needed. Orwell ended his article
by saying 'the succession of lower-middle-class novels which are his
greatest achievement stopped short at the other war and never
really began again.'

In 1942 Orwell described Wells's 'basic message': 'Science can solve
all the ills that humanity is heir to, but that man is at present too blind
to see the possibility of his own powers.'[3] And after Wells's death in
1946, writing of how the work of many good writers deteriorates as
they grow older, he went on, 'We value H. G. Wells for *Tono-Bungay*,
Mr Polly, *The Time Machine*, etc. If he had stopped writing in 1920 his
reputation would stand quite as high as it does: if we knew him only

by the books he wrote after that date, we should have rather a low opinion of him.'[4]

He chose to ignore Wells's technical books on history and science – the second written in collaboration with Julian Huxley – which were extremely well done and very widely read. He also seemed ignorant of Wells's early political books that had pointed the way to the welfare state just being set up. Yet Orwell's judgement as far as the fiction is concerned seems essentially right: Wells produced stories and novels of extraordinary brilliance and originality up to the period just before the First World War, and then seems to have stopped trying, with the result that his novels became disappointing. In February 1947, after Wells's death, Orwell wrote another piece in *Tribune* describing how Wells had told him he did not bother to point out misprints in reissues of his early work by Penguin, because he no longer took the faintest interest in those books, 'written so long ago that he no longer felt them to be part of himself'.[5] As far as I know no other writer has distanced himself so decidedly from his successful early work – but possibly the remark was meant only to shock and silence Orwell.

Wells had given his own account of his life in his *Experiment in Autobiography*, published in 1934, when he was nearly seventy. It is a book of great charm; it made me love Wells when I first read it, and led me to reread many of the books and stories I already knew, and look for more. It was soon clear to me that the books of his I most admired were all written – apart from the autobiography and the *Outline of History* (1920) – in the period starting in 1895, when he published his first story, *The Time Machine*, at the age of twenty-nine, and up to 1911 – which fits pretty well with Orwell's view.

Orwell praised him for his lack of literary vanity. He seems to have known little or nothing of Wells's years of poverty, his struggle to get an education, the serious ill health that dominated his existence from 1887, when he was twenty-one, to 1898, when he was thirty-two – or how success arrived suddenly in 1895, transforming his life. While his best books were written over the next fifteen years, it is that early period in which he overcame what must often have seemed insurmountable obstacles that were crucial in making him into the great writer who was the young H. G. Wells. And it was this that led me to decide to write about his early life – which turned out to be an even more complex and fascinating story than I had expected.

1. Two Accidents

Throughout his life Wells found happiness in sunshine, fresh air and open spaces. He was a mover and a traveller. He tricycled, bicycled and tandemed through the English countryside in the blessed period when the roads were shared only with horses, carriages and walkers. He relished long hikes in the Swiss and Italian Alps. He took great pleasure in living beside the Channel for ten years. Wide views and good light pleased him best. He disliked darkness, confinement and basements. He foretold the aeroplane and space travel with their extraordinary interest, pleasures and dangers, before they happened. It seems appropriate that the year of his birth, 1866, was also the year in which the Aeronautical Society of Great Britain was founded.

The love of light came partly from his childhood memories of the small terraced house in which he was born and lived his early years, mostly in the scullery and basement kitchen below the shop run by his father. Atlas House, it was grandly and unsuitably named, and it stood alongside other shops in the High Street of Bromley, a small Kentish town nine miles south of London. Oil lamps gave what light there was, and the whole house smelt of paraffin, which was also used to combat the bed bugs upstairs. His mother, who was forty-four when he was born, was already tired out by trying to clean and cook and look after two sons while his father, Joseph Wells, ran the shop unsuccessfully and spent few evenings at home. Officially he sold a rather odd mixture of crockery and cricket bats – but he cared nothing for the shop. He was an outdoor man, an outstanding cricketer – he had played for Kent, and was the first bowler in county cricket to take four wickets in four successive balls; and he had taught cricket in a Norfolk school. His other skill was as a gardener, and the single beauty of the house was the vine he trained up the back wall. At various times he had thought of emigrating, to Australia, to America, to New Zealand, but had not the willpower to carry through these dreams. He told his third and youngest son, Herbert George, whom he called Buss, that he liked to lie outside at night looking up at the stars.

His wife, Sarah, was the daughter of a Sussex innkeeper, and had been given some education: the Kings and Queens of England, the countries and capitals of Europe, but not the French she longed to learn. She became a pious Christian and deeply devoted to Victoria from the time of the Queen's accession in 1837 – Wells describes this as a form of feminism among women who hoped for something better after one dissolute and one undistinguished king. Perhaps so: he also attributes the awakening of his lifelong republicanism to his mother's absurdly exaggerated reverence for the Queen.

Sarah was fifteen in 1837. She was apprenticed to a dressmaker and learnt hairdressing well enough to get work as a superior lady's maid. In 1850 she was taken on by Miss Frances Bullock at Uppark, the great house on the top of the West Sussex Downs above Harting. The next year a new gardener, Joseph Wells, arrived and a friendship began and became something more. When Sarah left to nurse her sick mother and was suddenly orphaned, Joe gallantly insisted on marriage. There was a rapid wedding in November 1853, and they moved to Northamptonshire, where he found gardening work on the Shuckburgh Estate. There a daughter, Frances, was born in 1855. But Joe lost his job as a gardener and was persuaded by a cousin to buy his shop in Bromley – and so they were caught in the wretched house and unprofitable business. Neither of them had any idea of how to run a shop profitably, and neither made any effort to learn.

Two more children were born, both boys, Frank and Fred. Then Sarah's adored daughter died, aged nine, of appendicitis. After that a last male child, Herbert George, appeared. Sarah was worn down by hardship and grief. If she expected her new son to take the place of the departed Frances, she was disappointed. She called him Bertie. He was not to be a comfort to her – not for many years at any rate.

In his earliest memories of her she had already lost several teeth, her hands were distorted by years of housework, and she was always tired – of sewing and mending and keeping up appearances. She cooked but had never learnt to make food appetizing. She was often anxious, usually low-spirited, and also deeply religious and devoted to the Church of England. Her faith had been tested by the loss of her first and best-loved child, and her last child's failure to be another daughter was a further blow. She seems to have been a dutiful but never an enthusiastic mother. His brothers Frank and Fred were nine and four years older than him, and his early memories of them were of fighting, throwing a fork at Frank's face, breaking a window when he flung a wooden horse at them, and being half suffocated under pillows when they turned on him. Wells believed his mind developed almost as that of an only child – only later did he make friends with Fred and Frank.

Joseph Wells's failure in the shop was largely due to his having no interest in selling crockery and giving all his attention to the cricket goods. Apart from playing and teaching the game, he had memories of his earlier life as a gardener, and his father had been gardener to Lord de L'Isle at Penshurst Place. Hence the vine planted in a dustbin in the yard. He was knowledgeable about the natural world, pointing out plants and birds and knowing where to find wild mushrooms. He was a reader too, a frequenter of libraries and second-hand book-shops. He came of a large family, so there were uncles, aunts and cousins aplenty – in fact, Bertie's first wife was the daughter of Joe's brother William Wells, an unsuccessful draper who had died in the workhouse.

Cricketer, reader, dreamer, Joe proved a disappointment as a husband. He was rarely at home in the evening, when he preferred to go out to drink with friends. Keeping up appearances grew more difficult as the shop failed to flourish. Sarah, wanting her sons to have safe and respectable jobs, decided that their best chance would be to become drapers: why she decided this would be good for them is hard to guess. Disregarding her brother-in-law's disastrous failure, she seems to have thought working in a draper's shop was a safe occupation. Drapers were obliged to dress like gentlemen, which may have seemed desirable to her. And to become a draper it was necessary to start work as an apprentice at the age of thirteen and serve long hours, six days a week, for four or five years. Frank began his apprenticeship when Bertie was five, Fred when he was ten. Neither had any wish to become an apprentice, legally bound by contract to serve the draper, but neither had the strength to rebel, and so it was done. It made life easier for their mother, since they were mostly out of the house, and quieter for Bertie.

He was taught his letters by his mother and then sent to a dame school, with an admonishment not to mix with rough or common boys. He learnt quickly and soon took pleasure in reading. When he was seven, in the summer of 1874, fooling around the cricket pitch where his father was playing, a friendly older lad picked him up saying, 'Whose little kid are you?' and threw him up into the air – only to miss him as he fell. He landed on a tent peg, breaking the tibia in his leg: the tibia is the larger shin bone and walking depends on it. Bertie had his leg strapped between splints and was installed on a sofa at home. The young man responsible happened to be the son of the local publican, and both his parents felt guilty at what had happened, with the result that the publican's wife kept coming round with offerings of delicious food for Bertie for as long as he was immobilized.

Wells would say many years later that the accident changed his life for the better while he was convalescing. He had just become seriously interested in reading, and now his father took it on himself to supply him with books, fetching them almost daily from the local Literary Institute: geography, history, natural history, and the magazines *Punch* and *Fun* – known as the poor man's *Punch* – which he read and reread. Reading became his passion, and he was also blessed with a good memory for what he read and saw. This time of uninterrupted reading was crucial to his mental development.

He remembered too that Britannia, France and other countries personified in magazines as bare-bosomed and lightly clothed women first aroused sexual desire in him: 'When I went to bed I used to pillow my head on their great arms and breasts.' Eight seems an early start, but the effects were certainly powerful in his adult life when he pursued sexual encounters energetically and with an unhesitating sense of entitlement.

The tibia set badly and needed to be broken again and reset, an agonizing business – but it also gave him extra time with books. When, in September, he was able to get up and walk to his new school, Morley's Academy in the High Street, he went with a mind crammed with information about the world, and a great readiness to talk about what he knew. The pupils were a mixed lot, half boarders, from London mostly, the others locals. Thomas Morley was sometimes a good teacher – he liked Wells when he saw that he was interested in grammar and mathematical problems – but he was eccentric, often distracted by indigestion or anxiety. Sometimes, in the middle of a lesson, he would decide to shave, at other times he would simply fall asleep. He would hit boys with a ruler, and smack and cane them, but he was not a monster. His job was to turn out competent clerks and book-keepers, and at this he did pretty well. The only history lessons he gave were about English history, and the French he taught crippled the language for life for Wells – so he said, although he was able to read French as an adult. But at the age of thirteen Wells and a fellow pupil came joint first in all England for book-keeping. Wells had developed a strongly competitive spirit. He also accepted his mother's view that theirs was a middle-class family, and he looked down on the common boys who went to the National School as heartily as she expected him to.

Out of school he amused himself by playing war games, imagining himself as Napoleon or Cromwell while he walked the pebbly footpaths, fields and hills around Bromley, which at that time was still surrounded by unspoilt open countryside, with a pretty free-flowing river, fields and woods. Wells sent his cavalry against enemy armies and slaughtered them with relish – war games he would later encourage his two sons to imitate on a smaller scale in their nurseries. He also formed a secret society with a school friend, inventing a private language and an initiation ceremony that involved burning a finger in a gas jet. And he tells us that he was glad to have blue eyes and fair hair, and that he believed in the natural superiority of the English over all other nations, and expected them to be ruling the whole world presently.

By this time he had also become a non-believer in the Almighty. He says he was frightened of Hell as a small child, went through a period of detesting the Devil and then decided God must be hateful to have set up such a system – and went on to see that the whole story was a lie.

In October 1877 his father, pruning the vine high up on the back of the house, slipped from his ladder. Bertie and his mother found him lying in the backyard when they returned from church. His thigh bone was badly broken. He needed expensive medical care and would never be able to play or teach cricket again.

Bertie was just eleven. For two years the family lived on meagre fare – bread and cheese, half a herring for breakfast. Growing fast as he was, he became very thin – it seems quite possible that his growth was stunted. He still went to school but his fees were not paid – evidently Morley thought him too good a pupil to lose. His brother Frank generously gave from his small earnings for new boots for Bertie. Reading and solitary war games remained his chief entertainments, and, amazingly, he also produced, sometime between 1878 and 1880, a book of his own, handwritten and illustrated on almost every one of its ninety-six pages.

This was *The Desert Daisy*, the story of a war between the King of Spades and the King of Clubs, involving a considerable cast of characters including a prince bishop who steals the crown of his king, a king who becomes a pawnbroker, a youth of noble birth called Lionel Geffory de Thompson Smythe and the Desert Daisy herself, who digs Smythe out of the sand dune in which he has been trapped and marries him. The illustrations, one to each page, are detailed and funny, showing a ferocious bull, many fights, a sun with an expressive face. His images of the King's counsellors were drawn from pictures of current politicians Wells found in magazines – they include a recognizable Disraeli – and there is a donkey sitting comfortably among them. But the most sophisticated part of the book is the introduction, which announces this as a second edition and offers press notices of the first: '*The Naily News*: Charming book! "will be read when Shakespeare is

forgotten – but not before"'; '*The Telephone*, "Magnificent book"';
and another tribute, 'Beautiful book – Brought tears into the eyes of
the editor's grandma.' It also explains that the author, named as 'Buss',
after completing this work, was 'seized with a lingering malady & has
been obliged to retire to Colney Hatch [a mental hospital] where he is
forbidden to write again.' The work is consequently introduced by its
editor, H. G. Wells.

Many boys and girls embark on writing stories but few finish
them, and for a boy of twelve – or even thirteen – this was a substantial achievement. It shows that he had already a sophisticated sense of
humour, real skill as an illustrator and a surprising range of knowledge about book publication – some of it presumably gained through
conversation with his father, who brought him so many books and
evidently knew a fair amount about the process of publishing and
even publicity.

Writing was an escape from a family life that was becoming
increasingly difficult through poverty. Then by good fortune came
an invitation that opened a new world to Bertie. Uncle Tom –
Thomas Pennicott, a second cousin of his mother – had bought a
derelict waterside inn named Surly Hall on the Thames near Windsor. He rebuilt it as best he could and managed it well. The position
was beautiful, with tall trees along the bank, white and yellow water
lilies, forget-me-nots, dragonflies, songbirds in the trees. There was a
paddock where campers could put up their tents, a ferry, punts and
rowboats, and an eyot – as small islands in the Thames were known –
near by. Eton boys came in their boats in summer to buy drinks and
biscuits. Mrs Wells may have asked her cousin to invite Bertie: he
arrived hungry and was made very welcome, nourished, fed and
cared for, and entertained.

Uncle Tom was a widower with two pretty daughters in their
twenties, Kate and Clara. They, together with the chief barmaid,
made much of Bertie, a lively, good-looking boy, with his bright
blue eyes and ready smile; he became their Cherubino. They took an
interest in what he had to say, relishing his original and often unexpected remarks, flirted and accepted his devotion. For the first time

he found himself part of a congenial group as the girls encouraged him to express himself. They also put down plenty of good food before him, making up for the semi-starvation at home. They were accomplished young women, well read and musical, playing the piano and singing – this was something entirely different from the only music he knew, the strict, dull hymns heard reluctantly in church over the years. His cousins introduced him to music as a trans-forming experience.

There were books on the shelves at Surly Hall too, a complete Dickens, Eugène Sue's *Les Mystères de Paris* in translation, and the *Family Herald*, a popular magazine of household tips and stories. He would make summer visits here and visit whenever he could as long as it flourished. A day came when the great actress Ellen Terry, then in the full bloom of her beauty, arrived. She was studying a part and took a room for several days, enjoying the sunshine; and here she was visited by Henry Irving, whose company she had just joined. One day Bertie was allowed to take her out in a punt on the river, a new experience for both of them. He could not swim, but no one asked him if he could. The idyll was perfect.

Wells gives a bleak account of how Surly Hall later changed from idyll to nightmare. Uncle Tom had borrowed too much money, could not pay off his mortgage and lost his touch as a landlord. He disapproved of his daughters' lovers and quarrelled with both of them. The winters proved too cold and grey, and his daughters left. Kate would marry, but Clara was abandoned by her lover and took to drink. When she returned hoping for her father's forgiveness, he treated her harshly. She went out in her nightdress one night and drowned herself in the river. Her father died soon after. No one wanted to take over the inn, and it seems to have fallen into ruin. In time there was nothing left to show where it had been.

This grim story made part of his education, he says, showing him the unreliability of human happiness. Yet he hardly needed the warn-ing. He never drank or got into debt; and, when he rejected his mother's values and plans for him, managed to do so without breaking the bond of affection between them. He kept the skill he had just begun to develop as a writer too. Even when he faced illness, poverty and unhappiness, his driving will and intelligence kept him from despair. And he did not learn to swim for another twenty years.

Midhurst Grammar School

2. 'What else can you do?'

By 1880 Frank and Fred Wells were both living independently. This left only Bertie. Mrs Wells, having placed his two elder brothers as apprentices in drapers' shops, and seen them work their way through their years of servitude with reasonable success, could think of nothing better than to make the same arrangements for her youngest son.

He was nearly fourteen. He had left Morley's Academy in June, and was happily staying at Surly Hall when a message came from his mother informing him that she had arranged a period of trial apprenticeship for him at a superior draper's shop in Windsor. They had been told of his success in the book-keeping examination, and as a result he was to be put in charge of the till, taking and recording customers' cash payments. Uncle Tom drove him to Windsor and set him down in front of Messrs Rodgers & Denyer, opposite the Castle.

From the first moment, as he was taken up a narrow staircase to a dormitory he would be sharing with other apprentices, Wells hated everything about the place. He felt he was being imprisoned, deprived of all he valued – reading, writing, studying, painting, conversation with congenial people, freedom to walk the countryside. Now suddenly he had to work six days a week, dusting and sweeping before the shop opened, sitting at the cash desk all day, then tidying and refolding bales of cloth when the shop closed. He found no friends among the other apprentices. He made up his mind to behave badly, escaping from the till whenever he could to read in the basement, hiding behind bales or in the lavatory. His inattention meant that the figures on the cash sheet rarely corresponded with the money in the till, causing anxiety and extra work as it was checked. After a while he was suspected of fraud – wrongly, since he had no interest in the money. His uncle defended his honesty and he was cleared, but no happier. He did not satisfy his employers, he did not fit in, and after two months he was dismissed.

He went happily back to Surly Hall. His father did his best to get him work as a clerk with Hoare's bank – the Hoare family had a place near Bromley, and he had bowled for them in past cricket matches; but it was perhaps too long ago for him to be remembered, and no offer was made. Bertie enjoyed the rest of his summer by the river and reached the great age of fourteen. Now another 'Uncle' – Tom's brother-in-law – came up with something: Uncle Williams was headmaster of a boys' school in Somerset, in a village called Wookey, two miles from Wells, and he was in need of an extra teacher to help him out. When Bertie got there he found he was the only assistant.

Uncle Williams had travelled the world, working as a schoolmaster in the West Indies, losing an arm – he had a stump with a hook – and developing a sceptical and humorous view of things. He saw himself as a character, and he talked to Wells as man to man, letting him know a good deal about the more sordid aspects of adult life that he had been so far unaware of. He was a cheerful cynic, ready to laugh at bad behaviour, and also to suggest that laughter could be the best response to difficulties and disappointments. Wells was entertained by this new slant on life.

As to the teaching, Williams offered a few tips and let him get on with it. Wells found it much more interesting than shop work, even though he had to discipline a class of rough Somerset boys, some as big as he was and all speaking a rather different version of English. 'I fought my class' was how he described his efforts, driving in his lessons energetically, teaching them to read, to do sums, to learn something about weights and measures, as well as dates in history and basic geography. He showed he could devise a teaching programme and control an unruly group of boys – a remarkable achievement for a fourteen-year-old. He began to take some pleasure and pride in the work and grew more sure of himself and his own capacities.

It turned out to be a very short episode. Uncle Williams had got his position as headmaster under false pretences, and when it was discovered that he was without the required qualifications the school was closed. Wells was no longer needed. He travelled back to Surly Hall, and this was when he found it changed into an unhappy place. It was dark December, and the girls had quarrelled with their father.

Bertie went back to Bromley, where there had also been changes. His father was now there alone, keeping house as best he could – the reason for this being that Mrs Wells had made her escape from her miserable existence below the shop, announcing that she had found herself a perfect and well-paid situation. Her old employer and friend, Miss Frances Fetherstonhaugh at Uppark, the great mansion on the Downs, had invited her to become her housekeeper. She would be in charge of all the indoor servants and domestic arrangements in the house where she had once worked as lady's maid. It was a triumphant moment for her, and strengthened her belief that she knew best how to organize the lives of her sons.

Now installed at Uppark with her own sitting room and bedroom, she appealed to her employer and old friend for permission to bring her youngest, fourteen-year-old Bertie, to stay in the servants' hall over the Christmas period in 1880. Miss Fetherstonhaugh graciously allowed her to invite him. He would stay in the servants' quarters and sleep in one of the many attic rooms. It was the first of many visits made over the next eleven years, during which Uppark would contribute largely to Wells's education, literary, political, artistic and scientific.

His mother meanwhile had found him another apprenticeship, this time at a chemist's in Midhurst, the small Sussex market town eight miles from Uppark. Wells was immediately interested in the contents of the shop, eager to learn about everything and ready to help with the rolling of pills and pounding of strange mixtures in a mortar. His master, Mr Cowap, appreciated his enthusiasm and intelligence. He was an enterprising man himself and had devised his own cough linctus from undisclosed (and probably alcoholic) ingredients, and it sold well.

Mrs Cowap made a fuss of young Wells and was often in the shop teasing her husband and making them both laugh. Midhurst was agreeable too, with its pleasant, pretty streets and picturesque old buildings, beside the chalklands of the South Downs. He was enjoying himself so much that he asked Cowap about the length of study needed to qualify as a chemist; and, hearing that he would need Latin, he made his own arrangement to take lessons with the headmaster of the local grammar school. After only a few lessons he realized that his family could not possibly afford to support him over the long period needed to train as a chemist. So he gave up the idea, but went on studying Latin for the sheer pleasure of learning. 'It was a new way of saying things. It was like something I had been waiting for' – the remark of a true scholar.[1]

He had to leave Cowap, but he had impressed the headmaster of the grammar school, Horace Byatt, so much that he was allowed to become a boarder – the only one. At this time the government was encouraging science teaching by giving grants to teachers whose pupils excelled in examinations, and Byatt saw that Wells appeared so promising that he might do well enough to bring him rewards. But, before he could sit the exams, Mrs Wells had found another apprenticeship for him, with another draper, this time in Southsea, a residential district of Portsmouth.

So, still fourteen, in the spring of 1881, he left school again and started at Hyde's Drapery Emporium, signed on for four years. He arrived burning with resentment and dismay, feeling like a condemned prisoner. Hyde was, he said afterwards, an unusually good employer – he provided his workers with a reading room and small library – yet he added that his time as an apprentice in Hyde's shop was the unhappiest and most hopeless period of his entire life.

His description of the apprentices' day shows what torment it must have been for a boy with intellectual interests and ambition. Woken in their dormitory at seven, they went down to clean windows, dust and unwrap goods. At eight they washed and dressed, then had a breakfast of bread and butter. On to window dressing. Occasionally he was sent out to buy ribbons or other sundries: he always lingered for as long as he dared away from the shop. Mid-morning there was beer or tea, and then half an hour was allowed for lunch. Closing time came at seven in winter, eight in summer, followed by tidying, throwing wet sawdust on the floor and sweeping. A supper of bread and cheese and beer was served at eight thirty.

During this time he was urged by his mother to be confirmed – the Church of England ceremony in which he was supposed to assert his allegiance to the faith. Instead he argued with the Vicar of Portsmouth, telling him he believed in Evolution, not the Fall of Man. He became interested in pantheism and in atheism. When he could afford it, he bought a newly founded weekly called the *Freethinker* and enjoyed its blasphemous jokes. Persuaded by one of the girls working in the shop to accompany her to a service in the local Catholic church, he found the words being spoken to be 'horrible nonsense'.

At the shop he was never out of trouble. In his second year, dressed now in a black morning-coat and tails and promoted to serving customers, he did worse still. He failed to find what was wanted, and, if he did sell something, he was quite unable to wrap it up neatly. He knew that he must somehow contrive to get out but could not think of any way of escaping. At Bank Holiday weekends he sometimes managed to visit his brother Frank, working as a draper in Godalming, but, friendly as Frank was, when Bertie applied to him for advice, Frank simply asked, 'What else can you do?'

3. Uppark

It is a stiff, steep walk to Uppark from any direction. To visit his mother from Portsmouth, Wells would take the train to Rowlands Castle, with a five-mile trudge onwards up the hill. Setting off from Midhurst also meant a long walk: three hours through hilly heathlands to Harting and then the climb. Once faced with the great house, he did not of course go to the front door but made his way round the side to the steps that would take him down to the servants' quarters, where he would find his mother waiting for him. He probably remembered her telling him that she had worked there as a lady's maid years before his birth, in 1850. And she may have reminded him too that Miss Frances Bullock, whose maid she had been then, was now the owner of the great house, and went under a different name, as Miss Frances Fetherstonhaugh.

Uppark was to be of crucial importance to Wells over the next eleven years. To begin with it made a large contribution to his education. Later it became a place of refuge when his health was failing, where he was nursed, seen, prescribed for and advised by a first-rate London medical man, Dr William Collins. The same doctor made sure that he was again taken to Uppark when he suffered further breakdowns, and there looked after efficiently, nursed, kept warm and well fed and able to convalesce over many weeks and months. In this way Uppark acted as hospital, convalescent home and indeed almost as a home to him; it is not too much to say that his life was effectively saved there. The Wells family could never have afforded to pay Dr Collins, and were clearly not expected to. This long connection between the Fetherstonhaugh family and the housekeeper's son is a striking instance of support being given by privileged landowners to a sick young man with very little claim on them. Their generosity was a piece of extraordinary good luck for Wells – owed, of course, to the old friendship between his mother and Frances Fetherstonhaugh.

Standing so high up like a crown on the top of the Downs, Uppark makes an uncompromising statement of privilege to anyone approaching. It had been set there squarely in the 1690s, built for the Earl of Tankerville, Privy Seal to William of Orange when he became King of England. Its three storeys of red brick and stone in the Dutch style have nine tall windows across front and back and seven windows across each side, all commanding views over many miles of open countryside. The rooms inside are decorated with gilt and marble, fine and intricate plasterwork, Rococo pier glasses, tapestries, busts, hand-painted wallpaper and exquisite furniture – and hung with paintings. Outside there were, in Wells's day, stables, a dairy, a farm, a deer park, a picturesque ruined tower and gardens and walks in all directions. Much of its splendour remains.[1]

The Fetherstonhaugh family had owned Uppark since 1747, when Sir Matthew and Lady Fetherstonhaugh, an extravagantly rich couple, highly educated and well travelled in France and Italy, set about decorating the house they had inherited. Their son Henry was born at Uppark in 1754 and came into possession at the age of twenty, travelling home from Italy – he was making his grand tour – on learning of the death of his father. After a period of mourning the young heir set about enjoying himself and was soon entertaining the Prince of Wales and his companions. There was much hunting, shooting, gambling, drinking, love-making and feasting. An account of their amusements lists 'races of all sorts – fine horses – poneys – cart-horses – women – and men in sacks, with various other divertimenti fit for children of six foot high'. So wrote Mrs Montagu in 1784, adding that 'Poor Lady Fetherstonhaugh, Sir Henry's mother, fled from the riot.'[2]

Sir Henry brought the beautiful Emma Hart – later Lady Hamilton – to Uppark as his mistress. She was installed in a house on the estate and lived there for a year. When she found herself pregnant, she left with Henry's friend Charles Greville, with whom she lived in

London, where Romney's painting of her made her famous. Henry was generous to her then and later: when she was in need in 1806 he gave her five hundred pounds and tore up the IOU she sent him.

Sir Henry was a Whig, supporting Charles James Fox in Parliament – and setting up his bust in the house. But, although he became an MP, he never spoke in the House of Commons and declared it was in a degraded state, 'a complete farce', 'the shadow not the substance' of what the people needed.[3] He decided that the French did things better and formed a high opinion of Napoleon, whose bust is also on display in his house. Sir Henry spoke and read French, and returned to France in 1802, during the lull in the long war fought against Napoleon, and was able to take dinner with Talleyrand in Paris.

The Prince of Wales dropped Henry – no one knew why – and without the royal influence his life grew quieter. He took in an illegitimate daughter, born in 1805, to be brought up in the house – she was called Anne Sutherland and her mother's name is not known. He still gave shooting parties, but now also interested himself in farming. He called in the architect Humphry Repton to make improvements to the house. He planted trees, changed the principal entrance and added a portico, and a large, separate dairy. Bookcases were built – white and gilt ones for the saloon, beautiful but not big enough to hold all Sir Henry's books.

Then, in 1816, he suddenly considered selling his house to the Duke of Wellington, who was looking for a country place: the Duke was tempted, but decided the approach was too steep for his horses. 'I have crossed the Alps once,' he said, and withdrew.

Sir Henry visited Paris again, then began to feel life was losing its savour, until, on a fine day in 1825, he heard one of the dairy maids on the estate singing, and saw that she was pretty. On a whim, he proposed marriage. He was seventy-one; she was twenty; her name was Mary Ann Bullock, and she was the child of a labouring family that had moved from Surrey to Sussex. His proposal was accepted, and he sent her to France to be taught manners, reading, writing and embroidery. The wedding was solemnized in the house, with Sir

Henry's daughter, Anne, now nineteen, as a witness. There were no children but soon they took in Mary Ann's younger sister Frances Bullock, and entrusted her education to Anne.

What was called 'Society' never accepted Lady Fetherstonhaugh, and there were days when Sir Henry thought he had made a fool of himself. They were not on visiting terms with his social equals, but together they did good works locally, including setting up a school. Lady Fetherstonhaugh wore beautiful clothes, produced a prodigious amount of needlework, changed some of the wallpapers in the house, and nursed Sir Henry through his long last years. He lived to be ninety-one, dying in 1846.

Four years after his death, Wells's mother went to Uppark to be Frances Bullock's maid, both of them well aware that the maid came from a higher class than her mistress, since her parents had been inn-keepers. But Frances grew very fond of Sarah, who stayed with her for three years, and kept in touch with her afterwards; and when the young Mrs Wells's first child was born, a daughter, she named her Frances after her friendly patroness.

Sir Henry's widow, Lady Fetherstonhaugh, lived until 1874. Frances inherited Uppark and was granted arms – presumably because it was believed that the owner of so great a house and estate must bear arms. So the renamed Frances Fetherstonhaugh was officially absorbed into the aristocracy.

Frances Fetherstonhaugh and Anne Sutherland settled down together. It is said that they always dressed in velvet – usually black velvet – and sat in the same small sitting room on most days. Local clergymen called, and occasionally they invited guests for shooting parties, and people came: whatever the low birth and lack of breeding of the ladies, they were living in one of the most luxurious and elegantly furnished great houses in the country. There was also the consideration that Miss Fetherstonhaugh would one day need to decide who should inherit Uppark from her.

She acquired an agent to advise her on practical matters, a Portsmouth auctioneer called William King. He was hard-working, ambitious and active in good works, had become a magistrate, then an alderman, rising to be Mayor in the 1870s and again in the 1880s, and he finally achieved a knighthood. He lived in Southsea and came over regularly to advise Miss Fetherstonhaugh and keep an eye on things. According to Wells, it was Sir William who advised his mother to apprentice him to Hyde's drapery in Southsea.

Wells always entered Uppark down the steps to the servants' quarters, which occupied the whole of the vast semi-basement. Although intersected by dark corridors, all the principal rooms have large windows giving good light, and he found his mother's domain as housekeeper was a comfortably furnished room with its own fireplace and windows. The butler also had his private room, and there was a great servants' hall where they took their meals. Here gathered butler, housekeeper, footmen, housemaids, ladies' maids, valets and probably coachmen and other outdoor workers who came in during the day – as well as the servants of any visitors to the two ladies of the house. The room was used for gatherings including occasional parties and Christmas dances organized by the servants for their own pleasure. They had a lively time when they chose to.

Mrs Wells did not sleep in the basement but in one of the many attic rooms, reached up flights of steep back stairs. They are small but agreeable, warmed by good fireplaces and with windows looking out over views even more spectacular than those from the grand first and second floors occupied by the family and their guests. Wells, allotted a bedroom near his mother's, made it his business to explore this top floor of the house. He quickly found rooms full of discarded furniture and other unwanted objects to be examined, and among them a great many books. There was Plato's *Republic*, some Voltaire – evidence of Sir Henry's interest in French liberal thinking – Tom Paine's *Rights of Man*, Swift's *Gulliver's Travels*, Johnson's *Rasselas*. All of these impressed themselves on his thinking and imagination with their ideas, their political statements and their imaginative flights: the closed valley in which Rasselas lives would reappear in different form in the story 'The Country of the Blind', and the flying machine had many successors in Wells's stories; the brilliant oddity of Swift's invention would also be matched by him. Then there were volumes of engravings of works by Raphael, Michelangelo and their fellow painters: Wells brooded with delight over their 'sybils, gods and goddesses'.[4] Entranced, he stored his mind with what he read and saw, and his excellent memory kept it there.

When he came on a big box containing a jumble of metal pieces, he set about putting them together carefully, and found himself with a telescope. He told no one but simply set it up in the window of his bedroom and began to study the night sky. A treasure such as this might have been prescribed by rich parents for a fourteen-year-old endowed with exceptional curiosity, technical intelligence and persistence: to Wells it was given by chance, and he made extraordinarily good use of what he found.

That first Christmas of 1880 at Uppark Wells also decided to write a daily news sheet for the servants, for his own amusement and theirs. He called it *The Uppark Alarmist* – and since an alarmist is someone who frightens people with false information, it allowed him to make jokes. No copies have survived – a pity, as his jokes about what he saw of life at Uppark would be worth reading. The weather became so harsh that he was stuck there, snowed up into the middle of January: a piece of good luck. This gave him time to construct a miniature theatre and put on a shadow play – with cut-out puppets and candles – to entertain the servants further. It must have made for a far livelier Christmas than usual at Uppark. Probably no one so clever had been seen there since the death of Sir Henry.

By now Wells knew his way around. He undoubtedly opened and peered through one of the doors in the partition separating the back stairs from the main house, and caught sight of the bookshelves in the saloon, solidly packed with further neglected treasures: and when he saw the coast was clear, he darted in to extract a book or two.

Hateful as Southsea was to him, he escaped back to Uppark at Christmas each year, and there, either in 1881 or 1882, he had his first experience of sexual delight. It came about through the servants' dance. He had noticed a pretty kitchen maid called Mary and asked her to dance with him – in those days the waltz was danced, and the polka, as well as group dances like Sir Roger de Coverley. They made a good couple and enjoyed themselves so much that they stayed together until his watchful mother intervened, bringing other partners to him in such a way that he could not refuse them.

He never forgot the experience of dancing with Mary, or the colour of her dress. Years later he wrote, 'I can feel her heart beat against mine now, I can recall the lithe body in her flimsy yellow dress.' And, as he left the servants' hall where they had been dancing, and went along one of the dark passages, she darted out of a recess and kissed and embraced him. 'No lovelier thing has ever happened to me. Somebody became audible down the passage and she made a last dash at me, pressed her lips to mine and fled.' So Uppark gave him a sexual education too: 'after that I knew that love was neither filth nor flirtation and I began to want more of it.'[5]

The next day he left for Portsmouth in the dog cart on the frosty road to the station at Rowlands Castle. When he returned to Uppark, Mary was no longer working there. But she had inspired him to ask himself what it was he wanted of women. Reading Shelley – *Epipsychidion*, no doubt, a hymn to sexual freedom – he began to dream of 'free, ambitious, self-reliant women who would mate with me and go their way, as I desired to go my way'.[6] Had he read the story of Shelley's actual experience with women, it might have persuaded him to adjust this fantasy to the real world: as things turned out, Shelley's unrealistic dream led him and the women he loved into trouble.

He was also reading about politics. Later on, as he lay on the grass at Uppark beside the ruined tower in the summer of 1884, he absorbed some of the ideas in Plato's *Republic* – especially that the common interest must overrule the claims of private ownership – and found strong endorsement from Henry George, the American author of *Progress and Poverty*, at that time a world bestseller arguing that land must belong to the whole community.[7] Between them they left Wells ready to believe that socialism was on the way and that it would make everyone active and happy.

4.   'A bright run of luck'

As long as he had to return to Hyde's Drapery Emporium in Southsea, he remained wretched, knowing that his life was being wasted as he spent day after day folding and unfolding bales of cloth, serving customers, struggling with the parcels he never learnt to do up neatly. He escaped when he could to read, and stretched the time it took to make any errand he was sent on last for as long as he dared to make it. The passing months did not resign him to his fate but increased his unhappiness and resentment, as he saw his ambitions and hopes fading further out of reach.

Yet Wells was too strongly motivated to give up. He saw that he had to work out his own means of escape – but how? A glimpse of light came through a sympathetic fellow clerk who noticed him studying Latin and said something about schools employing ushers – apprentice teachers who were also still students. Wells thought about this and then sent off an appeal to the headmaster at the grammar school in Midhurst, Mr Byatt. Would he consider taking him on as an usher? To his joy Byatt wrote back, saying he might – but with no mention of pay. How could Wells proceed when he had wasted the money spent by his parents on his apprenticeship at Hyde's? When he raised the matter with his mother, she wept and told him to pray for help. Even his father failed to support his new plan.

Then Byatt wrote again, this time offering to pay him twenty pounds for one year, and twice as much for a second. He encouraged Wells further by asking him to come over, giving him a good dinner and suggesting cheap and agreeable lodgings near the school that he might share with another assistant master. Wells pointed out to his mother that a schoolmaster's clothes would cost half as much as what was needed for a draper's outfits, which had to be very smart – and, he went on, a schoolmaster had a prospect of rising to a good position in the world, while a draper's assistant had no such hope. It was a matter of urgency, he insisted: to become a schoolmaster, 'I must begin at once . . . Which would you prefer?' he asked her.

At this point he got himself into serious trouble at the shop for disobeying orders. Whether he had done it on purpose or only carelessly, the humiliating prospect of punishment made his current existence even harder to bear. By now he was so anxious and distressed that the idea of killing himself rather than having to face punishment came into his head.

He soon discarded that plan. But he saw that he could threaten his mother with the idea, took action and set up a dramatic situation. On the next Sunday morning – this was in July 1883 – he walked the seventeen miles from Southsea to Uppark and waited close to the path always taken by his mother as she returned from church in Harting at the bottom of the hill. As she appeared with her fellow churchgoers, he signalled to her, took her aside, and told her he was determined to leave the drapery and become an usher in a school instead. When she protested, he insisted that he was ready to kill himself unless she agreed: a life of torture, he said, was not worth living. Evidently he spoke with enough force to convince her that he meant what he said, and with this, surprisingly, she did at last give way. She agreed to pay the money necessary to cancel his indentures, drawing on her savings. He could leave Hyde's.

He walked back to Southsea and triumphantly announced that he would be leaving, and with his mother's agreement. His father withheld consent for some days, and Wells was urged to stay on to help with the summer sales. He refused, managed to persuade his father and left on the last day of July. His intention was to devote August to reading. On the train to Midhurst he found himself too excited to read, and instead, being alone in his carriage, he performed a celebratory song and dance. His rejoicing was fully justified, because now at last he was on the path towards becoming what he wanted to be, and was confident he could become – an educated man who could hold his own in any company.

★

The lodgings Mr Byatt had recommended were in North Street, a few steps from the grammar school, let out by the good-natured Mrs Walton, who ran a sweet shop on the ground floor; and there, before the start of term, he set himself a programme of work that filled almost every moment of his day. It allowed no reading of fiction or playing of games, and included a one-hour daily walk to be made at the speed of four miles an hour. He supposedly described a pro-gramme of this kind in a novel he wrote almost twenty years later, *Love and Mr Lewisham*, in which his hero pins up maxims on the wall of his room – 'Who would control others must first control himself', 'Knowledge is power' – alongside a list of French irregular verbs and a timetable that he called a 'Schema'. It listed 'French until eight', breakfast in twenty minutes, then learning extracts from Shakespeare for twenty-five. There was also Latin composition and literature. In the novel Mr Lewisham is distracted by a passing pretty girl, but in life Wells let himself be distracted by nothing. A bonus at his lodging house was that Mrs Walton served him meals of rich meat stews and puddings of fruit and custard. He described it as the first good food he had ever eaten, which cannot be entirely true, but was part of his sense of having at last escaped and arrived where he wanted to be. He needed feeding: he was about to be seventeen, and still small and skinny.

He had begun to understand what his own capacities were: to learn fast, to plan his work, to observe people about him, to know what he valued most, to fight for what he wanted and to win. He knew he enjoyed good conversation, difficult books, intellectual puzzles and challenges, and the beauty of the natural world – and that he hated unrewarding labour, dull company, religion, bad food, ugly suburbs. He noticed the world around him with exceptional vividness and thought about it, interested in the contrast between the familiar muddled suburban sprawl of Bromley he had come to hate, and the neat, coherent layout of Midhurst, with its medieval and Tudor buildings, small squares and gently hilly streets from which you rarely lose sight of the surrounding countryside of heathland, woods and fields, and the Downs tempting you upwards. He wrote later that all his memories of Midhurst were full of sunshine – it answered to his love of light, sun, open spaces and hills, and windows with views.

Not long before the start of term in September 1883 his fellow teacher Harris arrived. They took walks together, aiming at four miles an hour, just about managing to talk, their shabby clothes dignified by the mortar boards on their heads. Term started, and Wells was asked to teach in the main classroom, where Byatt presided and gave him advice on teaching methods. When Wells was not teaching, he was studying: physics, biology and anatomy, mathematics, chemistry, geology. Byatt gave him what were called special evening classes, for which he provided him with whatever textbooks he could find for each of these subjects; and, since he was not able to teach any of the science Wells was eager to learn, he sat writing letters while his usher worked his way through the books. In this fashion Wells managed to take in the outlines of the physical and biological sciences. By his own account he learnt without much difficulty, and did extra work on brain anatomy and electricity. Lightly as he described this process, it cannot have been an easy way to learn.

Still, he progressed steadily and with a determination to do well strengthened by a discovery he had made and kept to himself: that the Department of Education, hoping to encourage better science teaching, was offering scholarships for a four-year course at the Normal School of Science (later the Royal College of Science) in South Kensington, London, to those who achieved the best results in the May examinations – Normal Schools were teacher-training colleges where they could work for a university degree. Without saying a word to anyone at the grammar school or his family, Wells filled out the application form and sent it off.

He had to deal with an infuriating distraction when Byatt told him that every teacher in the school was obliged to be a member of the Church of England. Protest as he might, it was clear that he could not continue teaching without being confirmed and taking the sacrament. He was sent to the curate, another young man living in lodgings, and argued with him until he realized it was simpler to pretend to accept what he did not believe. The one good result as far as he was concerned was his mother's delight. He retained a sense of resentment and distrust of the Church throughout his life.

May came, he sat the exams, and soon heard that he had done outstandingly well in them – so well that he was awarded a studentship for a year to study biology under Professor Thomas H. Huxley at the Normal School of Science. He was to be given his fare to London and a guinea a week to live on there for a year, with a good chance of renewing the scholarship for a further two years.

This was an extraordinary achievement under the circumstances. Byatt heard of his success with mixed feelings. He was surprised and proud, but he did not want to lose his usher, and did his best to persuade him to stay for another year on a doubled salary. There was of course no chance that Wells would even consider this.

In July 1884 Wells wrote to his mother, 'We break up on the 25th July . . . Will there be any chance of a week at Uppark before I go to Bromley' (i.e., to his father) – followed by 'HOORAY!' He was at Uppark both before and after Bromley – he wrote again in late August to his mother, saying, 'I should like very much a short holiday at Up Park before I settle down.' There he enjoyed the summer weather and reading, much of it outside, lying in the grass. He also enjoyed his time with his father, now bearded and lame but still active, camping out in Atlas House, getting books from the Literary Institute, still selling cricket goods, and making rather better meals than his wife had ever managed. They got on well together. He made his son help about the house and one day took him to Penshurst to show him where he had been a boy. Wells was impressed both by his father's lack of worldly ambition and by his knowledge of the natural world, as he showed him sights he would not have found by himself: a trout in the river, and a kingfisher flashing by.

His brother Frank surprised him too. Wells's success in escaping from shop life had made Frank think about his own position and presently he decided that he would also throw up work as a draper. He had no high ambitions and simply decided to live without a formal job. Having developed some skills of his own, he embarked on an itinerant life, moving from place to place, first on foot, then on a bicycle, repairing clocks, selling watches, sometimes dealing in furniture. Rural England still allowed such freedom: cars had not yet arrived, and there was space in which to wander and camp out. Frank always kept in touch with his parents and younger brother, and did occasional odd jobs such as putting up shelves for them; and later, when Wells was married, he sometimes joined him and his wife for holidays – he went over to Boulogne with them, his first visit abroad.[1] He remained a bachelor, and was content to be poor and free, although he descended on his father when he needed somewhere to stay; and, as the years went by and things got more difficult, he effectively ended up living with him. Wells admired his refusal to pursue worldly success or money. He called his second son after him, and paid tribute to him in his novel *The History of Mr Polly*, the story of a small shopkeeper who burns down his own shop and escapes into a life of freedom in the English countryside.[2] Wells understood the impulse to escape well enough, not only writing about it but also occasionally succumbing to it himself.

His parents' failure to help him to get a higher education did not alter his affection for them. Perhaps he realized that such a thing was outside the scope of their imagination of what life could be; and, once he had achieved his object in getting to college, he simply forgave them. He had done it, they were proud of him, and that was enough – and he later wrote thanking them for their early care. He supported them financially as soon as he could, and then bought them a house. It was the behaviour of a model son.

In September 1884, as his eighteenth birthday approached, he arrived in London: a dirty city of smoking chimneys, steam trains and horse-drawn traffic – although the first cable tram was set up that year, and the inner circuit of the Underground's District Line opened in October. The lodgings his mother had found him through a relative were in Westbourne Park, within walking distance of the Normal School of Science, a five-storey building in Exhibition Road. He would be working on the top floor, in the laboratory given over to elementary biology, and attending lectures on zoology by Professor Huxley.

Huxley was a scientist of the greatest distinction, a friend of Darwin, whose work on Evolution he had defended strongly against attacks from the first. For Huxley, an anatomist and physiologist, accurate observation and logic were the two most important elements in scientific research and thinking. As a young man he had travelled with the Navy on a voyage of discovery to New Guinea and Australia, working on marine invertebrates. Later he had a chair in Natural History, and when Wells became his student he was the President of the Royal Society. He had rejected any belief in Christian doctrine, describing himself as an agnostic, saying he believed the problem of existence was insoluble. He was a good man as well as a brilliant one: happy to teach women, and working men, opposed to denominational schools, and dubious of the honours system. Young Wells was keenly aware of what it meant to be taught by such a man, and idolized him, describing his overseeing of the study of zoology as 'an acute, delicate, rigorous and sweepingly magnificent series of exercises'; and he took to his studies like a parched traveller at last reaching water.

The laboratory in which he worked was decorated with anatomical drawings and shelves of skeletons, skulls and wax models of developing chicks. There was a microtome – an instrument for fine cutting – and blackboards on the walls for the demonstrator; and the long tables on which the students were set to slicing up plants and dissecting rabbits, frogs, guinea pigs and mussels were lit by gas lamps. Next door to it was the small lecture room in which Huxley spoke.

Wells had entered a new intellectual world and a new social world at the same time, and now, for the first time, he found himself working alongside students whose minds were as agile and questing as his. Most had been to better schools than he had, and, while the majority came from middle-class families, others were as poor as he was – Richard Gregory's father was a boot-mender – and like him struggled to manage on the single guinea that was handed out to each of them

Royal College, Exhibition Road

every Wednesday. Wells saw two of his fellow students faint from hunger in the laboratory, and he regularly went without lunch himself on Mondays and Tuesdays. He got breakfast and high tea at his lodgings, but that left nine hours between.

He weighed little more than seven stone, his ribs showed, he had not much muscle, and he felt himself to be a poor specimen. But he quickly made himself popular. A. V. Jennings, son of a private schoolmaster, appreciated his clever and irreverent conversation, made friends with him and, realizing that he was half starved, took him out to lunch. Wells enjoyed the four-course meal but resolutely refused any further invitations out of pride. 'For a year I went shabby and grew shabbier, I was under-fed . . . and it did not matter to me in the least because of the vision of life that was growing in my mind.'[3]

It was the happiest year he had yet lived, because he was learning more than he had ever learnt before, about method, and about observation, and his brain was fully engaged. He was lucky, because his class was the last to be taught by Huxley, who fell ill with a depressive condition and gave up teaching – he was to die in 1895. But he had inspired Wells. Although he did not become an academic scientist himself, he learnt to look and think clearly, and to write precise descriptions not only of what he saw before his eyes but also of the extraordinary things he imagined.

Only his lodgings were unsatisfactory. The landlady of the house in Westbourne Park turned out to be both slatternly and provocatively flirtatious, and kept her house crammed with too many lodgers. Wells found the grubbiness and overheated atmosphere unpleasant. Although he craved sexual experience, he was hoping for something splendid, not the fumbling experiments going on in this overcrowded boarding house. He soon managed to move, this time to the house of a widowed Mrs Wells – Aunt Mary, who had been married to his father's brother – and her daughter Isabel, his young and very pretty cousin. They lived in the Euston Road, which meant a longer walk to college, but he was well looked after there, and happy. He and Isabel, who earned her living retouching photographs in a Regent Street shop, became friends and allies: he talked, she listened; he was excitable, she was calm and conventional.

Life at college was intensely interesting, still more so after he joined the Debating Society. Other students were drawn to Wells because he enjoyed talking – and he talked well, throwing out original and provocative ideas, and was happy to argue and fun to be with. He was loyal, and he inspired loyalty, and he took such friendships seriously. One of the most important was with Elizabeth Healey, a highly intelligent and well-educated young woman, daughter of a professor at the Normal School of Science and a few years older than him. It is likely she was one of the women students who 'disavowed sex' in their dress and behaviour – Wells's words. He enjoyed her company, took her views seriously and confided in her. She saw him as a brilliant thinker and speaker, always ready to attack shams and conventional ideas, and never ill-natured. She also admired his 'remarkable blue eyes and thick, tumbled brown hair'. They became friends for life – one of his very last letters was to her. Over the years they exchanged a great many long letters, discussing literature, morality and his various problems with health and work.

Another friend was Tommy Simmons, who shared his enthusiasm for socialism. Wells exchanged jokes with him, suggesting once that the best thing he himself could do would be to take religious orders, on the grounds that 'It would irrevocably damage the Establishment.'[4] Simmons became a journalist and in due course editor of *The Times Educational Supplement*. Richard Gregory and Arthur Morley Davies both collaborated on writing textbooks with Wells, Davies became a palaeontologist and Gregory became Sir Richard, and President of the British Association for the Advancement of Science. William Burton became a chemist and successful businessman. All these close men friends of his went on to succeed in their chosen careers, and many of them preserved his letters, seeing him as exceptionally gifted as well as a delightful and entertaining friend.

In the zoology exams at the end of the year, June 1885, Jennings and Wells both achieved a First Class. July and August were spent at

Uppark and with his father in Bromley. His scholarship was renewed, but he was not allowed to continue with zoology as he wished. He was obliged to study geology and physics, and found the way it was taught tedious – which meant he lost interest and performed much less well in his exams. The third year was still worse, because by then he realized he was more interested in literature, history and art than geology and physics.

He was always busy. He continued to speak at the college Debating Society, enjoyed addressing an audience and found he was good at it – despite the handicap of a high and sometimes squeaky voice. In his second year he gave the paper 'The Past and Future of the Human Race', in which he foretold a distant time ahead when men would have developed into hopping heads controlled by unemotional intelligence, living underground, with air brought down through metallic shafts from the frozen Earth above, all vegetation and animal life having long since disappeared.

His fellow science students relished this, not surprisingly. For us it is a significant moment to recall, knowing that from this first venture into forecasting the future would come his life-changing success ten years later with *The Time Machine*. He rewrote the talk in 1893 to be published in the *Pall Mall Gazette* as 'The Man of the Year Million', who will be all brain, with powerful hands, large lustrous eyes, no teeth or stomach; he will absorb nourishment from the fluid in which he swims ('avoiding the unwieldy paraphernalia of servants and plates', added Wells) and enjoy artificial lighting in his underground home.

He was using his mind for his own purposes, not following the programme he was expected to stick to, so that, although he got another First in geometrical drawing in the summer of 1886, he had only a Second in geology and failed in astronomical physics. What he called the 'bright run of luck' he had enjoyed between 1883 and 1885 was over. In September 1886 he was back at South Kensington to study geology: this was when he realized that, although he had enjoyed studying zoology, other science interested him less. Effectively he gave up working at his syllabus.

In December he set up *Science Schools Journal*, with an opening essay in which he wrote of the 'noblest specimens' of science students being gathered at the college, and how they excelled at acquiring and retaining systematic knowledge. He went on, 'Clearness of perception, imagination and order are alike *the* mental requirements of the scientist and the writer' – as though laying out instructions to his future self. But the authorities now decided he was not working hard enough, and three months later he was told he must hand over the editorship of the *Science Schools Journal* to his friend Burton.

He went with his friends to meetings of the newly founded Fabian Society (1884), which held open events at William Morris's house on the Mall. Here he heard Bernard Shaw and Graham Wallas speak – both of whom were to become his friends ten years later. He certainly read Shaw's magnificent *Manifesto*, the second Fabian pamphlet, two pages only, published in 1884, which begins: 'The Land and Capital of the nation is the birth-right of every individual.' It goes on to demand nationalization of the land (as a public duty). Also equal political rights for the sexes – which as yet had been entirely rejected. And it ends with the stirring statement that 'we had rather face a Civil War than such another century of suffering as the present one has been.'

These views of Shaw's chimed well with his – although he does not appear to have been interested himself in equal rights for women. In October he gave a talk on 'Democratic Socialism' to the college Debating Society. He was inspired by Plato and Henry George, and keen to pass on George's message that socialism would produce active and happy people; and that the abolition of any private property except what a man has earned would rearrange the world for the better. This was not a young man's passing belief – he remained a socialist to the end of his life.

But he did not take his cousin Isabel to Fabian meetings. Instead he taught her to ride a tricycle, and perhaps went with her for an occasional ride in Regent's Park, for which he must have cast aside the top hat and tail-coat he felt obliged to wear when going out with her on more formal occasions. Her views remained strictly conventional. She was not a reader, and not interested in politics. Her clothes were conventional too. Women's bodies at that time were kept covered by several layers of different materials from neck to feet, and in any case Isabel, beautiful and friendly as she was, kept his hopeful sexual advances under strict control. They were simply not allowed before marriage. Poor Wells: he felt that sexual desire was as natural as hunger and thirst, and should be a complete encounter of two mutually desirous bodies, but he had not yet found such an encounter. He was twenty in September, still weighing a good deal less than eight stone, still ill-nourished, and ashamed of his thin body, now just five feet, five inches tall.

So 1887 became a bad year. He had failed to get the degree he should have achieved easily. He described himself as 'probably the only completely unsatisfactory student turned out' by the Normal School of Science at South Kensington – this was years later, when he could joke about it, but at the time it was no joke. And yet what made him do so badly in his exams was not just his failure to interest himself in geology – for which he got a Second – or astronomical physics – which he failed – but rather that he had become interested in so many other things: learning to debate, to edit a magazine and to write articles and stories, looking at paintings, enjoying conversation with friends. The editorship of *Science Schools Journal* had been taken from him – but he had managed to place several stories with it, the new editor Burton being a friend – and he had more planned. With a mind exceptionally alert to new possibilities, he was always ready to set off on fresh paths. Taking on too much was the way Wells lived his life.

The drawback was that there was now no chance of returning to South Kensington for a fourth year. At the same time he learnt of his father's bankruptcy in Bromley: the shop was finally given up and Joseph Wells moved into a dilapidated cottage in Nyewood, three miles from Uppark, where he had to make do on an allowance from his wife. None of his sons was earning enough to help him out – so now the youngest must look for work. He found it by taking up that last resort of undergraduates who have failed to make the grade: he was going to the distant provinces to teach in a cheap private boarding school for boys.

5. Blood

The new junior schoolmaster set off by train in the summer of 1887 for the Welsh border town of Holt, on the River Dee, near Chester. Holt Academy was a private boys' school, but he would also be giving lessons to some of the girls in its sister school. Their term started in July. He took with him several stories he was working on and a partly written novel called 'Lady Frankland's Companion' – a wonderfully old-fashioned title – of which no copy has survived (he destroyed it in 1930).

He was greeted by a black-toothed headmaster wearing a tall hat, formal black frock-coat and white tie over dirty linen. It was soon evident to Wells that he was an alcoholic – and his wife too. There appeared to be no timetable. The schoolrooms had bare brick floors and dirty walls, many of the windows were broken and the desks and chairs were all dilapidated. There was nothing in the chemistry cupboard but a few broken bottles and test tubes. The boarders slept three to a bed. Meals were served irregularly. It was clearly a school that kept going on the Dotheboys Hall principle that the boys' parents were not interested in how they were treated, and were charged very low fees.

The room Wells was to share with another master lacked even a chair to sit on. But he could not feel too wretched, because for the moment the sun was shining warmly, the surrounding countryside was green and lush and the banks of the River Dee were beautiful. He was working on a story, and also cheered by meeting the French master, a colleague who quickly became congenial as he boasted of being an atheist, a socialist and a cuckold maker.[1] Better still, he met a young woman teacher on holiday in the area, fell into conversation with her, found she read Ruskin and George Eliot and persuaded her to spend time with him enjoying cultural conversations on a shady river bank.

He described her in a letter to a friend as 'a damoisel, beautiful, of extraordinary force of character, and higher culture'. Her name was Annie Meredith. Isabel slipped his mind for the moment.

August came, and his interesting friend Annie left. Disaster struck almost at once. Joining in a game of rugby with the older boys, he was tackled fiercely and knocked to the ground. He managed to stagger back to the house with a pain in his side, was violently sick and found he was urinating blood. In the night he became delirious, and the next day a doctor was sent for. He diagnosed a crushed kidney and a bruised liver, 'and my intestines & muscles between the ribs and the pelvis mashed up more or less' – so Wells wrote to his mother from his sickbed when he was able to hold a pen again, asking her to send him ten shillings. He was kept in bed for a time in his barely furnished room – but not for long.

The headmaster insisted that he should return to work. Soon he collapsed again with further symptoms: bronchitis, piles, more pains in the kidney. He began to cough blood, and when the doctor came again he produced a further diagnosis, this time tuberculosis in his right lung, and said he should be kept warm in bed and well fed. No further action was taken by the school beyond a suggestion that he should go home, and he was still lying in bed in what was now a cold room on his twenty-first birthday on 21 September, barely looked after. He had a visit from his college friend William Burton, newly married and working as a chemist for Wedgwood potteries in Stoke-on-Trent, who invited him to stay as soon as he was well enough. For the time being he was too ill to accept the invitation. So he remained in limbo at the school, sick and uncared for, and getting weaker day by day.

Meanwhile his mother, hearing from him of the threat to his lungs, went into action – not surprisingly, since a young Wells cousin, Lillie, daughter of his aunt Hannah, had recently died of tuberculosis.[2] It took a few weeks of persuasion from Mrs Wells to get Miss Fetherstonhaugh's permission to bring her sick son to Uppark: only 'the magic word consumptive softened the heart of Uppark towards me.'[3] At last, in November, she was able to tell Bertie he might come. With considerable difficulty he packed up his scant belongings and set off on the twelve-hour rail journey to London, then on to Sussex, stopping briefly at his father's cottage in Nyewood before arriving at Uppark. No sooner was he installed in an attic bedroom than blood began first to trickle and then to pour from his right lung.

Here at last his luck changed. A fashionable – and clever – young London doctor was staying in the house for some shooting, and, hearing of a patient, he naturally went to his bedside. Dr Collins sent for ice bags, laid Wells down firmly on his back and told him to stay there. The flow of blood was stopped. Under the direction of Dr Collins he was now at last properly cared for. The Uppark maids washed him and took his few clothes to be laundered, changed his bed carefully, emptied his chamber pot, and came and went with food and water. After a few days he was able to look about and appreciate that his room was full of sunlight, warmed by a good fire in the grate, and comfortably furnished with an armchair and a table.

As he began to recover from the painful and frightening experiences he had undergone, he had moments of self-pity, but above all – by his own account – he felt a deep exasperation at not having seen the world, at not yet having become famous and, worst of all, at being likely to die still a virgin. He knew what he wanted: fame and sex – but what hope was there of either? The fear of death was there too, of being stifled and shut up. And there was the constant anxiety that a cough would bring on another haemorrhage, 'the little tickle and trickle of blood in the lungs', the dread of tasting the peculiar tang of blood.

He says he told no one of his fears, and indeed, in a letter to his friend Arthur Davies informing him he was now a confirmed invalid, he managed to make a joke of his condition, saying that if God had sent all this to chasten him, God had certainly mistaken his man, and he repudiated God.[4]

Dr Collins continued to interest himself in Wells's case. In December he took specimens of his blood and urine to London for analysis: 'He has borrowed a phial of piddle – my piddle – and taken it up to London.'[5] Wells reported Dr Collins's warning that he might become a chronic invalid, and that he must stay indoors for a year, sitting down and keeping warm. At the same time he reassured him that, although he was still spitting blood, his lungs were not tubercular, merely 'disorganized'. Yes, he could kill himself by sitting between an open window and a fire for a couple of hours, but the real problem was the damage to his kidney, which might lead to diabetes – Collins was right about this and in due course it did. There is no doubt that he was an excellent doctor, but, from Wells's account at any rate, it was often possible to read his advice in different ways.

Wells's spirits rose and fell from day to day. He suffered agonies from having to paint his chest with iodine, a prescribed treatment that produced burning irritation and sore patches. 'Damn! Damn! Damn! Damn! God Damn' (and more) he wrote, but conceded the iodine did him good and his cough was eventually cured. His college friends kept loyally in touch, and his replies varied from complaints that he could look forward to nothing but a maimed existence to jokes and letters of advice.

When Simmons said he was thinking of marriage, Wells offered his instructions on choosing a wife: 'she may be religious but she must not be *too* religious . . . she must have perfect health, an unmistakable preference for you over any other, especially children.' She should be 'at least good looking', truthful and a good dressmaker, cook, housewife – all these more important than a pretty face, or charm, or talent.[6] It was a lowering list: what woman would wish to be chosen by the man who wrote it? And what about sex, which he longed for so desperately from his invalid bed? However desperately, it seems to have remained unmentionable.

He asked Davies about the London Library and learnt that it was too expensive to be thought of. He also contrived to keep sending stories to magazines in London and collected large numbers of rejection slips. 'My only chance now for a living is literature . . . I think the groove I shall drop into will be cheap novelette-eering.'[7]

And he was reading. All the Uppark books were reasonably accessible again, of course, Burton nobly sent more, and even the local curate lent him novels. He got through classics, Hawthorne's *The Scarlet Letter* and Blackmore's *Lorna Doone*; and recent fiction,

Stevenson's *Treasure Island* and *Jekyll and Hyde*. He persevered through a good deal of both Rousseau and Emerson, and found new pleasure in poets ranging from Spenser – whose 'glades, tangled underwoods, enchanted castles, and glistening streams' charmed him – to Heine, Keats and Whitman.[8] He was inspired to try his hand at sonnets of his own, and to write letters in Whitmanesque style. He sent some of his attempts at verse to Healey, who wrote back pointing out that he had not begun to understand about metre. Never mind – he was reading poetry and fiction with attention to language as well as pleasure.

He went on spitting blood, carefully throwing the 'gore-laden tissue' straight into the fire to save his mother from panic. But when Christmas came he ventured to get up and go downstairs. His father and brother Frank were allowed to come to Uppark for three days – 'We infested the house,' wrote Wells apologetically – and he himself managed to dance and sing in the servants' hall, before being firmly put back to bed in the afternoon.

There were still days when he saw only a bleak future. 'I shall never join the marching column again,' he wrote. 'My youth went long ago' – this to Healey.[9] But then there were others when he was able to take himself out to walk in the thawing snow on the Downs and through the beech woods, risking disapproval from Dr Collins. In February he managed a seven-mile walk.

Thinking over the past three years of his life, he must have asked himself whether his great fight to get an education had done him much good. He had failed in his studies, he had not begun to establish himself in a career, and through no fault of his own he had been injured so badly that he was likely to suffer serious after-effects for the rest of his life. He had not even found a woman willing to make love with him. And he decided that everything he had written until now was worthless, and resolved to burn just about all of it and start again.

Dr Collins told him he might hope for a complete recovery – except perhaps for the damaged kidney – if he kept very quiet for a year or so. But what sort of quiet life could he hope for with no means? So in February he wrote to Collins asking him if he could put him in contact with anyone in London who might offer him a job, since Collins knew the Huxleys, Bernard Shaw and others who must surely employ assistants. He added that neither Miss Fetherstonhaugh nor William King, her agent, was able to do anything for him: not too surprisingly in the case of King, who had found him the apprenticeship in Southsea he had spurned. And he pointed out that visitors to Uppark were for the most part 'military gentry, clerical dignitaries or that fortunate independent class whose only business is to live happily' – a neat encapsulation of the people he occasionally encountered.[10] Dr Collins wrote a friendly reply, but he also made it clear that he was unable to help him find a job. Wells would have to work out his own way of living without straining his health. It is a puzzling response from the generally sympathetic doctor, but it may be that he felt it would be wrong for him to recommend a patient for a position – given that he knew nothing of Wells's abilities.

Wells understood that he would have to work hard to learn to write well – to revolutionize himself, as he put it. He had, in fact, started writing a new story in January, 'The Chronic Argonauts', built around the idea of time travel, and sent it off to the *Science Schools Journal*, where his name was well remembered. It told of a time-travelling machine, the Chronic Argo, made by a Dr Nebogipfel living in a remote Welsh village. Although Wells described it as a romance, it drew on current discussions among scientists of multi-dimensional geometries, with the suggestion that Time might be a fourth dimension, or that there might be a further dimension of space. He was not alone in wanting to explore such ideas. Oscar Wilde made a ghost disappear into 'the fourth dimension of space' in his story 'The Canterville Ghost', published in 1887, and Wells had heard, and read, a paper entitled 'The Fourth Dimension' given at his college in the same year.[11]

The first instalment of 'The Chronic Argonauts' made its appearance in the *Science Schools Journal* in April, and on 7 April 1888 Wells left Uppark at last, stopping briefly in London on his way to take up William Burton's invitation to stay with him and his wife in Stoke-on-Trent.

At the Burtons' he suffered another haemorrhage. They did not panic, called a doctor and looked after him well, and he recovered. Once better, they found him an amusing if not always easy guest, shabbily dressed and moody, but ready to be interested in Stoke. Burton was doing well at Wedgwood and pleased to show him the Potteries and the Staffordshire countryside. Wells began to plan a novel set there, but in the end managed only short stories – one, 'The Cone', is an effectively horrible account of sexual jealousy and revenge in a Stoke foundry.[12]

From the Burtons' he wrote to Davies, sending him a list of the work of the last year:

		£ s. d.
Item 1 Short Story	Sold	1. 0. 0.
Item 1 Novel. 35,000 words	Burnt	0. 0. 0.
Item 1 Novel unfinished. 25,000 words	Burnt	0. 0. 0.
Item Much comic poetry	Lost	0. 0. 0.
Item Some comic prose	Sent away, never returned	
Item Humorous essay	*Globe*, did not return	
Item Sundry stories	Burnt	
Item 1 Story	Wandering	
Item A Poem	Burnt	
	etc., etc.	

adding 'Total income (untaxed) £1.0.0.'

Yet below this he added a remarkable comment: 'Some day I shall succeed, I really believe, but it is a weary game.'[13] The 'Wandering' story was presumably 'The Chronic Argonauts'. Two more instalments made it to the *Science Schools Journal*, but he offered no more, having lost confidence in the story. Later he wrote that, if a young man brought him a story like 'The Chronic Argonauts', he would not encourage him to go on writing. But one of the long letters he addressed to Elizabeth Healey from the Burtons' house had a P.S. reading 'The Chronic Argonauts is no joke. There is a sequel.'[14]

Spring had arrived, and promised summer. There came an afternoon in June when he took himself for a solitary walk in the sunshine and lay down in a bluebell wood, absorbing the warmth and beauty of the flowers. As he lay there something changed in his mind. 'I have been dying for nearly two-thirds of a year,' he said to himself, 'and I have died enough.'[15] And with that he announced to the Burtons he would be departing for London the next day.

He had two halves of a five-pound note from his mother. With this he set off, telling no one what he was doing, to seek whatever work was going. He took a cheap lodging in Holborn and failed to find a job of any kind. He had nothing worth pawning – his socks were in holes, his waterproof collar was disintegrating, and his brain was entirely preoccupied by the struggle to find some way of supporting himself. Hungry and lonely, he sent off a postcard to his old college friend Jennings, who came to the rescue at once. He was lecturing in biology and gave Wells work copying diagrams for slides sold to medical students. Better still, Jennings got him a reader's ticket for the British Museum Reading Room, which was always warm, and also open seven days a week. Sundays were bad for the lonely in London, stretching miserably, the only places of refuge St Paul's Cathedral – and, once you had a ticket, the Museum Reading Room, with its comfortable chairs and comforting, headachy air.

With some money in his pocket at last, he wrote to his cousin Isabel. He was invited to return to lodge with her and his aunt, now living at No. 12 Fitzroy Road near Primrose Hill, and affectionately welcomed. Now he made the brilliant discovery that he could earn further small sums by writing quiz questions for cheap papers like *Tit-Bits* – a weekly magazine founded in 1881, costing a penny – and quickly realized he could earn slightly larger sums by submitting answers that brought prize money. He visited his father, who was drinking too much – Wells described him as an alcoholic savage – although he seems to have returned to relative sobriety after this, and there were no further complaints from his son.

At last Wells began to put on weight. He spoke in his old college Debating Society (subject: 'Are the Planets Habitable?'). He thought of joining the Fabian Society, but hesitated. He was very far from any steady job or financial security. At Christmas 1888 he chose to return to Uppark: whether to show off his improved health, or simply because it was a sort of home, safe, warm and familiar.

6. 'For a young man to marry . . .'

At Fitzroy Road the relationship between Wells and his cousin Isabel was resumed. They now called it an informal engagement. She was as lovely to look at as ever, and it was a mixture of pleasure and torment for him to be living in close proximity to a girl he found acutely desirable. She neither reciprocated nor even acknowledged his sexual longing except as something to be kept at bay: only a wedding made sex permissible. He had 'a gnawing desire to marry' – that is, to possess her sexually – but he could not afford marriage. Instead he had to live with the distress and humiliation of unfulfilled lust. One experience with a prostitute did nothing to cheer him up. He had no idea that love-making may need care and practice. What he wanted was a passionate engagement of two bodies, 'flame meeting flame'.[1]

A year before he had commented on a friend's marriage in one of his many letters to Elizabeth Healey: 'for a young man to marry, who admires Shelley, indicates mental weakness; for a young man to marry who is not rich indicates considerable mental decay.'[2] In the autumn of 1888 he had taken up the subject again to Healey, giving his view that engagements were 'a device of Mrs Grundy'. He went on, 'I object to marriage as a general thing. The way in which two people after half a dozen weeks intercourse will bind themselves to burden and bore each other for the rest of their days, is perfectly disgusting to me . . . 99 per cent of marriages end in revolt or passive endurance.'

His views and his behaviour were in conflict. Driven by sexual pressure, he decided he had no alternative but to go through the forms he despised. Isabel remained obliviously conventional in her attitudes and wishes, looking forward to a church wedding, which was not considered necessary by Wells. Later he wrote a scathingly funny account of how women force men into conventional weddings: 'when a woman says you must do this or that – must have a cake at a wedding, for instance, you must do that. It is a kind of privilege they have – the categorical imperative.' Wells chafed and worried, and there was no immediate prospect of marriage.[3] It continued, 'Why should a sane healthy woman be covered up in white gauze like the confectionery in a shop window?' And later, in his novel *Tono-Bungay* (1909), he wrote a devastating account of a formal London wedding.

Happily, he at last found steady and enjoyable work as a science teacher in an excellent private school for boys, Henley House School, in Kilburn. The job advertised was to teach science, maths, drawing and scripture; and when he went for an interview the headmaster, John Milne, took to him at once and saw his quality. When Wells explained that he could not teach scripture because he was not a believer, Milne accepted this without fuss. He even invited him to become a resident master, which Wells turned down, explaining that he would be working in all his spare time for his Bachelor of Science degree from the University of London External Programme, and for a teaching diploma. Milne was again understanding.

Unlike many headmasters Milne genuinely liked boys – he had three sons of his own – and set out to cultivate their characters without crushing their individuality or imagination; and at the same time he was supportive to his teachers. This made the school a cheerful place. 'There was a great deal of laughter and happiness at Henley House,' wrote the biographer of his youngest son, A. A. Milne.[4] Wells began teaching there in January 1889 and was paid £60 a year.

Milne's sons soon shared their father's liking for their new schoolmaster. A. A. was only seven when Wells began to teach him, and in his view Wells went rather too fast as he led the boys swiftly into algebra, then to fractions and on to quadratic equations; but most of his pupils enjoyed the lessons and learnt well, and A. A. liked Wells even as he struggled. Since there was no equipment for science, he taught it all from the blackboard, and also extended the boys' knowledge by taking them on expeditions: to the Zoo and the Tower, to the South Kensington Museum (it became the Victoria and Albert Museum in 1899), and to Primrose Hill to examine the strata. There is no doubt of his being an unusually gifted and effective teacher.

Mrs Milne organized the school lunches and, having noticed how very thin the new teacher was, she encouraged him to eat heartily. As he ate, he admired the vases of flowers she put on the dining tables, something he had never seen done before. Flowers spoke to Wells: he liked to be sent them – 'half a dozen primroses . . . even better than a poem', he remarked of some. His mother posted parcels of snow-drops to him. Flowers were part of the appeal of Uppark – in April 1890 he told her he was coming to visit her there to spend 'a couple of nights and see the wild flowers'.

He now put aside his disapproval of formal engagements, and he and Isabel became officially engaged. He asked his brother Fred for a loan of his evening clothes so that he could celebrate by taking Isabel out to an ''aughty art sworry' at the South Kensington Museum, for which he needed to be formally dressed. He calls her 'the young woman whom it is his exalted function to "take around" and "trot about"'. He goes on, 'You will see that we have married' – a joke to shock his brother, or a piece of wishful thinking.[5] He does not give Isabel a voice in his letters, and perhaps she did not have much to say: she does not emerge as a character. But, when it came to sex, and marriage, she could impose her will on him.

In the same month the household moved along Fitzroy Road, to No. 46. He was preparing for another University of London examin-ation, which he took in July, achieving Second-Class Honours in zoology. He was also 'writing fitfully at various schemes for stories, though I have been at it for two years or more, now, there is all to learn in the art of fiction. But, failing death, I mean to learn it, & that learnt, to write and print, and printing, to succeed and sell.'[6] A won-derfully accurate forecast to have made.

Yet again, he makes you wonder how he managed to take on so much. Although he said he did not want a seaside holiday, he was persuaded by Isabel and his aunt to spend a few days in August at

Whitstable on the Kentish coast. He kept working, because he was writing a thesis on Friedrich Fröbel, while also preparing for more exams, to get a teaching diploma from the College of Preceptors.[7] Wells did extremely well in the exams, carrying off three prizes, and with this success Milne raised his salary and let him cut down his teaching hours at Henley House. He was twenty-three in September, still slim, now sporting a wispy moustache – and he had reached his final height of five feet, seven and a half inches.

More work opportunities came in the new year – 1890 – when he was invited to Cambridge for an interview with William Briggs, the pioneering organizer of the University Correspondence College – effectively the precursor of the Open University. Briggs offered Wells good money to take on correspondence tuition in biology, and also to give classes in London, in a laboratory in 'Booksellers' Row', as Wells called it, off St Martin's Lane. This was irresistible. Wells soon saw that he was being asked to do little more than push his pupils through exams, giving them a 'sterilized abbreviation' of what Huxley's course had taught him. But, in spite of his doubts about the value of such cramming, he was a conscientious teacher and his students appreciated his classes, his lectures and demonstrations. He was remembered as a painstaking and sympathetic teacher.[8]

The tutoring work was much better paid than school teaching, and John Milne, ever understanding, allowed him to cut down his hours still further. In March he was elected Fellow of the Zoological Society; at Easter he took himself to Uppark to see the flowers – and his mother. In May Milne proudly printed Wells's examination successes in the school magazine. Although he had lost him as a teacher – Wells resigned in June – their friendship remained. The autumn was taken up with further exams, Wells at last achieving First-Class Honours in zoology, then sitting more papers for the College of Preceptors.

But in December he had once again to pay the price for all his hard work and success. Although he had put on weight – he had reached eight stone, five pounds – he had also overstrained his strength, and an attack of influenza led to congestion of the right lung and another

haemorrhage. He was out of action and in danger again. Someone let
Dr Collins know, and he immediately arranged for Wells to be taken
to Uppark to be nursed. He was there for a month. Dr Collins
reassured him, telling him he still believed in his ultimate recovery.

Rest, warmth, reassurance, good care and relative solitude gave him
time to think, and to set down some of his thoughts on science in an
essay called 'The Rediscovery of the Unique'. In it he laid out his
belief that Charles Darwin and Alfred Russel Wallace had led all scientists away from the 'clockwork thought of the 17th and 18th
centuries':

> The neat little picture of a universe of souls made up of passions and
> principles in bodies made of atoms, all put together so neatly and
> wound up at the creation, fades in the series of dissolving views that
> we call the march of human thought. We no longer believe, whatever
> creed we may affect, in a Deity whose design is so foolish and little
> that even a theological bishop can trace it and detect a kindred soul . . .
> we have no reason at all to expect life beyond this planet.

For Wells, religious faith provided no better answer to the question
'What is life?' than either biology or physics did. At the same time he
concluded his essay with a paragraph warning against expecting too
much of science, in elegant and lyrical prose:

> Science is a match that man has just got alight. He thought he was in
> a room – in moments of devotion, a temple – and that his light would
> be reflected from and display walls inscribed with wonderful secrets
> and pillars carved with philosophical systems wrought into harmony.
> It is a curious sensation, now that the preliminary flutter is over and
> the flame burns up clear, to see his hands lit and just a glimpse of him-
> self and the patch he stands on visible, and around him, in place of all
> that human comfort and beauty he anticipated – darkness still.

He sent the article to Frank Harris, editor of the *Fortnightly Review*.
Harris was impressed and printed it in July 1891. Oscar Wilde praised
it, and Wells was invited to see Harris. He sent him another article,

'The Universe Rigid', an outline of a four-dimensional space–time system, which Harris found totally incomprehensible. But the contact had been made, and in September Wells sent Harris some of his serial story 'The Chronic Argonauts', which he was rewriting, asking for advice on publication.

Before that, in May, he had again suffered congestion of the right lung and another haemorrhage and had to cut down his working hours. Dr Collins prescribed Uppark once more, so for three weeks he was able to rest and enjoy its pure and bracing air and the views over Sussex in its green summer glory. The life of the household was not lively. Of the two old ladies, Miss Sutherland was now eighty-five and Miss Fetherstonhaugh seventy-four; and her agent, now Sir William King – he had been knighted in 1889 – was less disposed than ever to favour Mrs Wells as housekeeper. As she approached seventy, she was losing whatever grip she had on her position in the household. Wells was aware of the situation and warned his brother Fred later in the year, 'It will strengthen the Mater's position if we stand off from Uppark this Christmas.'[9]

His three-week stay in June 1891 was his last. For eleven years he had come and gone, even calling Uppark home to one friend: 'I had to come home to save my life and now I am living, artificially heated like an incubating chick,' he had written to Davies from Uppark in 1887.[10]

He had enjoyed and learnt from everything it offered him. There was the beauty of the landscape where he could feel ecstatically 'I was Pan – the great Pan – one with the brown earth, the blue ever changing sky – the rich grass and the distant hillsides.'[11] There were the books, a priceless collection for him to read at his leisure, in the attic or carefully snitched from Repton's gilded bookshelves in the saloon. There was the luxurious elegance of the saloon, there were the several parlours, the drawing room and dining room, all glimpsed occasionally over the years. There were the gardens in which he delighted, and the Christmas parties when he danced and celebrated with the servants. Above all, it was the place where he was nursed and fed when his life hung in the balance, brought back from death's door to be able to work, teach and write – and now to be married at last. He gave thanks where he thought them due: 'I thank God I am not as other Pulmonaries; I weigh 8 stone 8 lbs as against 8.4 a fortnight ago & 8 when you saw me. I cough not neither do I ache. For which, & for other mercies, let me thank GOD (& Collins).'[12]

He did not see Uppark again for more than forty years. In November 1936 he visited it at the invitation of Admiral Sir Herbert Meade Fetherstonhaugh and his wife, Margaret, daughter of the Bishop of Peterborough: Uppark had passed to them in 1931. Wells wrote to his brother Fred, 'the old place is very like it used to be and the park and gardens hardly changed at all.'[13] He seems not to have known that Lady Meade Fetherstonhaugh was already embarked on the process of cleaning and restoring the much neglected interior of Uppark. Hers was a work of cultural heroism that he would have appreciated, given his view that, even though such houses relied on a toiling class to maintain them, out of them 'came the first museums and laboratories and picture galleries, gentle manners, good writing and nearly all that is worth while in our civilization today'.[14]

Isabel had agreed on a date for their marriage and found a house for them to rent for thirty pounds a year in Wandsworth, brick-built with eight rooms on three floors, and a small garden.[15] Wells was twenty-five in September 1891, and he moved into the house in preparation for the wedding, which took place on 29 October, at Wandsworth parish church, All Saints, in the High Street. Their witnesses were Isabel's mother, who was very happy, and Wells's brother Frank, who burst into tears in the vestry. No friends or further family appear to have been invited, or turned up. It was a modest occasion, and, whatever Wells's objections to the ritual and fuss, it was full of joyous anticipation for him.

   There was no honeymoon and no flame meeting flame. Instead, a miserable fiasco – a reluctant young woman, embarrassed and afraid, succumbing to an uncontrollably ardent husband who gave her no pleasure but forced himself into her, reducing her to wretchedness and tears. This may not have been such an unusual start to marriage, although disappointment was possibly commoner than distaste and tears. He dried her tears, but he felt her reaction showed she did not love him. And so it was a still more bitterly wounding experience for him than it was for her.

Wells remained profoundly attached to Isabel – she never entirely lost her appeal for him – but he wanted to escape from the humiliation of his wedding night. Almost at once he embarked on infidelities: if he was not to have love as he craved it, he would opt for variety and sexual adventures. The most interesting fact about his early married life, as he wrote himself, was that he had been almost entirely faithful to her during the six years of their engagement – and that as soon as they were married he embarked on 'an enterprising promiscuity'.[16]

This set the pattern for the rest of his life. He had more sexual disappointments, and he also met women who responded as he hoped, flame meeting flame. He was extremely attractive to women – his last lover said his body smelt deliciously of honey – and when he set out to charm he could be the best of companions, fun to be with, inventive and generous. He also became rich, which makes it easier to meet and woo women. Throughout his life he had long and passionate affairs, and he also enjoyed many casual sexual encounters. Would all this have been different if Isabel had responded as he hoped? Probably not: but the young Wells who had served six years for his bride was transformed then and there into the Wells who felt entitled to seek and enjoy sexual intercourse whenever, wherever and with whom he pleased.

7.   More Blood

Some sort of attempt was made at marriage. Isabel was 'the head of the household', Wells joked, running things at home while he commuted into London to teach his students comparative anatomy in the laboratory at the tutorial college in Booksellers' Row. When he was at home their conversational exchanges were not much better than their attempts at sex. She could not understand why he was always questioning what she regarded as normal attitudes, why he complained about existing institutions and expressed exasperation with conventional views: 'making a fuss', she called it. Talk dried up as a result. Then, although he was eager for his friends to meet her, she was reluctant, on the grounds that they were clever and knew how to talk, and she did not. She was not a reader either. In any case he spent much of his time at home absorbed in work, turning out articles for the *Educational Times*. He had also taken on the task of writing two science textbooks.

Still, they took exercise together. He joined the Cyclists' Touring Club, bought tricycles and persuaded Isabel to join him in energetic tricycling at weekends. He mentions that they smashed up one machine and bought another, and managed to make a twenty-five-mile trip in May 1892. None of these adventures did much for the emptiness between them. In December 1893 he told Davies – who was also getting married – that 'I have been in very great trouble all the past year', because his own marriage had been 'a very great mistake'. He said he still loved his wife tenderly, 'but not as a husband should love his wife' – without further elaboration.[1]

A new friend, Walter Low, cheered him. They had met through William Briggs and the tutorial work: Low was two years older than Wells, a member of the Fabian Society and formidably clever. He was the son of a Jewish scholar who had been driven to leave

Hungary by anti-Semitism in 1848, one of a large and gifted family that had lost its money. Forced to leave school at sixteen, he had by sheer hard work and private study got himself degrees in French and German; he had also taught himself Norwegian and translated two novels by a Norwegian writer.[2] He was a literary intellectual of a kind Wells had not met before, and the friendship quickly became important to him. The two of them made time to walk the streets of London together, sharpening their wits as they talked before taking the evening Underground to their respective homes. Low lived in West Kensington and was also married, with three small daughters. He taught Wells a good deal about journalism and reviewing techniques, for which Wells was grateful.

Both of them suffered from the fact that, for all the hard work they had put in, they had not yet been able to get on to the ladder of success, but were still struggling – and both were ambitious to become good writers, and well aware of the difficulties of combining hack work with that ambition. Low was being given fifty pounds a year by Briggs to edit the *Educational Times*, a weekly he had set up for the College of Preceptors. And since Low was allowed another fifty pounds for payments to contributors, he decided that Wells could write all the contributions, and paid him the fifty pounds accordingly. Soon Wells was also editing Briggs's house journal for the students, the *University Correspondent*.

Although he and Low did not talk about their private lives in any detail, Wells had the impression that Low was also finding that marriage was not all he had hoped for – that for neither of them relations between the sexes were living up to what romantic literature had led them to expect. Low had been obliged to marry his wife, Alice, a colonel's daughter, when she became pregnant. He and Wells were dissatisfied with their lives.

Of the two books Wells was working on, one – *Honours Physiography* – was written in collaboration with his friend Richard Gregory, already embarked on a distinguished career: they sold it to a publisher outright for twenty pounds, taking half each. Both books were aimed at the type of students he was teaching, and the other, *A Text-book of Biology*, was all his own work. He called it hack work, but it is sharply written and reads well. Assuring his reader that a well-boiled rabbit is easy to take apart, he insists that you need to see the bones, and lists the instruments necessary for dissection. Frogs, dogfish and other creatures and plants are dealt with, and the specialized vocabulary required for such investigations is given. He recommends further reading, and provides a section on Evolution. For the first edition, published in July 1893, he drew the illustrations himself – he had them redone for the second. The book evidently filled a need and remained in print for thirty years.

In November 1892 Mrs Wells was given notice by her mistress, with a cheque for £100. She at once started looking for another position, but she was too old and too deaf, and she had no success. For the moment she clung stubbornly on at Uppark. In December the tutorial college moved to better premises in Red Lion Square, and a new batch of students arrived. There were several young women among them and one, a slight, fair-haired girl in mourning, caught Wells's attention and held it. Amy Catherine Robbins, she was called, and she was quick and clever, and planning to become a teacher. Delicately pretty, with fine features and dark eyes, she was also ready to talk freely, about her studies and, as Wells soon discovered, about the issues of the day: socialism, the emancipation of women, marriage, politics. She was only twenty and she seemed a new type of woman to him, open-minded and adventurous.

She had just lost her father in upsetting circumstances – he had been run over by a train at Putney Station, and it looked as though it might have been suicide. She was now living with her widowed mother. Wells soon found out that they both took the District Line, and they began to travel together when they could. They talked and talked, as perhaps neither of them had ever done before so freely with a newly encountered member of the opposite sex; his friendship with Elizabeth Healey was kept up almost entirely through letters, and after five years he still addressed her as Miss Healey; and his encounter with the attractive schoolteacher in Holt had lasted barely more than a week. Amy Robbins was the first well-educated young woman with whom he formed an intimate face-to-face relationship.

Meanwhile, life continued as before, with family problems. Christmas came, and brother Frank spent it with them. In January 1893 their mother was again told she must leave Uppark, which she did finally in mid-February, taking refuge with Wells and Isabel until April, then rejoining her husband in his cottage at Nyewood. In April brother Fred, dismissed by the draper who employed him, took up their spare bedroom, hoping to find a job in London. Wells proposed various possibilities but nothing worked out. Wells then suggested he might emigrate to South Africa to make a new career there. Fred thought about it.

Wells was now effectively the head of the family. He opened his first bank account. In April he took Isabel to visit his parents, whom he was helping financially. In May everything changed again. On the evening of the seventeenth, having worked late with a geology student after his day's teaching, he set off for home at about nine. This is what happened:

> . . . hurrying down the slope of Villiers St to Charing Cross Underground Station, with a heavy bag of specimens, I was seized by a fit of coughing. Once more I tasted blood and felt the dismay that had become associated with it and when I had got into the train I pulled out my handkerchief and found it stained brightly scarlet. I coughed alone in the dingy compartment and tried not to cough, sitting very still and telling myself it was nothing very much, until at last I got to Putney Bridge. Then it had stopped. I was hungry when I got home and as I did not want to be sent to bed forthwith, I hid my tell-tale handkerchief and would not even look at it myself because I wanted to believe that I had coughed up nothing but a little discoloured phlegm, and I made a hearty supper. It was unendurable to think that I was to have yet another relapse, that I should have to stop work again. I got to bed all right. At three o'clock in the morning I was trying for dear life not to cough. But this time the blood came and

seemed resolved to choke me for good and all. This was no skirmish; this was a grand attack.

I remember the candle-lit room, the dawn breaking through presently, my wife and my aunt in nightgowns and dressing-gowns, the doctor hastily summoned and attention focused upon a basin in which there was blood and blood and more blood. Sponge-bags of ice were presently adjusted to my chest but I kept on disarranging them to sit up for a further bout of coughing. I suppose I was extremely near death that night, but I remember only my irritation at the thought that this would prevent my giving a lecture I had engaged myself to give on the morrow. The blood stopped before I did. I was presently spread out under my ice-bags, still and hardly breathing, but alive.[3]

A better piece of descriptive prose would be hard to find. There is a sort of exhilaration to the telling that fixes every detail in the reader's mind, as though experiencing it yourself. After reading it for the first time, I felt I knew exactly what it is to haemorrhage from the lung until you are nearly dead. I also saw that Wells could write as well as any of his contemporaries, and better than many.

The doctor ordered starvation for a week. Wells found himself with a brain cleared of bother and a beautiful sense of irresponsibility. Nothing mattered, he knew – he might write or he might die – but there would be no more teaching. His first thin slice of bread and butter was a great event.

A week later Fred left for South Africa. Wells sent a letter to Healey letting her know he could not go on teaching but was not dead yet, although still lying on his back. Another letter went to Amy, telling her he must now write for his living – and asking her to visit him. By 28 May he could sit up.

He agreed with Isabel that they should go to Eastbourne for two weeks' convalescence. Once there, he happened on a book by J. M. Barrie in which he found advice to aspirant writers – not to aim too high, not to try to be original or give their theories of life, but just to write about ordinary things and simple events – which is what readers want. Obediently, Wells wrote 'On the Art of Staying at the

Seaside' – and sold it to the *Pall Mall Gazette*, which had until now turned down everything he offered. The piece appeared in August and he was launched. 'In a couple of months I was earning more money than I had ever done in my class-teaching days. It was absurd.'[4] Sixteen of his pieces appeared that year. It happened that Barrie read one of them, found it entertaining and asked the editor of the *PMG* who had written it. They wanted more from him, Wells asked to be given some reviewing as well and found himself earning still more.

In July his *Text-book of Biology* was published. In August he agreed with Isabel that they should move to Sutton in Surrey, to be able to breathe the fresher air of the North Downs, although still in a suburban semi-detached. He heard that Amy had achieved a First in her examination results. She was also, at his request, redrawing the illustrations for the *Text-book of Biology*, which was to be reissued in December.

In October he was ill again, just avoiding another haemorrhage. He wrote to Amy, 'this lung of mine is the greatest affliction ever human being had . . . I am resolved I will have very little more of this annoyance. I will breathe with gills. Perhaps it would be easier to go abroad after all. I have a horrible vision of the rest of my life, flying from England.'[5] He also told Milne that he was thinking of moving abroad, 'somewhere colds cease from troubling in winter', and living by his pen.[6]

In mid-December he took Isabel to visit Amy and her mother in Putney. At this point Isabel decided he was in love with Amy and told him he must choose between them. Wells said afterwards that he chose Amy because they were such good companions and both keen to turn accepted moral notions upside down. They were pioneers, they did not believe in marriage and had no intention of marrying. All that was doubtless true, but he was also in love with her. He asked Isabel to divorce him and she agreed. It all happened with amazing speed. He left with a trunk of belongings, Isabel moved to Hampstead, and that was that.

He told his family and friends that the separation from Isabel was entirely his fault, and together he and Amy defied Mrs Robbins's attempt, backed by various male relatives called in to speak to Wells, to make them at least wait for a decent period – until he was divorced and they could marry. But they had no intention of marrying, they said, and in January 1894 they moved together into rooms in North London, at No. 7, Mornington Place, Camden Town. He did not let his parents know until February.

The two lovers saw themselves as partners, but there was never any doubt about which of them was the dominant force. He disliked Amy's names – Amy Catherine – and told her he was going to give her a different name. First it was 'Euphemia' – which was probably a joke – then it was 'Jane'. Jane suited her, he said. She herself did not much like Amy, but it was a high-handed act by Wells: it was not a matter of pet names, of which they had many – Bits, Miss Bits, Snith, Bins and Mr Bins for him. If she had reservations she put them aside – she still called herself Catherine to some friends – but a pattern was set, of his wishes determining the course of their lives.

8.   *The Time Machine*

There was no honeymoon or even a holiday: this was to be a work-ing life. Their rooms were in a house built so close to the main line railway into Euston that the air was never free of smoke from the trains, floating in black flakes that settled on clothes, on hair, on skin, on everything. They had two rooms, divided by folding doors, a living room at the front and a bedroom behind – no bathroom, just a tub on the floor to wash in. Their papers and books were kept in boxes. Jane made toast on the open fire, her fair hair put into a neat plait when she got up in the morning. Their landlady brought them up simple meals, and they ate at a small table lit by a paraffin lamp. The table was cleared for Wells to work on. He was writing columns and reviews, preparing a lecture on science teaching and starting on a new story about a vivisectionist. He wrote to Simmons saying, 'My short stories are going at last' – but he had less than a hundred pounds in capital (a substantial sum, however, by today's values). Jane was working too, studying for her degree. They entertained themselves by playing chess, and by walking in Regent's Park and on Hampstead Heath; concerts and theatres were beyond their means, and they saw few people. They talked and talked, the best of com-panions, in love and happy to be together, but both had to work hard and neither was very fit. The doctor they consulted prescribed red wine for Jane as a tonic.

During their first month Wells had a summons from William Henley, renowned as a poet, critic and editor, who had seen his work in the *Pall Mall Gazette* and wanted something from him for his paper, the *National Observer*. Wells cut up what he called 'the old corpse of the Chronic Argo' – the time-travel story he had written seven years earlier, and of which two instalments had been printed in the *Science Schools Journal* in the spring of 1888. He tinkered with it again, and

Henley ran it anonymously. It made almost no impression and ended after seven instalments, when Henley left the paper. But he maintained his interest in Wells, and was a friend well worth having, and himself a great example of triumph over adversity. He had been crippled early by tuberculosis of the bone, spent years in hospital and, now in his fifties, made a striking figure as he got around on one leg with a stick – Robert Louis Stevenson's Long John Silver was modelled on him. He was a good poet, best known for 'Invictus', with its grandly inspiring final lines,

> I am the master of my fate:
> I am the captain of my soul.

Fortunately for Wells, who was working on yet another version of his 'Chronic Argonauts', Henley was also about to become editor of another magazine, the *New Review*.

When Wells finally wrote to his mother in February, he told her he had separated from Isabel, blaming himself but giving no further explanation – he simply said, 'I am with very nice people here.'[1] In March he and Jane moved to No. 12 Mornington Road, now Mornington Terrace, still in Camden. While they were there, he had a science fiction story published under his name for the first time (in the *Pall Mall Budget*, an offshoot of the *Gazette*): it was called 'The Stolen Bacillus' and described a moment of imminent disaster for mankind – and then turns into a tease. He had no difficulty selling his short stories and he kept writing, and by the summer he was turning out from six to ten columns a month and getting two guineas a column.

In June he wrote to Elizabeth Healey informing her that 'I have done something rather dreadful – at least from the current feminine point of view' – saying he and Isabel had parted but not mentioning Jane. He suggested to Healey that such behaviour might make her want to end her correspondence with him – to which she replied at once with her usual friendliness.[2] Later he asked her for news of Isabel – to whom he had introduced her during their marriage – saying she told him little in her letters, and then suggested Healey might visit her, because he thought she needed friends. Whatever

Mornington Terrace

bitterness he had felt about the failure of their marriage, he went on feeling responsible for Isabel, and caring for her.[3]

Only in August did he write to his parents about 'Miss Robbins', and in doing so he told them that his intention was to marry her as soon as the divorce came through. This seems to be the first mention of marriage; perhaps he and Miss Robbins were already suffering from the disapproval of landladies, and Mrs Robbins is likely to have kept up pressure for marriage. He also told his father about his work, and assured him that, although things were 'a little tight', he expected them to get easier – and that he would continue to do his filial duty to his parents. This was a generous promise, because he did not yet feel secure financially. He added that his health was no longer giving him any trouble – no doubt because by then he and Jane had taken themselves to Sevenoaks to get away from the London heat. Her mother joined them there, evidently reconciled to the situation – perhaps at this point with the promise that they would marry.

He was working hard on what he now called *The Time Machine*. But there were distractions. The divorce writ arrived in the post for Wells, Jane put it in a drawer, and their landlady, who already disapproved of them, sneaked a look at it. After that Wells found himself writing, often in the late, hot, summer evening, against a background of shouted remarks about her disreputable lodgers, aimed at her neighbours over the garden wall, to which she added loud complaints addressed to Wells himself through his open window. Mrs Robbins fell ill, and Jane was upset and unhappy. For a writer the conditions could hardly have been more unpropitious. But he kept going and just managed to get to the end of his story.

Back in Camden in September, he sent the manuscript to Henley. As soon as Henley read it, he assured Wells that it was 'so full of invention . . . that it must certainly make you a reputation', and paid him a hundred pounds down. Then for a few months things continued much as before, with reviewing for Frank Harris's *Fortnightly Review*, negotiations to publish old articles in book form, a lecture on science teaching. But Wells had decided that *The Time Machine* was going to make or break him. He wrote to Healey telling her it was 'my trump card and if it does not come off very much I shall know my place for the rest of my career. Still we live in hope.'[4]

It did come off, with more éclat than could possibly have been expected. In January 1895, a freezing month of ice and snow, just as his divorce came through, the first instalment of *The Time Machine* appeared in the first issue of Henley's *New Review*. There was a stir of admiration and interest as soon as it began to be read – which did not prevent Wells from discovering he was about to go bankrupt, and saving himself by putting on a spurt of article-writing.[5] Then, in March, a notice in the *Review of Reviews* called Wells 'a man of genius'. In May Heinemann in London and Henry Holt in New York published it in book form: Heinemann paid an advance of fifty pounds and a royalty of fifteen per cent. Soon paperback editions appeared – ten thousand copies in England – and translations into French and other languages began to be set up.

This is no surprise to those who know it: I doubt if anyone forgets their first reading of *The Time Machine*. It presents a future world in vivid and often horrifying detail, through the description of a 'Time Traveller' – an English scientist living in suburban Richmond – as he relates his experiences to a group of friends, all professional men, comfortably gathered in his drawing room for conversation, as they usually did on Thursdays. He has quite a story to tell them. He has built a machine that will carry him into another dimension, past or future time, and after its first test what he has to tell of the way in which Evolution has changed mankind and the environment amazes his group of friends – as it amazes the readers of Wells's story. Bleak as it becomes – the human race has divided into two groups, one playful and idle hedonists, the other underground workers who prey on them – the force of the writer's imagination and the power of his narrative make reading it an irresistibly thrilling experience. And whether it was seen as an allegory or a myth, or simply as an extraordinarily effective adventure story, it was one that posited a world without God – something that the great majority of readers accepted readily and without comment, so compelling is the narrative. Not all did – the editor of the *Spectator* wrote of 'the religious factors in human nature which [Wells] appears to ignore'[6] – but the overwhelming response was simply to hail it as an extraordinary achievement and a work of genius. It has never lost its power, and has remained in print ever since. With it, Wells was on his way to becoming a world-famous writer. He had written a story that gripped and entertained readers, and then changed the way they saw and thought about the place of man in the scheme of things. If Darwin's account of Evolution encouraged a belief in progress and improvement, Wells offered a grim prospect for the future of mankind.

In that same January 1895, as the first instalment of *The Time Machine* appeared, Wells was invited to try his hand as a theatre critic by Harry Cust, newly appointed editor of the *Pall Mall Gazette*, which had recently been bought by William Waldorf Astor, the richest man in America, now settled in London. Success in journalism is often a thing of chance: Astor wanted to spend money on newspapers, and Cust was a great figure about town, a brilliant conversationalist, an Old Etonian, a Cambridge graduate, lover of many ladies, one-time barrister and MP – so why not editor of Astor's paper? And Cust, hearing good things about Wells, summoned him to his office and held out two tickets for the Haymarket. Wells felt he had to come clean about the fact that he had been to the theatre only twice in his life, to which Cust responded, 'Exactly what I want – you won't be in the gang.'[7]

The tickets were for the opening of Oscar Wilde's *An Ideal Husband* at the Haymarket. Wells knew that a male theatregoer was expected to wear a dress suit, something he did not possess. Undaunted, he hurried to a nearby tailor and persuaded him to make him one in twenty-four hours, and so, correctly attired, he appeared at the Oscar Wilde first night, and again two days later for another, Henry James's *Guy Domville*. This time he recognized Bernard Shaw, the only man in the audience wearing an ordinary brown suit: Wells had heard him speak at socialist meetings ten years earlier. Henry James's play was a flop, he was booed and hissed, and went out into the night white-faced. But what an occasion: Wells and Shaw fell into conversation and left together, both for lodgings in North London. Shaw was ten years older than Wells, had failed as a novelist, enjoyed his first success in the theatre with *Arms and the Man* in 1894, and had another good play, *Mrs Warren's Profession*, banned. He was still a bachelor, and he talked to Wells like an elder brother. It was the start of a friendship that was sometimes bumpy but would last for fifty years – Shaw would outlive Wells by four years.

As a theatre critic Wells lasted little more than two months. He caught a cold and started coughing blood again, so prudently asked to review books instead, which could be read at home. He was soon in better health, and paid due tribute to the theatre with his 'Sad Story of a Dramatic Critic' – a preposterous account of a critic who finds himself infected by what he has seen on stage, gesturing, posing and enunciating as actors do – and losing his exasperated girlfriend as a result.[8]

He was already reviewing for Frank Harris, and now more batches of novels arrived in Mornington Street – in March he complained of fourteen being delivered at once. As well as the usual dross, he covered many brilliant books over the next two years, including two by Conrad, *Almayer's Folly* and *An Outcast of the Islands* ('perhaps the finest piece of fiction that has been published this year, as *AF* was one of the finest published in 1895').[9] Also a collection of short stories by Henry James (*Terminations*), Stevenson's unfinished last novel, *Weir of Hermiston*, Grant Allen's *The Woman Who Did* and work by Barrie, George Gissing and Stephen Crane, the dazzling young American author of *The Red Badge of Courage*. He hailed Thomas Hardy's *Jude the Obscure* as 'a book that alone will make 1895 a memorable year in the history of literature', and returned to it in a second notice, describing Jude's voice as that of 'the educated proletarian' and welcoming the account of his failure to get near any higher education as 'a tremendous indictment of English universities'. He must also have seen it as a painfully realistic account of the conflict between sexual fulfilment and the pursuit of education, a subject he would soon take up himself in a novel to be called *Love and Mr Lewisham*.

*

In the midst of his new success Wells lost a good friend: while he had escaped his unsatisfactory marriage and put a foot firmly on the ladder of success, Walter Low had no such luck. An attack of flu in the bitter winter weather, when he was already run down but still working as hard as ever, weakened him further; pneumonia followed, he got no proper medical care and died, in February 1895. He was only thirty. No doubt Wells was reminded of his own vulnerability as he grieved for his friend. He offered some financial help to the family, and wrote to Healey, mentioning Low's three little daughters and saying that the death seemed 'the most ghastly travesty of all the good I had thought of the world . . . However, it is no good howling.'[10] He remembered Low with respect and affection, and years later met his remarkable eldest daughter Ivy.[11]

Wells's spirits naturally rose through the spring of 1895 as the favourable reviews of *The Time Machine* piled up. On a good day he even told his friend Simmons that he was 'in a gorgeous state of cockiness'.[12] He offered to take his mother to the theatre, suggesting *High Life Below Stairs*, a farce about servants once played by Garrick, to remind her of her years at Uppark: whether they got to see it we don't know. In April he and Jane went to the seaside in Devon for a working break. In May, when *The Time Machine* was published in book form, they moved to a rented house in Woking in the outer suburbs of Surrey, to have cleaner air and more space.

For some years he had been a keen tricyclist, and now he bought himself a bicycle and taught himself, with many bumps, scrapes and bruises, to ride it. He used the experience to write another short comic novel, *The Wheels of Chance*, about young Mr Hoopdriver, a shop assistant who decides to use his ten days of summer holiday to bicycle through Surrey, Sussex and Hampshire, and encounters an adventurous middle-class young woman needing help to escape from the married man she has rather too innocently run away with. It is a story about social class as much as bicycling, pitched between fun and melancholy – a light read, but an enjoyable and even original one. In real life Wells acquired a special tandem on which Jane could sit in front while he did the pedal work behind her.

A collection of his own early humorous columns called *Select Conversations with an Uncle* was published in June by John Lane, and more publishers and editors now approached him with offers and requests. He kept working at what seems an impossible rate, producing stories so varied one might easily think they came from a team of writers. His scientific education led him to speculation and fantasy that kept readers excited and amazed. He was already at work on *The Island of Doctor Moreau*, published in April 1896. It is centred on a brilliant and evil scientist who plays God, cutting up and reconstructing the wild animals he has brought to the isolated island he inhabits, his aim being apparently to transform them into semi-human creatures: they worship and fear him. Some early reviewers found *Doctor Moreau* disgusting and perversely sensational, while others saw it as a parable criticizing the presumption of science or even a criticism of the dealings of God in allowing his creation to suffer. Hostile reviews did not stop it selling. Wells's fiction reads like reporting of things seen, touched and heard. *Doctor Moreau* is an upsetting story and I still hesitate before returning to it, but when I do I find that its narrative power holds me again, in spite of my reluctance.

There was a period when he was turning out seven thousand words a day.[13] This was while he was engaged on *Doctor Moreau*, reviewing novels and writing another novel, *The Wonderful Visit*, about an angel who flies over a Sussex village somewhat resembling Harting, the village at the foot of the hill on which Uppark stands.

And it was from Uppark that news of a death came in June: that of his mother's old employer, Frances Fetherstonhaugh, who died in the great house at the age of seventy-eight. She had chosen as her heir the suitably well-born Colonel The Hon. Keith Turnour, who was granted the Fetherstonhaugh arms and lived quietly at Uppark for the next thirty-five years, during which Wells made no attempt to revisit the place that had meant so much to him.

*

In September *The Wonderful Visit* was published – with a dedication 'To the memory of my dear friend, Walter Low'. Low would have been entertained – it is a witty story. Wells may have been inspired by Ruskin's remark that an angel appearing on Earth would be shot on sight, and he took a tone quite unlike that of his science fiction, partly comic and partly sorrowful. 'I set out to jest,' he told Walter's brother Sidney, 'and the deeper applications are by the way.'[14] The angel flying over Sussex is shot down by a vicar who happens to be an ornithologist keen to add to his collection, and he falls to Earth with a broken wing, to become the guest of the vicar. Everything has to be explained to him, and in explaining himself the vicar is led to confess that he scarcely believes any of the things he tells his parishioners, about life or death or behaviour; and that he does what he does only because 'it would never do to alter' anything he has always said and done. The angel finds it very strange that the vicar does and says things he does not believe in, and the vicar begins to doubt himself.

Other people the angel meets are upset by his logical thinking and his views, which are clearly those of a dangerous socialist. Wells does not spare the grand inhabitants of the big house, and the angel finds himself most at ease with the vicar's little housemaid. In due course the angel is dealt with. Readers eager for Wells's science fiction were disappointed, but another writer, Arnold Bennett, as yet unknown to him, later praised his moral and imaginative gift for seeing things afresh as no one had seen them before. He described the book as 'the most perfect and delightful thing he has yet accomplished'. Bennett saw that Wells's intention was 'to criticize the social fabric, to demand of each part of it the reason for its existence, and in default of a reply, to laugh it out of existence'.[15]

Wells and Jane moved briefly back to Camden to be married at St Pancras Register Office on 27 October 1895, with Richard Gregory as witness and no fuss. They then returned to Woking. Wells remained healthy and had now reached a good weight, just over nine stone. He was thinking up his next big science fiction story, *The War of the*

Worlds. Jane made fair copies of his work, and soon he was also sending some to a paid typist. He would not acquire a typewriter until 1899, when he bought one for Jane, declared it unusable and immediately learnt to use it himself, just to show he could. At the end of 1895 he reckoned he had earned between five and six hundred pounds, and could expect to make more in 1896.

9. 'Uncommonly cheerful and hopeful'

In January 1896 Wells started work on a short novel about the invasion of Earth by Martians seeking more space: *The War of the Worlds*. He had thought about the possibility of there being life on Mars from time to time, and now his brother Frank gave him the idea for a story. They were talking together about Tasmania, and the disaster the arrival of the Europeans had been for its people, who were annihilated – and this led Frank to suggest that Wells might describe what would happen to the human race if creatures from Mars, wanting more space, should arrive on Earth to colonize it.

So Wells was inspired to begin on his story. His Martians are nothing like humans – more like brains in tall metal walking machines – and they are not friendly, as is quickly made clear. They are out to destroy human beings. He enjoyed placing their first arrival on Earth and the subsequent action not too far from the Woking house in which he and Jane were currently living, and mischievously told Elizabeth Healey how he had set out to 'completely wreck and destroy Woking, killing my neighbours in painful and eccentric ways – then proceed via Kingston and Richmond to London, which I sack, selecting South Kensington for feats of peculiar atrocity'.[1] His story is much more than mischief, of course. The behaviour of the invading Martians is unpredictable and horrific, as they lay waste to much of Surrey and kill its inhabitants, en masse and individually. One of the many great descriptive passages is of the panic-stricken crowds fleeing along the main roads out of London as the Martians reach town – it reads like a forecast of the crowds fleeing from Paris in 1940. Wells lets us see London almost three dimensionally and engages our emotions with what seems effortless skill. The virtuosity of the narrative and, once again, the scope and detail of the imagination that drive it on make this every bit as compelling as *The Time Machine*.

As he embarked on writing *The War of the Worlds*, he had a letter from a newly established literary agent, James Pinker, offering his services. Although Wells was already signed up with the agent A. P. Watt, he sent Pinker an outline of the story, and Pinker saw at once how remarkable it was. Wells let him take over, and he set to work immediately on fixing good deals for serialization in England and America. This became a very slow process, because Wells kept rewriting throughout 1896 – while working on several other projects – and serialization did not begin until 1897. He even added a new episode for the first English edition, in January 1898, introducing the character of the Artilleryman, who believes that civilization is finished – 'Cities, nations, civilization, progress – it's all over' – and proposes an underground opposition to fight the Martians. He is an interesting character, with his faith in single-minded violence, but an irrelevance as things turn out. The book is strongest on mass reactions and terror. As one critic remarked, you experience the story 'not as romance, but as realism'. The last pages are among his most brilliant – fiction using scientific knowledge to produce its effect, and a poetic imagination that engages the imagination and the heart of the reader.

An early review described Wells as a writer working in the tradition of Swift and with the skill of Defoe – higher praise could scarcely be given.[2] Another reviewer wrote of the imaginative vigour of the story, its fidelity to life and subtlety in suggesting, and not obtruding, moral ideas. There were some unfavourable notices too: an early American review objected to the journalistic style in which it was written and predicted that it was doomed to be quickly forgotten. The public saw otherwise. Like *The Time Machine*, *The War of the Worlds* has never gone out of print – and has attracted ever more admiration as the years have gone by – and not a few screen versions, none of which get near Wells's narrative skill.

To many it must have looked as though Wells had established himself as a writer with enviable speed and ease. The truth was of course not that. He was thirty in September 1896, and only after this did he have a room of his own in which to work, for the first time in his life. It says much for his determination and for Jane's discretion. Early in

1896 he settled his parents into a pretty house at Liss, six miles from Uppark – he told Fred it had seven rooms and a garden and would be comfortable for 'the old folks'; and he thanked them for his success and assured them they were responsible for the beginnings of it, having given him paper and pencils and brought him books. Given that they had done their best to deprive him of the education he had so passionately desired, these were generous words. He was also planning to instal Frank in a shop of his own, his pursuit of freedom not having turned out as well as he had hoped. But in one respect at least Frank had triumphed: Wells dedicated *The War of the Worlds* to him with an acknowledgement that he owed the idea to him.

From month to month his professional life was growing more complicated and demanding. He did not simplify it by using several agents. A. P. Watt was currently handling *Doctor Moreau* for him, but for now Pinker was in the ascendant. Born in the 1860s like Wells, he had little formal education and had acquired literary tastes and experience as a magazine editor publishing short stories – which no doubt brought Wells to his attention. He started building a list, working from a showy office off the Strand, and he quickly did well: a photograph depicts him seated at his desk, cigarette in mouth, spotted bow tie, sharp haircut and smart suit, with a book open in front of him. He had an eye for promising authors and a readiness to make friends with them: Joseph Conrad, Henry James, Oscar Wilde, D. H. Lawrence, John Galsworthy, George Gissing all became his clients. His home was in Worcester Park, Surrey, where Wells's friend and patron Henley was a neighbour, and presently Henley himself advised Wells to let his work be 'Pinkerized'. The next thing that happened was that Pinker found a house for Wells, close to his own in Worcester Park, and persuaded him to move again in October 1896. Wells was scornful of most of his new Surrey neighbours, 'amateur poultry fanciers and dog lovers', but it was here that at last he had a study, as well as half an acre of garden. The house was named Heatherlea, and they acquired their first servant, a part-time gardener.

Wells did not become a grateful client of Pinker – or of any other agent. The effect of his long struggle to achieve success was to strengthen the sense of entitlement that made him ruthless in his dealings with agents and publishers. So he continued to use Watt as his agent as well as Pinker, and gave both agents a difficult time by dealing directly with publishers whenever he felt like it. He did not look on Pinker as a friend, and often complained of his bad management. Watt and Pinker put up with his behaviour, each ready to work hard for him, charging the same ten per cent: but he was never pleased with either of them, always believing he could do better.

Later this year he wrote to the publisher J. M. Dent himself saying he did not intend to bind himself to any one publisher, and outlining his current plan: *Wheels of Chance* was published in September by Dent; a collection of short stories was to appear early in 1897 by Methuen; in September 1897 a 'sensational story' (*The Invisible Man*) was already with Pinker; and for spring 1898, 'a scientific romance' (*When the Sleeper Wakes*) was to be serialized in England and America and then published by Heinemann.[3]

This represents a load of work so heavy it is hard to think how he managed to get through it. He was seizing his chance, determined to establish himself and believing the best way was to bombard the public with new offerings. The effect was not all good, but he seemed unable to put anything aside.

When the Sleeper Wakes, which he told Pinker was to be 'the culmination of my career', was a poor piece of work and did not do well. He rewrote it later, using the central idea of a man who sleeps for two hundred years and wakes to find society entirely changed, very much for the worse: fascist government, London grown huge and horrifying, flying machines fighting. Wells was never satisfied with it and told Arnold Bennett it was 'a big confused disintegrating thing' and later that it had 'a broken back and a swollen rump'.[4] And, although it has not been a favourite, it became remarkably influential, since both Aldous Huxley in *Brave New World* and George Orwell in *Nineteen Eighty-Four* were partly inspired by it. Huxley disliked Wells's writing and set out to parody it – 'I am writing on the horror of the Wells Utopia,' he wrote. Orwell, who, as we have seen, adored Wells's early work as a boy and disliked his later work, completed his horrifying *Nineteen Eighty-Four* three years after the death of Wells – when he was dying himself.

All the while Wells's productivity remained extraordinary. It did not depend on any fixed pattern of work. He tended to be at his desk in the late afternoon and the evening, often up to midnight, but he wrote longer hours when he had to, and sometimes early in the morning – and took time off when he felt like it. Ideas came into his head, some to be quickly made into short stories, others to develop slowly, worked, reworked, changed, abandoned, redrafted. Keeping track of his writing is difficult, and it is sometimes quite hard to believe he could possibly be working on so many different projects at once. As well as being published by four different English publishers in 1895, in 1896 he gave *Doctor Moreau* to Heinemann and *The Wheels of Chance* to Dent.

He also produced at least a dozen short stories good enough to be collected and reprinted in book form. One of the most brilliant, 'The Star', describes a near-miss by a passing star whose gravitational pull as it gets closer and closer to the Earth floods much of it and wipes out most of the population. Narrowly missing the Earth, it moves away, leaving chaos, death and a changed world. But the remaining population quickly adapt to their new condition, and Martian observers comment that not much has changed. Wells's account makes it both unforgettable and wholly believable.

In December 1896 he told his brother Fred he felt 'uncommonly cheerful and hopeful, not only for myself, but for the whole blessed family of us'.[5] During this year he had also been working on a long science fiction story, *The Invisible Man*, set in the present in rural England and London – a highly effective and sinister account of what it would be like to be invisible. It began to be serialized by *Pearson's Weekly* in May 1897, and was published in book form in September, a few months before *War of the Worlds*, to only moderate success. But it has always found readers and brought in a steady small income – which became a large one when in the 1920s it was filmed.

He had also started on something entirely different, *Love and Mr*

Lewisham, a novel he described himself as 'a sentimental humorous story', when it was, in fact, rather more than that. It took him years to write, from September 1896 to July 1899, when he was still revising it, and he sometimes fell into despair as he struggled: 'the more I read it the less I think of its chance of any sort of popularity,' he told Pinker in January 1899.[6] But when it finally appeared in volume form in June 1900 – after serialization in English and American papers – Henry James described it as 'a bloody little chunk of life, of no small substance' and wished it 'a great and continuous fortune'. It is indeed partly a chunk of Wells's own early life, concentrating on the struggle between two needs – for sex and for education – and the humiliations of looking for work and being found wanting. It is laid out so unflinchingly that you want to rescue Mr Lewisham as he destroys his own prospects by preferring early marriage to higher education. On his way he encounters a fine comic character – Chaffery, his wife's stepfather, crooked in all his dealings; he works as a medium, conning credulous seekers who want to speak to the dead. Chaffery is self-important and self-justifying: 'I am a sort of Robin Hood,' he says as he cheats and steals, and 'Lies are the mortar that binds the savage individual man into the social masonry,' he goes on to proclaim, citing Shaw and Ibsen. And when he absconds abroad with money filched from a friend, he remarks that there is 'more than a touch of the New Woman about me'.

This was Wells's first go at realism – 'practically my first novel', he told Edward Garnett (it was his second).[7] He became proud of it: 'I have toiled and attempted more in writing this book than I have ever done before and it has become something organic and personal in a way that my books certainly haven't before,' he wrote to Gosse.[8] And to Healey he wrote, 'there is really more work in that book than there is in many a first class FRS research.'[9] It achieved nothing like the success of his science fiction stories, but it is a decently written and touching novel as it follows the history of a young man who fails to fulfil his promise because he falls in love and opts for marriage rather than dedication to original work. It was a warning he had no need to give himself, of course.

By a curious chance another first novel, *A Man from the North*, was published in 1898 with the same subject of a poor young man with intellectual ambitions who abandons them for marriage and mediocrity. It was by Arnold Bennett, a journalist slightly known to Wells: Bennett had written him a fan letter in 1897, enclosing his own review of *The Invisible Man*. Bennett, born in 1867, was a year younger than Wells and had grown up in Staffordshire, 150 miles north-west of London, and done very well at school in spite of a stammer. He should have gone on to a university, but at sixteen his father, a solicitor, required him to start work in his office. Bennett made up his mind to leave, took himself to London in 1891, and soon had an editorial job on a magazine. His fan letter had made a good start to his friendship with Wells. But it was only in 1900 that Wells and Jane noticed that the plot of Bennett's *A Man from the North* had the same theme as *Love and Mr Lewisham* – that of a clever young man distracted from continuing with his education by falling in love and getting married. There was no question of plagiarism, since *A Man from the North* had been written in 1896 and published in 1898 – but Wells called it 'your Mr Lewisham' to Bennett.[10]

Intrigued by this coincidence, Wells invited Bennett to come for a weekend. He accepted – and he got on with both Wells and Jane – and from then on they kept in touch, reading each other's work, reviewing it and offering private criticism, mostly praise, although they could be startlingly rude. In 1903 Bennett wrote to Wells about his *Mankind in the Making*: 'the mere writing of a lot of the book falls short of even a respectable average . . . I was continually . . . irritated by the bad technique of the writing . . . sundry examples of bad grammar, scores of bad punctuation, hundreds of striking inelegance and not a few of an obscurity.'[11]

And Wells told Bennett, 'You are always taking surface values . . . you don't penetrate . . . You have probably never been in love. I doubt if you ever weep . . . You prefer "style" to beauty. You are not a poet, you are not a genius. But you are a dear delightful person.'[12]

Both took all these attacks calmly, although Bennett objected to being called 'a dear delightful person' – and their friendship was too important to both for them to quarrel; and, while Wells moved on to directly political writing and activity, Bennett stuck to literary criticism and fiction.[13] When he produced his masterpiece, *The Old Wives' Tale*, in 1908, Wells hailed it at once, saying – rightly – that there were few novels in their period to put beside it.[14] Over the years they paralleled one another in becoming rich, famous and respected for their work; they respected one another too, and remained always the best of friends.

While they were at Worcester Park, the Wellses' social life was expanding. His French translator, Davray, visited him in April 1897. A schoolfriend of Jane's, Dorothy Richardson, with ambitions to become a writer, became a frequent visitor, observing them somewhat sardonically: she noted that Wells had a Cockney twang to his voice, and that they both tried too hard to make clever conversation. Wells was kind to her, encouraged her to write, found her attractive – and they flirted. The Wellses gave Saturday tea parties, with croquet – Wells always enjoyed getting his guests to play games. He was invited to writers' dinners in London and met some well-established names, Kenneth Grahame, Jerome K. Jerome, Conan Doyle and Grant Allen, famous for his novel *The Woman Who Did*, about an unmarried woman who chooses to have a child – Wells reviewed it badly and Allen at once sought him out and very sensibly made friends with him. But the most important meeting was with George Gissing, a greatly gifted novelist and classical scholar, nine years older than Wells.

Wells had praised Gissing in a critical essay in 1895, saying that his novel *Eve's Ransom* was remarkably well done and 'we must needs read it to its bitter end for the grim interest of it that never fails.' He went on to say with some truth that Gissing was a writer whose genre was 'nervous exhaustion'. After reviewing another of Gissing's books Wells invited him to Worcester Park in December 1896; Gissing accepted, and the friendship was formed. Wells admired Gissing's 'splendid leonine head' and his manner of speaking, while Gissing liked Wells's 'wild face and naive manner' and was astonished by his self-education as well as his great talent.[15]

Wells and Jane soon learnt that Gissing, for all his gifts, did not know how to take care of himself: his life was a sequence of misfortunes. He married disastrously unsuitable women: both his two English wives were uneducated, the first became an alcoholic, the second was violent and descended into insanity. His lungs were weak and his health was poor. Fortunately he had a good doctor who was also a loyal friend, whom he introduced to Wells: his name was Henry Hick. Gissing worked as hard, or harder, than Wells: he had written *New Grub Street*, his eighth novel, 220,000 words long, in two months – that is 4,000 words a day – hard to believe anyone could achieve that.[16] It describes the lives of men and women who write for money and never make much, always hard pressed, never able to live comfortable lives. He was writing of course about his own situation – the book was full of savage truths, he said. Wells, acknowledging its truth from his own experience, admired it. Gissing had little success with his early novels and sold *New Grub Street* outright for a hundred and fifty pounds, but by the time he met Wells his reputation was growing and he was beginning to make some money, albeit not much.

Gissing and Jane got on well, and they all agreed to holiday together in Devon in May 1897, after which Gissing suggested they should join him in Rome the following spring. For him, as a classicist, Rome was a near-sacred place, and he had already visited it with rapture in 1888. Neither Jane nor Wells had as yet so much as crossed the Channel but they could now well afford to. They were tempted, and agreed to think about it.

Wells had something else on his mind that summer. Isabel – his first wife – asked him to visit her to discuss an extension she hoped to make to the poultry farm she was running, which he might finance. This was at Twyford, then a small village in the Thames Valley. He bicycled over and they spent the day happily walking and talking, relaxed and friendly together. Her mother was in the house, and he was to stay overnight. This was understood, but during the evening he was suddenly overcome with grief at the thought of his separation from Isabel. She was as beautiful as ever, he wanted to recover her, and when he was alone with her he implored her to let him make love to her. She was taken aback and refused, going off to bed in her room, which was next to her mother's, while he slept elsewhere in the house. He got up before dawn and prepared to leave without any goodbyes, but she came down early too, to light the fire and make him some breakfast. 'How can things like that be, now?' she asked him – since he was after all married. Wells was in such a state that he began to cry, took her in his arms and held her, sobbing like a disappointed child. Then he left and bicycled away, overcome with grief and feeling that nothing worth while remained in the world.

We know this because he described it himself years later – after her death in 1931. He could not be sure which summer it had been – it might have been 1898 although 1897 is more likely – but the strength of his desire and distress so many years ago was as sharp in his mind as ever. After that meeting he had set out to clear his imagination of her, without much success.[17] Some years later he heard she had remarried, concealing it from him, and he was again overwhelmed, this time by a storm of jealousy. He then destroyed every photograph he had of her. His brief account of these responses to her withdrawal from him is one of the most affecting passages in his autobiography, perhaps because it shows how deep and persistent his feelings could be even as his life was ever more demanding and successful – as he worked at frenzied speed on book after book and story after story, negotiating with publishers and agents, moving house, making new friends, supported by an adoring and efficient wife. But all the while, beneath this activity and success, some part of him was unchanged and vulnerable.

Gissing set off for Italy in September 1897, having parted finally from his second wife, and leaving two small sons whom he loved but could not manage to care for. Once in Rome he heard from Wells that he and Jane were coming in March, and set about finding them a comfortable hotel and preparing to show them the city. Knowing Rome from his earlier visit, he made a good guide – but for the fact that he valued only secular and pagan Rome, Christianity and Christian art being of no interest to him. Wells recalled friendly arguments as he showed them the great sights, omitting the Vatican and St Peter's – and presumably many other churches – as deplorable blots on the ancient city.

Wells took himself to see some of these and decided the Catholic religion was not all bad, since at least it aspired to be international. They made excursions out of town, to Tivoli and along the Appian Way, sometimes joined by Conan Doyle and other friends of Gissing as they talked, walked and enjoyed the Italian wine. It was a good introduction to foreign travel – 'a wonderful time for our untravelled eyes' – and the Wellses continued on their own to Naples and Capri before going north to Florence: there they were faced with bread riots, violently put down by the police, and news of more in Milan, so they hurried home through Brussels, where they found more rioting.[18] Back at Heatherlea in mid-May, Jane wrote to thank Gissing, telling him they were both 'extremely brown and well', and inviting him to visit them.

Wells settled back to work. He wrote to Heinemann, publishers of *The Time Machine* and *The War of the Worlds*, telling them he was sick of them letting his work 'fizzle in obscure corners' and was ending his relationship with them. Who were his publishers now? Pinker seems to have made a deal with Harper in New York to publish *Love and Mr Lewisham* simultaneously in America and England in 1900, after serialization – but a copy exists dated 1899 and published by Frederick A. Stokes, another New York publisher – so there is some doubt about exactly what Pinker had arranged, or whether Wells had interfered in some way. Wells presented a copy of the English first edition to Richard Gregory, with the words 'and the Lord bless and keep him', and Gregory responded gratifyingly by comparing it to *Jude the Obscure*. Wells also inscribed a copy for Isabel, 'I M Wells from H G Wells'.[19]

Gissing arrived back in England in June 1898 and went to stay with the Wellses. Wells taught him to ride a bicycle, with many falls and much laughter, and Jane served him good food. In July Gabrielle

Fleury, a Frenchwoman eager to translate *New Grub Street* into French, who had been seeking Gissing for some time, tracked him down to Heatherlea and was invited to lunch. Wells described her as well read, refined and intelligent, and indeed she had lived among intellectuals and writers in Paris. Gissing was greatly impressed by her as 'a sweet and intelligent creature' and within days was writing her love letters and arranging to meet her again after leaving the Wellses'. He had to explain to her that he could not marry her legally, but soon it was agreed that he should live with her in Paris, with the consent of her parents. In May 1899 he went through a secret – and of course illegal – wedding ceremony in Rouen Cathedral in the presence of Gabrielle's mother. Wells was one of the very few friends informed. Gissing thought he had achieved secure happiness at last, at forty-one: sadly, he was wrong.

Wells, at thirty-two, was at last growing plump. He took to wearing Jaeger suits, pure wool, comfortable and fashionable. But even now, as his imagination produced one astonishing idea after another, as he kept up his equally astonishing output, and as the world applauded, he still felt ill at ease in his body: 'until I was over forty the sense of physical inferiority was a constant acute distress to me which no philosophy could mitigate,' he wrote.[20]

10.   A House by the Sea

After Gissing's departure Wells and Jane agreed they would bicycle to the south coast, where he would at last finish writing *Love and Mr Lewisham* – he needed to make some money. They dispatched a trunk to await them at Seaford, a small resort in East Sussex, near Eastbourne, and set off on 29 July 1898. Gissing's friend Dr Henry Hick, who lived at New Romney, had invited them to look in on him and his family during their trip.

As they started, Wells had a fresh cold and was feeling less energetic than usual, but they pushed on to Lewes and then Seaford. Once there, he saw he was 'secreting ink'. Jane went out and bought a thermometer and found he had a high temperature. She sent a telegram to Dr Hick and he replied, suggesting they should come to him at once. It meant a short journey, but with several changes of train on little country lines, exhausting for Wells, who was now suffering from agonizing thirst as well as severe pain. Hick took one look at him and had him put to bed in his own house. It seemed likely he had an abscess on his kidney and would need a surgeon.

He and Jane remained with the blessedly kind Hick family until September, Wells carefully nursed, and cheered by letters from anxious friends. While they were with them, Mrs Hick gave birth to a daughter and Wells became her godfather – and wrote her a story, with illustrations: 'The Story of Tommy and the Elephant'.[1] Gissing wrote to Jane saying he regarded Wells as 'the friend of a lifetime; I can't do without him'. The surgeon came from London, examined Wells and said no surgery was necessary because there was now virtually nothing left at all of the troublesome kidney. Very slowly, Wells began to get better.

In August two distinguished visitors arrived and took tea with the Hicks and the Wellses: Henry James, now living along the coast at

Rye, and his guest Edmund Gosse, author, translator, critic and literary fixer. They bicycled over from James's house and showed themselves to be very friendly. Wells remembered seeing James in the theatre in January 1895, but this was the first time they had exchanged words, and he was charmed. J. M. Barrie then also appeared and told Wells stories of his early years of poverty when he claimed to have lived almost entirely on buns. Only later did Wells realize that they were all emissaries of the Royal Literary Fund, a body that helps writers who are in financial difficulties.

Fortunately Wells, for all his anxieties about money, was still solvent. Pinker was doing his stuff, and the Hicks continued to provide accommodation, medical care and general support. Hick told Wells his health demanded that he leave Worcester Park and never try to live in London or the suburbs again: he must make his home on sand or gravel, or by the sea, he said, and preferably in a place both high and sheltered. The Wellses took this excellent advice seriously and decided to look for somewhere along the coast. Wells gave his bicycle to Hick, being unable to take any exercise for fear of troubling the abscess that remained on the site of the vanished kidney.

In any case he was so weak that he had to use a wheelchair. He was still with the Hicks on his birthday on 21 September, and only at the end of the month were he and Jane able to move into a boarding house in Sandgate, a seaside village west of Folkestone, and look for somewhere to settle. They found a minuscule two-storeyed house at the end of a terrace, No. 2 Beach Cottages. It is still there, a charming cottage facing the sea and indeed so close to it that the roof is sometimes sprayed by waves when the tide is high and the wind brisk. Jane enjoyed swimming – Wells had not yet learnt to swim – and she wheeled him energetically along the beach when he wanted to go out. Here he managed to finish his first draft of *Love and Mr Lewisham* – and started on 'The Wealth of Mr Waddy', which, he assured Pinker, would become 'the finest thing I ever wrote': a Dickensian comic novel he never finished, but that transmuted into *Kipps*.

While his energy was returning, his moods fluctuated dramatically. In late November he told Pinker he was 'near breaking point'

Sandgate

and that he saw nothing but removals, unrest and worry ahead, no steady growth of reputation – adding for good measure that he expected to die miserably. He also recorded the loss of several back teeth and a patch of hair on the top of his head, and complained of being allowed no alcohol or tobacco. But he went on writing, revising *Love and Mr Lewisham*, and producing more short stories. And he began to appreciate Sandgate: 'this place is a lovely place and everybody ought to live here,' he wrote, twice in the same letter. He was right, because it is an exceptionally agreeable village, set under the cliff, with a very long High Street behind a very long beach, and unpretentious but pleasing houses and shops. It is also conveniently placed, with Folkestone next door, offering its urban luxuries and easy access to France and London. He and Jane began to think they might remain in Sandgate and to discuss the possibility of having a house built there for themselves.

Wells never went back to Worcester Park. In February 1899 they found a bigger house to rent in Sandgate, this one a good solid middle-class three-storey brick semi-detached, named Arnold House.[2] They took a three-year lease on it. Jane went back alone to Heatherlea to pack up its entire contents and have everything sent to their new address. They were now living in a quiet cul-de-sac between sea and cliff, with a small ruined castle at one end of the road, and their garden going down to a sea wall with a gate on to the beach. The rooms were of a decent size, and there were enough of them to give Wells a study and visiting friends a bedroom – there was even a servant's room next to the kitchen, with a side entrance. The whole house was full of light and on good days sunshine: just what Wells needed. In March they moved in; they were to stay for two years.

In May *When the Sleeper Wakes* was published – in London and New York – Wells gave an inscribed copy to Dr Hick. He was still forbidding his patient smoking, drinking and exercise, and Wells described himself as 'an elderly invalid' – but he was working again, reviewing, still 'punching about', as he put it, the last five chapters of *Love and Mr Lewisham*, which would at last begin to be serialized in November, and struggling with 'Mr Waddy'. He sent Pinker two short stories about men who plan to go to the moon – which later became a particularly lively and entertaining novel, *The First Men in the Moon*.

It was a good moment to buy a typewriter for Jane. His own writing had deteriorated 'to a state unfit for the human eye to look upon' – except of course in Jane's eyes, since she would be typing out what he had written.[3] Jane learnt quickly once she was allowed to try it, and from now on she typed all his work: it is to be hoped she had her own study. She had long since given up working for a degree. But throughout his illness she had grown in strength and confidence and shown herself well able to take command of the practical organization of their lives. Wells said later that he lived in all his households as a paying guest, and Jane made it easy for him to choose that role.

He was now recovering steadily. Their new neighbours, Arthur and Florence Popham and their children, were friendly and intellectually congenial – they had family connections with members of the Fabian Society. Although Wells was still meant to be cautious about exercise, the Pophams taught him to swim at last, and he learnt to enjoy the water as well as the sight of young women on the beach wearing bathing suits, even though they still covered shoulders and thighs: his drawing of Jane beside the sea shows her in such a suit. At once he began to think of a novel about a mermaid. It became *The Sea Lady*, an account of a conventional and hard-working young man who is distracted from his duties and responsibilities by the allure of the sea and one of its tantalizingly beautiful inhabitants. It is a fantasy in the genre of *The Wonderful Visit*, and it makes an entertaining parable, although far too long for its subject. Wells should have cut it severely, but he clearly relished describing his hero escaping from the demands of a respectable working life and a serious-minded fiancée.

Joseph Conrad sent a letter of sympathy when he heard of Wells's illness. He was living nearby, in a farm lent to him by another writer, Ford Madox Hueffer – later Ford Madox Ford – and he proposed to visit Wells. Conrad was deeply grateful for Wells's praise of his work – Wells had chosen his novella *The Nigger of the 'Narcissus'* as the best book of 1897, and Conrad believed that its success was the first event in his writing life that really counted.[4] They also shared an agent in Pinker, who would certainly have encouraged Conrad to approach Wells – he liked his clients to be friends.

Conrad took to driving over in a pony trap, and he and Wells would lie on the beach talking for hours in the sunshine. Wells says Conrad was baffled by many aspects of English culture: 'What is all this about Jane Austen?' he asked. He could not understand what Wells was doing writing *Love and Mr Lewisham*, or why Wells was interested in social and political issues, and apparently indifferent to style. Wells for his part distrusted the artistic persona he saw Conrad adopting and found his writing sometimes overwrought – but for now they remained on cordial terms. In 1906 Wells chose Conrad's autobiographical *The Mirror of the Sea* as one of the best books of the year, alongside Henry James's *The Golden Bowl*, its elaborate prose acceptable to Wells at this point. Then in 1907 Conrad dedicated *The Secret Agent* to Wells – a perfect novel in which Conrad proved he could achieve greatness with simplicity.

The Wellses were now thinking seriously of building a house of their own. He had savings of over a thousand pounds. Dr Hick, having looked after him for many months, did him a further favour by introducing him to his brother-in-law Charles Voysey, an architect of brilliant and original gifts, much influenced by the ideas of Ruskin and William Morris. His houses were solid and handsome, with tiled gables, bow windows and fine details, full of light and easy to live in. Wells had his own strong views about architecture – he gave his interests in *Who's Who* for 1899 as 'detailed description of his various illnesses, and architecture'. Voysey understood that he wanted something quite unlike the usual seaside villa.

They found a narrow sunny site high up on the clifftop at the eastern end of Sandgate, where their house would have views over the sea as far as France on a clear day, and with enough space for a garden on several levels. There were negotiations with the owner of the land – it belonged to the Earl of Sandwich – and problems finding a builder willing to work on such a difficult site. In March 1899 Voysey submitted his design, showing bedrooms, bathrooms, living rooms, study and loggia all on one floor – this because Wells thought he might need to use a wheelchair for many years. So it was to be a long house. It was also strikingly handsome and unlike any other house in the district, with brick walls to be roughcast and painted white, windows set in stone, the roof high-pitched with deep tiled gables. There were discussions and revisions to the plan, a builder was found, and Wells signed the contract in February 1900: he was to pay £1,760 for the house – of course in the end it came closer to £2,000. Voysey made a habit of signing his houses with heart-shaped decorations, but Wells objected to these and asked for spades instead, and so it became Spade House. You can still see what a superb building he made for the Wellses, both as a work of art and as a machine for living.[5]

Among the many writers Wells was meeting the most exotic was Stephen Crane, an American who had published his first story at the age of sixteen – he was born in 1871 – worked as a reporter, won fame with a novel about the experience of a soldier fighting in the American Civil War – *The Red Badge of Courage* – and lived a life packed with incident and scandal. He came to England in 1897 with Cora Taylor, whom he had met in Jacksonville, Florida, where it was alleged she had been running a brothel, after leaving two husbands. From then on she lived with Crane as his wife, showing him deep devotion. Crane and Conrad met and took to one another, and Pinker became Crane's agent. Conrad praised Crane for his 'incomparable insight into primitive emotions', and Wells described him in a review as the best writer of their generation: so a friendship was easily made.

By 1899 Crane needed all Cora's care: his health was deteriorating and he had tuberculosis. He and Cora were lent a large, ancient and partly derelict manor house near Rye, called Brede Place, and, in spite of his illness and their lack of money, they decided to throw a four-day party there to celebrate the arrival of the new century. Crane's idea was that they would write and put on a play, Wells was to help with it, and he and Jane were invited over on 27 December.

Spade House

The play was to be called 'The Ghost', and was meant to have specially made scenery and an orchestral accompaniment – all on a splendid scale – although nothing turned out quite as intended. Wells saw that Crane was full of ideas but wholly impractical: he had the walls and ceiling of his bedroom painted scarlet, with a red carpet, while the other bedrooms in the house were left unfurnished. Many distinguished guests had been invited and came from London as well as locally, and some truckle beds had been hired for the occasion, although by no means enough. According to Wells, the play was enjoyed by its authors and cast and hardly understood by the audience. The house was candle-lit and there was dancing. Wells got guests to play a game in which they ran races on broomsticks, and Crane tried to organize a game of poker which no one took seriously. Those who chose to stay overnight had to huddle down where they could and wander around the garden to find somewhere to relieve themselves, for lack of plumbing in the house. Breakfast was served at midday, with beer.

Crane had pretty well run out of money. He kept talking obsessively of the various stories and reporting jobs Pinker was signing him up to do, yet he was clearly so weak that it seemed unlikely he would be able to produce anything. And so it turned out.

This was Wells's introduction to bohemian living, and, although he liked Crane and later described the party as an extraordinary lark, it was a lark that ended ominously. In the small hours of the night after the play, Crane fainted and had a lung haemorrhage, which he tried to hide. He told Cora he didn't want anyone to bother about it, but she very sensibly asked Wells to get help, and he at once rode off on a borrowed bicycle in the cold, wet dawn to find a doctor in Rye – perhaps his first bicycle trip since his illness.

Tragedy took over from farce. The Cranes stayed on until May, Stephen getting steadily worse. Cora decided to take him for treatment to a spa in the Black Forest in Germany. On 17 May 1900 she summoned Wells to visit them in Dover, where they were staying in the Lord Warden Hotel – the most expensive in Dover – with a servant, a doctor, two nurses and a dog. Henry James had already sent them fifty pounds. They crossed the Channel on 24 May, travelled to Basel and on to Badenweiler,[6] where Cora sent messages to Pinker asking for money. Crane died within a few days, on 5 June. Cora took his body back to New Jersey for burial and then returned to Jacksonville and her old business.

Before the party Wells had written to Healey, telling her how habitable he found Sandgate, and also asking her, 'How do you face the intricate problems, the warring desires, the tragic circumstances of life? Let me know how things go with you.'[7] His question contained the implication that he was facing his own problems and warring desires. Some were to do with his work, and he was able to solve one quickly: he abandoned his attempt to write about Mr Waddy and rechristened the character and the proposed book 'Kipps'. This released whatever was blocking his progress, and *Kipps* became one of his most successful novels.

Other problems were to be dealt with when, in February 1900, he signed the contract for building their new house. Now he confessed to Healey his fear that building a house was a symptom of incipient 'Middle Age'. Still, he was well enough to exercise, and in May he was even able to set off for a short cycling tour in northern France, achieved without trouble. He would still occasionally complain of 'my beastly kidney', but he was never to suffer from a seriously disabling illness again. The diabetes that afflicted him from 1933 – as predicted by Dr Collins – did not keep him from any of his usual activities. During the summer, as the house was being built, Jane and Wells talked about whether they should have children: possibly another symptom of incipient middle age. They came to an agreement, and in October Jane conceived, even as they were supervising the planting of eight hundred daffodils and many trees in the garden of Spade House. Wells made daily visits to the site to oversee the installation of a pergola, summerhouses and a rock garden, as well as a tennis lawn and smaller sunken lawns below.

On 8 December Wells sent a postcard to Arnold Bennett from Spade House to say they had moved in: 'No carpets no dining room table or chairs, little food but still – *there*!'[8] His next communication with Bennett was to say, 'Mrs Wells and I have been collaborating (and publication is expected in early July) in the invention of a human being.'[9]

Before the new human being could arrive, on 22 January 1901, Queen Victoria died. She had commanded his mother's passionate loyalty, standing only a little lower than God in her mind from girlhood on, and Wells noticed that in her last years his mother dressed in a black bonnet and black silk dress as like the Queen's as possible. But to Wells the Queen's death was a signal that things were going to change. In November 1900 he wrote to John Galsworthy, who had recently sent him a book: 'I'm an extensive skeptic, no God, no King, no nationality.'[10]

He also wrote to Graham Wallas, whom he had heard speak at the earliest open meetings of the Fabian Society at William Morris's house in 1886, and now met again – he was married to the sister of their neighbour Mrs Popham. Wallas's essay 'Property under Socialism', published in 1889, spoke of the need for nationalizing basic services, while suggesting that a perfect socialist society could come only when the whole world accepted such a system. All this was intensely interesting to Wells – Wallas was also a free thinker and an educationalist – and they rapidly became good friends. Wells was embarking on a book of essays on the future, telling Healey that it was 'designed to undermine and destroy the monarch, monogamy and respectability – and the British Empire, all under the guise of a speculation about motor cars and electric heating'.[11]

The book would be *Anticipations*, serialized from April 1901 in England and America, published in November and reprinted five times in the next year. It was his first non-fiction bestseller. Pinker, who had suggested the idea of such a book, was naturally overjoyed. Beatrice and Sidney Webb, at this time the most distinguished and influential activists for social reform, and leading members of the Fabian Society, were both enthusiastic. Bernard Shaw thanked Wells for sending him a copy, recalling their conversations of 1895. The Director of the Museum of Natural History, Ray Lankester, gave it a

long review, saying he was haunted by it, finding it both an indictment of existing society and also an offering of hope for the future:
he invited Wells to dinner and they became friends. Churchill also
wrote, and Wells replied, telling him that he – Churchill – belonged
to a class that had scarcely changed in a hundred years, whereas Wells
would find his great-grandparents as alien as contemporary Chinese.
'I really do not think that you people who gather in great country
houses realize the pace of things.' And he assured Churchill, 'Liber-
alism is as dead as Adam.'[12]

With *Anticipations* Wells was making a claim to forecast the
future; he called it a prospectus, a view of how things were to
develop in everyday life: in transport, social activities, education,
warfare. He said he felt free to attack existing institutions such as
the monarchy, the ruling class and the universities because he was
himself a complete outsider – and he did attack them. He wrote of
the future dominance of motor vehicles and the spread of roads and
suburban living, and predicted tank warfare, while surprisingly
underestimating what would happen in the air. More important
was his vision of a society in which scientists, doctors and engineers
would form an elite, and this educated class would work towards
forming a world state, 'the new Republic', in all likelihood speaking one language only.

In his original version he advanced another suggestion: that once
sexual activity were to be separated from reproduction – as it clearly
could be – there would be no more moral aspect to it than to a game
of golf or chess. He suggested the possibility of special cabins, or
'love rooms', easily accessible and sound-proof, where partners could
be stimulated by diverse electrical means to reach orgasm. Paying for
the use of such a cabin could give income to the state, and sex would
become a sport like any other. Wells did not give any details of how
the electrical stimulant would work, and it took a later generation to
name it the 'orgasmotron', and Wilhelm Reich to devise an orgone
accumulator in 1939 and go on to sell 'orgone boxes' to American
intellectuals, among them Saul Bellow and Norman Mailer.[13]

The old idea of God, mysterious and arbitrary, would disappear along with sexual guilt. The human race would become fine, efficient and beautiful, and the 'people of the Abyss', or what he called 'base and servile' men and women, and those who could not keep pace with the higher types – Wells indicated they might include Black, Asian and other non-white ethnicities – would have to die out. Today's reader, having lived through the twentieth century, starts back in shock and horror from these calmly advanced suggestions and finds it extraordinary that they seem to have been accepted at the time.

John Carey's account of them, written in 1992, reminds us of Wells's extreme and now unacceptable position – and he also points out that Wells managed to remain in two minds about much that he wrote, and that his fiction offered a wholly different attitude from his political theorizing. Wells's heroes – Mr Polly, Hoopdriver, Kipps, Bert Smallway – are as far as can be from the coolly efficient, beautiful elite he proposed for the future of humanity.[14] Wells spoke the truth in his fiction and sometimes got things badly wrong in his political and social prescriptions. Indeed, he soon retreated from this racist position altogether. Within two years of publishing *Anticipations*, he was writing approvingly of a multiracial society in *A Modern Utopia*: 'my eye is caught at once by a young negro, carrying books in his hand, a prosperous-looking, self-respecting young negro in a trimly cut coat of purple-blue.' He went on to write with particular admiration of the African-American population of the United States when he visited it for the first time in 1906.

There is some comedy in his prospectus too, if unintended. He foresees married couples bringing up families of three or four children without any domestic help, because they will be living in automated flats heated by electricity, and with filtered air free of dust. They will wear shoes that don't need cleaning and sleep in beds that take only five minutes to make; everyone will leave the bathroom clean after using it, and cooking meals will be no more than a pleasant amusement – he says nothing about shopping for food or peeling the potatoes. Nor has he anything to say about laundry, and he suggests that a small garden will be no trouble at all as long as bedding out plants are avoided. His assumption is that highly educated wives will not want domestic help because they will have a distaste for 'vicarious labour'.

Like many idealistic men planning utopias, he brushed aside reality. Meanwhile Jane was preparing to give birth, for which there could be no vicarious labour. Wells complained to Healey that 'This house will be infested with doctors and nurses in a week or so and until the end of August very probably.'[15] Against the prospect he had recently, and secretly, rented a room in a pretty farmhouse in Aldington, about twelve miles away, and was preparing to retreat there to work. He remained at Spade House while Jane went through a difficult labour on 17 July – there were moments when he feared for her and the baby boy's survival. As soon as it was clear they were both safe, he sent off a telegram to her mother, and then left sharply the next day on his bicycle, leaving no information about where he was going or for how long. He was away without sending word home until 5 August, although he told a new friend, Edith Nesbit (author of *The Railway Children*, *The Treasure Seekers*, *Five Children and It*), about his farmhouse room, warning her not to give the address to anyone else – she had a holiday house herself at Dymchurch, not far away. After returning home briefly – Jane had been upset, and had then apologized for being upset – he departed again for a bicycle tour, seeing his parents and taking in Tenterden, Bodiam, Brighton, Worthing, Petersfield, Hastings, Winchelsea – and getting home again to Spade House in mid-September.[16]

It was not unusual at that time for men to leave home when their wives were engaged in caring for a new baby. All the same, Jane was clearly unhappy, disconcerted and even frightened by what happened. She decided she must keep him happy by not complaining or putting the slightest emotional pressure on him. It was now accepted between them that Wells needed to be free to behave as he liked, and Jane would never allow herself to make a fuss.

Wells felt he was entitled to this, rather as he felt entitled to treat his agents badly. And it was not just a matter of disappearances and failures to keep her informed. In his *Experiment in Autobiography* he

writes of a 'compromise' he and Jane made – 'after 1900' – that went
much further than this. He persuaded her to accept that he needed to
have affairs with other women, on the grounds that she was 'fra-
gile' – which seems to have meant she had less enthusiasm for sex
than he did – while he, as his health was restored, craved for a great
deal of what he called the 'complete loveliness of bodily response' –
which was not perhaps what the 'love rooms' of the future would
have encouraged.

This was not a compromise, of course, but a formal agreement
between them, by which Jane agreed not to be jealous of what he
called *passades* – meaning light-hearted sexual encounters – while he
in exchange seems to have assured her that the marriage would never
be in danger. And presumably both agreed there would never be a
divorce. The agreement worked in the sense that they remained married until her death. And yet the scandals, the loneliness and
humiliation he subjected her to over the years, as he pursued public
and long-drawn-out love affairs with other women who did their
best to monopolize him, bore him children and tried to persuade him
to get a divorce; the other homes he set up with them, which caused
him to remain absent abroad for very long periods of time, leaving
Jane to put a good face on the situation – all this hardly bears thinking of.

For now, he was on top of the world, his books being translated into
Russian, French, German, Italian, Norwegian, Hungarian, Czech
and Danish. In France all the bookshops displayed his work in their
windows. An invitation to deliver a lecture at the Royal Institution
came early in 1902. Wells wrote to Graham Wallas to tell him he had
joined the National Liberal Club, at that time said to be a hotbed of
radicalism, in its large and splendid building on the Embankment –
he described it with relish later in his novel *The New Machiavelli*. He
also wrote to his old friend Richard Gregory, 'We'll have a Republic
in twelve years – or at any rate we may have if only everyone will
buck up. The amount of latent treason I am discovering is amazing.
I shall talk treason at the R.I. [the Royal Institution – Wells was to

talk there on 24 January 1902]. I am going to write, talk and preach revolution for the next five years. If I had enough money believe me to keep me off the need of earning a living I would do the job myself.'[17] He never lost his enthusiasm for revolution and republicanism.

11. Fabian Friends

In December 1901 a letter had come to Wells from Sidney Webb, expressing admiration for his book *Anticipations*, and introducing himself as one who, like Wells, had sometimes gone to talks at William Morris's house 'in the old Hammersmith Socialist Society days'. He had been, as Wells probably knew, an early member of the Fabian Society, and he mentioned that he and his wife Beatrice were good friends of Bernard Shaw and Graham Wallas – all now on the Executive Committee of the Fabians, and both known to Wells. He went on to say he was eager to discuss Wells's ideas with him, and Wells responded by inviting the Webbs for a weekend at Sandgate.

Wells had been excited and impressed as early as 1886 by hearing William Morris, Bernard Shaw, Hubert Bland, Graham Wallas and other socialists speaking at Morris's Hammersmith house: 'by the time I came to London Fabianism was Socialism', and he was already a socialist himself.[1] But he had left London to teach and then suffered injury and illness, and only when he was back in London in the autumn of 1888 did he again think of joining the Fabians, as he told Elizabeth Healey. And yet he did nothing and forgot about it again.[2]

Now at last, in 1901, he felt he might be ready. The Webbs accepted Wells's invitation. A few days before their visit, on 10 January 1902, Wells had a letter from Edward Pease, Secretary of the Fabian Society and another of its founders. He told Wells they were 'the pioneers of your New Republic', as described in his new book *Anticipations* – and at the same time complained that the Fabians had no new ideas and needed someone else who could think ahead: clearly Pease was dissatisfied with the current situation. Wells replied, saying he was looking forward to thrashing out all sorts of things with Webb. He also asked Pease where he stood on the monarchy: 'the centre of base and vulgar habits, and ideas, the keystone of the real control of the country by fools, fanatics and society women'. Pease's response to this is not known. Wells wrote to him again on 29 January 1902, after meeting the Webbs, whom he described as 'wonderful people'. But he still did not join the Fabian Society – and he knew almost nothing of how it had started or developed.

The history of the Fabian Society, which began very modestly and went on to become an important political institution over the years, was this. Edward Pease had been since 1882 (when Wells was an apprentice draper in Southsea) at the centre of the small group that would become the Fabians. As a Quaker, Pease believed that socialism was common sense and private property wrong, and that reform could be brought about peacefully – and he became one of a group calling itself 'The Fellowship of the New Life' whose intention was to live on a communistic basis. The members set out to subordinate the material to the spiritual, aiming to perfect their characters, engaging in manual labour and agreeing to share all domestic work. Tolstoy was an inspiration, and they were for the most part pacifists and vegetarians. Members included Ramsay MacDonald – the future Labour Prime Minister – Olive Schreiner, the South African novelist, Havelock Ellis, a progressive doctor with a particular interest in sexuality, and Edward Carpenter, friend of Walt Whitman and pioneering activist for gay rights. Also Emma Brooke, a keen feminist who had been one of the first students at Newnham College, Cambridge, in 1871. William Morris recommended that they should try living together in one house – 'Fellowship is Heaven,' he told them. But, after a brief attempt at sharing a house in Bloomsbury, a woman member amended Morris's words to 'Fellowship is Hell' – and they broke up.

Meanwhile Charlotte Wilson, another Newnham student, from 1871, now with a stockbroker husband prepared to fund her ideas, set up in 1884 what began as the 'Karl Marx Club' and then changed its name to the 'Hampstead Historical Society'. Its meetings were held in a large old Hampstead farmhouse called Wyldes – it is still standing at the edge of Hampstead Heath – and which was described by

Bernard Shaw, who attended enthusiastically, as 'the birthplace of middle-class socialism'. Sidney Webb, Sydney Olivier, Annie Besant, Edward Pease, Graham Wallas, Hubert Bland, Edith Nesbit, Olive Schreiner, Havelock Ellis and Edward Carpenter – almost all of them future Fabians – were regulars. Emma Brooke acted as Secretary. In 1886 Charlotte Wilson founded a monthly newspaper, *Freedom: A Journal of Anarchist Socialism*, with Peter Kropotkin, whom she had invited to come to England after he had fled from arrest in Russia and then France.[3]

While attending the Hampstead Historical Society, Edward Pease decided to set up another, more formal club in January 1884, with the intention of holding discussions and lectures that would actually lead to promoting political and social reform; he set out their aim as being to make the rich poorer in order to make the poor richer. The twenty earliest members of this club numbered civil servants, clerks, would-be journalists, writers, architects and politicians, almost all of whom were also attending the Hampstead Historical Society – which seems to have gradually faded away. But Charlotte Wilson joined the Fabians in October 1884 and was the only woman elected to its second Executive Committee in January 1885 – she left it in April 1887, while remaining a member.

The name 'Fabians' was taken from a third-century Roman general, Fabius Cunctator, known as 'The Delayer' from his successful strategy of avoiding pitched battles as a means of keeping the invader, Hannibal, at bay. It turned out to be a good name, simple and memorable – the current group meant to avoid violence even as they worked for reform – and of course the name signalled that many of them had received a classical education.

At the same time almost all the newly named Fabians regarded themselves as socialists, Tolstoyan or Marxist, and Charlotte Wilson and Emma Brooke were both active in promoting the cause of women's rights. Brooke, who was for eight years Secretary of the Fabian Hampstead Group, delivered the paper 'State Maintenance of Motherhood' and published an article in a journal edited by Annie Besant, pointing out that all women's wages were conditioned by the fact of their sexuality, which is a saleable thing, whether as wives or as prostitutes. Wilson also wrote papers on anarchist communism published in *Justice*, the paper of the Democratic Federation, and interested herself in women in prison.

Shaw, not yet a playwright and still penniless, joined in May 1884, and wrote into the minutes of the society, 'This meeting was made memorable by the first appearance of Bernard Shaw.' He gave his first talk within two weeks of joining. His proposals – state ownership of most businesses, state support for children, and equal rights for men and women – were at once published by the Fabians as their manifesto. He ended it with a ringing and memorable cry, not approved by all his fellow members: 'We had rather face a Civil War than such another century of suffering as the present one has been.'

Later in 1884 and the spring of 1885 two outstandingly clever young men – Sidney Webb, who had been born into a lower-middle-class London family and got himself an excellent education through scholarships, passing effortlessly into the first division of the civil service, and Sydney Olivier, public school and Oxford educated and now rising rapidly in the Colonial Office – became members, followed by Graham Wallas, another Oxford graduate who, like Olivier, had rejected his Christian upbringing for secularism.

According to Olivier, Sidney Webb could memorize a whole page at one reading. He made his first address to the Fabians in March 1885 and enrolled as a member in May.[4] In December he decided he was a socialist, announcing a little belatedly in February 1886 that he was no longer sure that capitalism could be morally justified.

In 1888 Webb and Olivier joined Shaw on the Executive Committee, alongside the brilliantly forceful Annie Besant – already the Vice-President of the National Secular Society. She was forty-one, divorced, and had written in favour of birth control and spoken against the House of Lords and capital punishment.

Shaw and Besant were the stars of the society at this point, both compelling speakers and unstinting in giving their time and energy to the Fabian cause – but Besant left in 1890 when she became a Theosophist, after which she moved to India.[5] Another committee member was the journalist Hubert Bland, whose wife, Edith Nesbit, saw the society as divided between the practical and the visionary, which gave it 'an excitement it might otherwise lack' – Nesbit went on to write her immensely and permanently popular children's books.

The Fabians published general educational pamphlets as well as strictly political ones: Shaw wrote on Ibsen; Morris, who was a supporter but not a member, on Gothic architecture and on communism (he died in 1896); Olivier wrote on Zola; Annie Besant on school board policy; Sergei Stepniak, a Russian revolutionary in exile in England, on Tolstoy. Aylmer and Louise Maude, translators of Tolstoy, were also Fabians.

In 1886 there were 67 members of the London Society and two years later there were 861. They were generally opposed to private ownership of land and industrial capital, and almost entirely middle class and highly educated. There were further groups in Bristol, Edinburgh, Birmingham, Manchester, Sheffield, Bournemouth and many other towns in Britain – and one as far as Bombay. An American group was formed in 1895 – but lasted less than a decade.[6]

Olivier served as Secretary to the Fabians from 1886 to 1890, when he was appointed Colonial Secretary in British Honduras: he returned faithfully to the Fabians between each of his later colonial postings. Graham Wallas contributed 'Property under Socialism' to *Fabian Essays in Socialism* in 1889. Shaw and Besant both delivered many very well-received public talks. In 1887 they all joined in setting up a mock Parliament – Henry Champion, an ex-army officer, was Prime Minister, Webb Chancellor of the Exchequer, Wallas President of the Board of Trade, and Olivier Colonial Secretary. That November many of them were caught up in the violence in Trafalgar Square when thousands of protesters against coercion in Ireland, and unemployment in England, gathered, some armed with knives and pokers, to be attacked by police and soldiers – this became known as 'Bloody Sunday'. Among the Fabians present were Shaw, Charlotte Wilson and Annie Besant, who tried to protect the protesters from police violence – while Shaw confessed he 'skedaddled' before it. Besant went on to assist the protesters with their legal defence.

Then, in 1888, Besant, along with other Fabians, gave solid support to a strike by women employed to manufacture matches in the
East End of London – underpaid and endangering their health working with phosphorus – and with this they were successful, helping
the women to form a union and win their fight against exploitation.
It was an important and notable victory.

Besant, Olivier, Shaw, Webb, Wallas and Bland were on the
Executive Committee in 1888, and Webb took the lead in discussions
about 'the Basis and Prospects of Socialism' and wrote many essays
for the cause. It was at this time that Wells thought of joining – but
he was at a low ebb, looking for a job, writing essays for magazines
and working on the story that was to become *The Time Machine* –
and he spent Christmas at Uppark. Things got better for him when
he found a teaching post in London early in 1889 and became officially engaged to his cousin – but he was still too busy to think of
the Fabians.

The year 1889 was the one in which Beatrice Webb later said the
Fabian Society started a true 'Progressive movement'.[7] A volume of
Fabian Essays edited by Shaw was a success that Christmas. But in
November 1890 they lost Annie Besant. At about the same time Webb,
Wallas and Shaw met Beatrice Potter – then a handsome, brilliant,
rich and well-connected 38-year-old with an established reputation as
a researcher and writer on social questions. She had been indifferent to
the Fabians until she noticed Webb's essay in the volume of *Fabian
Essays* sent to her in 1889, which interested her because he had 'the
historic sense'.[8] She invited some of the Fabians to visit her and got a
teasing reply from Shaw, who thought she despised them as 'a rabble
of silly suburban faddists'.[9] He was wrong about this.

She approached Webb in January 1890 for information relating to
the research she was doing for a book on the co-operative movement.
He introduced her to Wallas, and in January 1891 she wrote in her
diary, 'Both pressed me to join the Fabians: refused lest it should
injure my chances as an investigator.'[10] But she was persuaded to join
privately, asking for her subscription to be entered only by her ini-
tials. Later that year the Fabians installed themselves in their first

office, at No. 276 the Strand, from which they now issued leaflets and books.

Beatrice Potter found Shaw, who at this time sported a two-piece yellow Jaeger suit, a 'marvellously smart witty fellow . . . Above all a brilliant talker – and therefore a delightful companion' – although she later told a nephew that 'the first time they were alone together Shaw simply flung himself on me'.[11] Wallas seemed to her a lovable man, demonstrating a scrupulousness so selfless as to be almost weak; and she decided that Shaw, Wallas and Webb made up 'the Fabian Junta'; and that Webb 'insinuates ideas, arguments, programmes, organises the organism'.[12] 'Webb taught us to work,' wrote Wallas.[13]

Webb fell in love with Beatrice Potter. She saw him as an entirely unsuitable wooer with a 'tiny tadpole body, unhealthy skin, lack of manner, cockney pronunciation and poverty' – 'an ugly little man with no social position and less means',[14] but she also saw that his brain and his capacity for work were formidable; and, with so many interests in common, and the same hopes of reforming the worst aspects of English society, they got on very well together. In June 1891 they went on holiday in Norway with Wallas, and there she asked Sidney what he planned to do in life – to which he replied that his greatest wish was to take part in a government that would replace capitalism by a socialist administration of his own devising. And with this he won her agreement to marry him, if not her love.

It was a private engagement, and she told him frankly that she was not in love with him and there was no question of marriage while her father still lived. In July she wrote in her diary, 'We are both of us second-rate minds, but we are curiously combined. I am the investigator, and he the executor.'[15] By September she was 'more confident that our marriage will not interfere with our work' – surely the coolest reason ever given for being prepared to marry.[16]

She knew that marriage to a man of his modest background would not please her family or friends, so there was no wedding until six months after her father's death, which came in January 1892. In February the Fabians held their first annual conference and issued a manifesto, written by Shaw, and Sidney Webb left the Colonial Office and stood as a Progressive candidate for the London County Council. He won, and he and Beatrice were married in July. Her father had left her enough money to guarantee her an income of a thousand pounds a year – the money came of course from private land and industrial capital, but she took it, intending to put it to good use. She and Sidney were both ferociously hard and productive workers. At the same time they lived the conventional life of her class in many ways, entertaining and going out, and travelling – they were to go round the world twice. And they astonished the world as the marriage she had been so reluctant to make became an outstandingly happy and affectionate one. It also led to Beatrice Webb becoming one of the most powerful figures in the Fabian Society.

In the autumn of 1893 the Webbs and Shaw decided not to support the Liberal Party but rather to encourage independent and Labour candidates to stand for Parliament at the next election. The Webbs now moved from the Hampstead flat where they had begun their married life to a terraced house in Grosvenor Street on Millbank, with views over the river and within easy reach of the London County Council offices where Webb worked. Here they were able to employ secretaries and to entertain. She chose William Morris furniture and wallpaper – for political rather than aesthetic reasons, she said – and people came to her dinners for the talk, not the food or the wine. She became a vegetarian and ate little of anything herself. In the summer she would rent a country house for three months – and of course they employed a cook and a maid as well as secretaries. Her income allowed all this.

Sidney had no interest in music, literature, the theatre or art, but both enjoyed bicycling quite as enthusiastically as Wells did, and Beatrice became a 'graceful and intrepid' bicycle rider, observed 'scudding down one of the back streets of Pimlico . . . with both hands behind her back, steering by the pedals'.[17]

Webb and Shaw published an article in November 1893 accusing the Liberals of failing to help the unemployed or to make sure workers were fairly paid. The article ended, 'Pending the formation of a

Labour Party, the working classes need not greatly care which party divides the loaves and fishes,' and urged the Trades Union Congress to raise a parliamentary fund and run fifty candidates at the next election. This led to resignations from the Fabian Society – and in March 1894 Beatrice Webb declared herself happy to make their house 'the intellectual headquarters of the Labour movement'.[18]

During this period Wells had been struggling with the bad health that forced him to give up teaching and try to earn his living as a writer – he believed he might have to move abroad to save his lungs. He also decided to leave his wife and live with his pupil. Then – at last – in January 1894 he began to have success with his stories. But he still had not a spare ounce of energy to think about political action of any kind.

In the summer of 1894 Shaw enjoyed his first success in the theatre, with *Arms and the Man*. At the same time the Fabians received an unexpected inheritance of ten thousand pounds from an old supporter, Henry Hutchinson, who also appointed Sidney Webb to be the Chairman of the trustees of the fund. The Webbs decided it should be used to set up a London School of Economics and Political Science. There were arguments with their fellow trustees about their use of Hutchinson's money, but the Webbs got their way – a signal that the Fabians were to be primarily devoted to education rather than to direct political activity. The London School of Economics – thereafter the LSE – opened in October 1895, first as a night school. By 1900 it was officially recognized as part of the University of London, giving degrees and doctorates. It became, and has remained ever since, one of the most successful colleges in London.

Emma Brooke, still a keen Fabian, decided to pursue further education at the LSE later in the 1890s – but before that she had already published several novels and achieved a remarkable success with one, *A Superfluous Woman*. It was anonymously published at first: a study of a society beauty who falls in love with a Scottish peasant farmer but marries a rich aristocrat, under pressure from her aunt and guardian, only to find that her children are all born with appalling mental and physical defects as a result of her husband's venereal disease. The story is partly seen through the eyes of a sympathetic but ineffectual doctor. It is both melodramatic and sentimental – Brooke was not a gifted writer – yet it had an extraordinary success and was reprinted many times – the reason no doubt because its theme was relevant to the real experience of many women whose husbands infected them with gonorrhoea or syphilis, a fact well known to doctors but never discussed publicly. *A Superfluous Woman* was soon republished under the author's name. Beatrice Webb did not disguise her poor view of Brooke's writing, but Brooke remained a loyal Fabian and became, in 1908, a founding member of the Fabian Women's Group – and wrote many more feminist essays and novels – now largely forgotten. Charlotte Wilson was another founding member of the Women's Group.

In the late 1890s the Fabian Society went through a quiet period, losing members and confidence and finding it hard to know how best to deal with a changing political situation as the trades union movement and socialist groups flourished and moved towards creating the Labour Party. The Webbs decided to travel, and from March 1898 to January 1899 they were away, visiting America and Australia. They arrived back to find Shaw married (in 1898) to a very rich and agreeable wife, Charlotte Payne-Townshend, who had nursed him through an illness and convinced him that he could entrust himself to her care – and income – permanently. And, although Charlotte had many reservations about the Fabians – 'a parcel of boys and old women thinking they are making history, and really making themselves ridiculous' – she joined the society in 1896 and gave handsome donations to them and to the LSE. The Shaws and the Webbs became and remained close friends.

In 1900 the Labour Party was formed, and in January 1901 Queen Victoria died. The Fabians fell out about the Boer War, fought from 1899 to May 1902, the Webbs being in favour of the Empire, Ramsay MacDonald supporting the Boers. As a result MacDonald resigned, and a very large majority voted with the Webbs and supported the status quo.

Wells, whose brother Fred was in no danger in Johannesburg, showed little interest in the war in South Africa. Wells was now in touch with Graham Wallas and giving vent to his political opinions in letters to friends, declaring he had 'No God, no King, no nationality'[19] and 'I am going to write, talk and preach revolution for the next five years.'[20] His new book, _Anticipations_, with its revolutionary message, was serialized from April 1901 and published in book form in November. It went into eight impressions and was acclaimed on all sides, by Churchill and William James and by Sidney and Beatrice Webb. It was at this point that the Webbs made up their minds to bring Wells into the Fabian Society.

12. Joining the Club

Beatrice Webb wrote a long account of her first meeting with Wells, in January 1902, in her diary. She said he told her his mother had been housekeeper to 'a great establishment of 40 servants – his father a professional cricketer attached to the place' – it seems Wells improved his father's situation somewhat – and that he had been left with 'a hatred of that class and of its attitudes towards the "lower orders" '. And she noted that he was likely to be 'a good instrument for popularising ideas', and appreciated his intellectual vivacity. She was harder on Jane, whose dress, manner and accent she described as carefully moulded, and her intelligence as mediocre; there was 'an ugly absence of spontaneity of thought and feeling', she thought, and felt her constant company might be 'somewhat stifling'. But Mrs Webb's snobbery was strictly for her diary, and she proceeded to send invitations to Jane, to visit her and to write her friendly letters. She developed warmer feelings in time – and in any case she knew the importance of maintaining good relations with people she was working with to achieve a desired end.

Wells was as busy as ever. On 24 January he delivered his lecture 'The Discovery of the Future' at the Royal Institution, to a large audience, many of them of course Fabians. He talked of how it was possible to predict the future, and of his confidence that world government would become a reality, that the human race was entering on greater progress, and the 'blood and character of the race' would be improved; and, although his high voice was sometimes inaudible and he spoke too fast, it was a very successful occasion and he received many more invitations to speak. The lecture was published, and applauded by William James for making 'a sudden daylight break through innumerable old blankets of prejudice'.[1] A different view was given by Joseph Conrad, who thought Wells failed to take account of 'human imbecility'. After 1907 they were no longer communicating. Conrad told Hugh Walpole he could not read Wells, and Wells said Conrad found him philistine and stupid.[2]

Wells now started writing a follow-up to *Anticipations*, to be called *Mankind in the Making*, in which he attacked the monarchy, deplored the decline of republican thinking and pointed out the bad effects of a society in which power is inherited, by the crown and the aristocracy. In March 1902 he dined with Churchill, who was never a republican but was at this time active in plans for social reform, which meant the two men saw eye to eye on a good many subjects. Churchill held professional writers in high esteem, passionately enjoyed Wells's stories and read him closely enough to argue with some of his ideas. Wells's respect for experts, for example, was distrusted by Churchill, who thought people wanted to live comfortably rather than being made perfect. And when Wells sent Churchill his 1905 novel *A Modern Utopia* he asked Wells to keep to story-telling: 'I am always ready to eat your suet and have eaten all you have ever prepared; but I must have the jam too' (what he called the 'suet' was social preaching; the 'jam' was the more pleasurable story).[3] The dinner in 1902 established a friendship between the two men that survived disagreements and lasted throughout their long lives.

Later in March Wells sent off a crusading letter to Graham Wallas, giving his views on sex: 'Year by year Christian training scales off me and I get more and more purely physiological with regard to sexual intercourse. A man or woman ought to have sexual intercourse. Few people are mentally, or morally or physically in health without it,' he told Wallas, adding, 'emotions can be controlled . . . We've got to rationalize the sentiment in these affairs.'[4] Wallas, recently and happily married, was not the ideal recipient for these ideas, and if he responded to them his reply has not survived.

He did, however, reintroduce Wells to Bernard Shaw, who had also been impressed by *Anticipations* and was eager to renew his acquaintance with the young man he had first met at the theatre in 1895 and seen only occasionally since – Wells had been sending him some of his stories and Shaw thought well of them. Shaw asked Wallas to arrange a meeting, and Shaws and Wellses were both pleased and became good friends. Shaw was amused by Wells and liked both him and Jane, and he would sponsor Wells formally when he finally joined the Fabian Society a year later.

Wells half joked that he was 'awfully afraid' of Beatrice Webb on first meeting her – as indeed he should have been, since she was the most brilliant woman of her generation, and eight years his senior: not only exceptionally intelligent but well born, well connected and now seeking him out. Later he wrote in a fictional account of her, 'She had much of the vigour and handsomeness of a slender impudent young man, and an unscrupulousness altogether feminine' – and he added, 'she manifestly liked me.'[5] She walked with a stride, she smoked, she enjoyed talking politics with clever men – and she still had a face to turn heads, handsome, with a Roman nose, deep-set black eyes and dark hair springing up from her brow, and often disordered. She wore her clothes carelessly, but when dressed up she had 'a gypsy splendour of black and red and silver all her own'.[6] He found her sometimes aggressive but also imaginative and possessed of a great capacity for ideas. If there were a few reservations on both sides, there was also an undeniable spark between them. He would give her name to the beautiful, well-born heroine of his best novel, *Tono-Bungay* – although her character bore no resemblance to that of the great Mrs Webb.

When the Boer War ended in May 1902, shipping was no longer under strain, and Fred Wells was able to return to England for a holiday, warmly welcomed and offered a bed at Spade House. Wells had planned to take a holiday in May in order to miss 'the bloody coronation' of Edward VII, but the coronation was postponed when the King went down with appendicitis, and did not take place until 9 August, when Wells again left the country, this time for Paris.

Before that, in June, Wells and Jane went to Switzerland, leaving their son Gip with his nanny. In July 1902 Wells's *The Sea Lady*, the novel he had started to think about in 1899, after moving to Sandgate, was published (by Methuen), and, although it was greeted with praise from Arnold Bennett, it failed to sell. It draws on Wells's enjoyment of the sea, bringing a mermaid to disrupt the life of young Mr Chatteris, who is embarking on a serious political career encouraged by his sensible fiancée. The conflict between duty and reason on the one hand and imagination and desire on the other is played out and finishes with Chatteris disappearing into the waves with his mermaid in his arms. It does not read as a warning against such bewitchment but delights in it – which might have alarmed his new political friends had they bothered to read it. In September *Mankind in the Making* was serialized in the *Fortnightly Review*; he attacked the 'stupendous sham' of monarchy and aristocracy, with their 'complete air of unshakeable permanence' – and was to return to the subject many times without ever finding much support.

Dauntingly well informed and intelligent, the Webbs mixed with a wide circle of politicians, editors, philosophers, aristocrats, bishops and even what Beatrice called 'the brilliant but silly Souls' – the society ladies who liked to meet and entertain clever people. In fact, they knew everyone – including Arthur Balfour, nephew of the Conservative Prime Minister Lord Salisbury, who, finding himself falling asleep during Cabinet meetings in the summer of 1902, simply handed the prime ministership on to his nephew. Balfour took office on 12 July 1902. Beatrice entertained him, flirted with him, argued with him, admired him and called him 'Prince Arthur'; and he invited the Webbs to stay, and they went, not entirely to Sidney's approval but greatly to Beatrice's enjoyment. She liked to be in the political swim.

In September 1902 Sidney asked Wells to become one of the founding members of a new dining club to be called the Co-efficients – it had been Beatrice's idea but was to be exclusively male. There would be twelve members – politicians, philosophers, editors and writers – who would meet monthly to discuss the topics of the time, such as local government, education and the Empire. It was a flattering invitation for Wells, and he accepted unhesitatingly – this was when he took a flat in Clement's Inn, close to the Fabian offices, allowing him to spend more time in town.

So he found himself dining alongside Bertrand Russell and debating informally with leading politicians. Russell had not heard of Wells until then but found his point of view more sympathetic than that of any of the other members, who included Edward Grey, Richard Haldane, Leo Amery and Alfred Milner. Leo Maxse, editor of the right-wing *National Review*, was another member, as was Charles Masterman, academic and journalist, who went on to write *The Condition of England* (1909), a book strongly influenced by Wells's ideas, and to become a Liberal MP and a privy councillor; and William Pember Reeves, a liberal New Zealander now settled in England and the High Commissioner for New Zealand. Wells found Masterman, Reeves and Russell the most congenial in their views. A few other writers were invited later, among them Henry Newbolt (poet of 'Play up! play up! and play the game!'), who became a friend of Wells.

They began to meet in December 1902. Russell walked out after a fierce argument with the Imperialists, saying he would rather wreck the Empire than sacrifice freedom – and he went on to take up the cause of votes for women, which was not a subject discussed at Co-efficient dinners.[7] Wells spoke for republicanism in November 1904, and the crippling effect of monarchy – and found that this was considered 'a barely pardoned eccentricity'. He saw that he and Russell were the most 'irresponsible' members – he enjoyed presenting his own unorthodox views, and querying the educational dominance of Oxford and Cambridge, where virtually all the other members had been educated. He also acknowledged that he learnt a great deal from listening and arguing with such well-informed and powerful men. The club continued until 1909.

Beatrice Webb was also arranging social occasions for her protégé, to introduce him to more people likely to be useful to him. In November 1902 she invited him to dinner to meet Balfour, the Prime Minister; Herbert Asquith, the Liberal politician who would become Prime Minister in 1908; John Burns, the trades unionist politician; the Shaws; and Lady Elcho – one of the 'silly Souls', who found Wells interesting and took to inviting him to Stanway, her house in Gloucestershire. On this occasion Mrs Webb thought Wells tried too hard to be clever – although Wells himself told Jane he felt he had talked well. In any case their friendship flourished, and they exchanged letters and visits. Early in 1904 she sent him a chapter on prison reform from the book on local government she was writing with Sidney. Wells told her he was working on his *A Modern Utopia* and then became personal, saying he was engaged in 'quite a lot of intricate thinking about these Webbs' and going on to accuse her of being a 'faceted' person who could be sensible but then liked to take up 'some palpable absurdity such as the monarchy or the established Church, and produce beautiful upside-down reasons for regarding it as the most perfect of human institutions'.[8] Beatrice was indeed a Christian who found comfort in the Church, but she was not offended, and after another visit to Sandgate she wrote in her diary, 'We like him much – he is absolutely genuine and full of inventiveness – a "speculator" in ideas – somewhat of a gambler but perfectly aware that his hypotheses are not verified. In one sense he is a romancer spoilt by romancing.'[9]

Wells wrote telling her she was a reactionary with an anti-radical creed. This was good-natured teasing, and he was invited back to stay and take another 'little dinner'. The little dinner was again with the Prime Minister, Balfour, the Bishop of Stepney, Maud Pember Reeves (wife of William) and a clever young Tory lawyer – the discussion covered the hereditary monarchy, the Church, the board school, the public school and university, the 'Governing Class', training in science and the device of popular elections. It was a success – afterwards Beatrice told her sister Mary that Balfour had let himself go and said to her on leaving that he had had a most delightful evening – satisfying her vanity as hostess fully. 'And Oh! my "Pictuer" dress did look so charming.'[10] This was the worldly Beatrice who loved entertaining the great and presiding over witty talk, and confessed in her diary that she had spent twenty-one guineas on an evening dress. While she thought Balfour had looked aged and out of health, she had clearly charmed him. And Wells had charmed her:

when he was next in London she sent a note, 'Won't you turn up for lunch tomorrow? Don't answer'[11] – indicating that he was to be a friend who could call informally when he liked. She was enjoying her social life too much, Sidney felt, and in June he stopped her from going to more parties, telling her 'You won't be able to work in the morning.'

Wells was also in contact with another, very different Fabian family, that of Hubert Bland, a founding member of the society who had remained its Honorary Treasurer ever since – somewhat surprisingly, since he declared his dislike of democracy, converted to Roman Catholicism and held generally conservative views. A big, assertive man, he sported a frock-coat and single eyeglass, and he wrote a popular newspaper column for the *Manchester Sunday Chronicle*; and his more successful wife was Edith Nesbit. Edith liked Wells, and he reciprocated, and admired her books too. The Blands had six children and lived in a large house in Eltham (in South-East London), with a smaller place at Dymchurch on the south coast, not far from Sandgate, and here the Wellses first visited them in the autumn of 1902, and he and Edith exchanged warm compliments on each other's work. The Blands were also friends of Dr Henry Hick and his wife, and very hospitable and jolly. Soon Wells was going for weekends of charades, badminton, picnics, cigarettes and good food. Also some surprises: as Wells came to know them, he discovered that only three of the children were Edith's: one had been fathered by Bland on his mother's companion, and two more on Edith's friend Alice Hoatson, who lived with them. Wells's advanced views on sexual behaviour did not run to approving of Bland, who told Wells he was 'an experimentalist in illicit love' – Wells chose to call him 'a sort of Tom-cat man'. The children had grown up ignorant of these complications and all believed that Edith was their mother – that is, until their late teens, when they were told the truth.

Wells disliked Bland but was enchanted by Edith and her attractive teenage daughter Rosamund – she was in fact Hoatson's daughter – and was very ready to join in parties and other pleasures. In the summer of 1905 he turned up uninvited at Dymchurch, with a suit-case, and stayed for a week, working on a book. Rosamund, now nineteen, had literary ambitions and had already published some sim-ple children's stories – *Cat Tales* and *Bunny Tales* – and Edith told Wells that she would have to earn her own living, and hoped it would be by writing – could he advise her? Rosamund then went to stay at Spade House, the Wellses were kind to her, she adored the little boys – by then there were two, Gip and Frank – and all went well. She also became an enthusiastic founding member of the Fabian Nursery, set up in April 1906 while Wells was in America – another was Amber Reeves, daughter of Maud and William Pember Reeves: two clever young women with literary taste and an ambition to write. Amber had the advantage of a good education and parents who could afford to send her to university, and she was already studying at Cambridge. Rosamund had an admirer in Clifford Sharp, the young journalist who set up the Fabian Nursery, and who hoped to marry her.

For Wells, who would be forty in September 1906, the admiration of attractive and high-spirited Fabian girls was intoxicating. At some point he and Rosamund agreed to take a clandestine trip to Paris together – possibly in March 1907 (although the date is not certain). Wells was already sexually involved with the writer Violet Hunt – they were occasional afternoon lovers on a free-and-easy basis – and he wrote a note to her on 7 March, remarking, 'And I have a Pure Flame for Rosamund who is the Most – Quite!' Whether it was a pure flame or not, Clifford Sharp grew jealous of Wells, who was advising Rosamund not to marry him. When Sharp found out that Rosamund was planning an escapade with Wells, he told Bland, and the two of them confronted her with Wells on the platform at Pad-dington, poised to take a train on their way to France. Bland struck Wells a blow and forced Rosamund to go home with him.

Edith then wrote to Jane, complaining of Wells's behaviour. Shaw tried to calm everyone down. Wells defended himself to Shaw, writ-ing, 'Damn the Blands! All through it's been that infernal household of lies that has tainted the affair and put me off my game.' And further, 'You show the judgement of a hen. You write of Bland in a strain of sentimental exaltation, you explain his beautiful romantic character to me – as though I don't know the man to his bones. You might be dear Mrs Bland herself in a paroxysm of romantic invention. All this twaddle about "the innocent little person". If she is innocent it isn't her parents' fault anyhow.'[12]

He followed up this ungentlemanly sneer at the girl he had been proposing to take to Paris with a boast about his own superiority over Shaw in the matter of sexual relations: 'You don't know, as I do, in blood and substance, lust, failure, shame, hate, love and creative passion.' Shaw was always more amused by Wells than disapproving. Wells also accused Bland of incestuous feelings for Rosamund, who had described her father's behaviour to him.

To run ahead: despite Wells's advice, Rosamund did marry Clifford Sharp, in September 1909. He was a protégé of the Webbs and would become the first editor of the *New Statesman* in 1913. He was also an alcoholic, his life disintegrated, and he left the *Statesman* in 1928 and died in 1935. Rosamund remembered Wells with affection, and some years later wrote to him, calling him 'the H. G. who writes unforgettable, and darling things, the H. G. one loves, and always loved and couldn't misunderstand. This was once my H. G. and I think in some deep place in me is still my H. G.'[13]

Wells finally made up his mind to join the Fabian Society in February 1903. At this point the Secretary, Pease, admired him as a man of outstanding genius, believing that 'his energy and attractive personality added radiance to the Society only equalled in early days.'[14] But Wells was still not ready to concentrate on Fabian matters, although he went on a walking tour in Switzerland with Graham Wallas in the summer of 1903, talking politics and sociological questions: Wells disconcerted Wallas by engaging in flirtations, and more, with women he met in the hotels they stayed in. This was during Jane's second pregnancy: she gave birth to another son, named Frank for his uncle, in October 1903. Wells had more rooms built into the house for nurseries, and added a bay at the back.

He was generous to friends, sending twenty-five pounds to Conrad on hearing he was in difficulties in November 1903. He was also reluctant to live too formally, telling Jane that December, 'I really don't see why we shouldn't wait on ourselves at table . . . Model housekeeping isn't our business, but model literary production.'[15] This letter was sent to her from his London flat, written after dining with the Webbs the night before, and he assured Jane – at home with the new baby – 'The Webb household outshines yours – it does. Simply because the Webbs are compared with us limited & stupid & vulgar people. My house is not made with hands, my success, our success is not to be measured by material things, our reality is dreamland & the unseen.'[16] These are fine words, but the insults he throws at the Webbs seem oddly inappropriate – Sidney and Beatrice Webb limited, stupid, vulgar? Was he writing faster than he could think, putting down the first words that came into his head to please Jane? Or was he drunk on the Webbs' good wine?

13. Pressure

However busy Wells kept, he took friendship seriously. In December 1903 he was presented with a crisis to which he responded, at first reluctantly, then with generosity and energy. A telegram came on the 23rd from Gabrielle, George Gissing's French common-law wife, saying, 'Come and see me.' He replied, 'What for?' On the next day, which was Christmas Eve, she wired again, saying that Gissing was dying and entreating him to set off in haste. They were living in the Basque Country, at Saint-Jean-Pied-de-Port, a small town above Saint-Jean-de-Luz – a long journey from England. Wells had a cold and asked another friend of Gissing, Morley Roberts, to go, but he replied saying he was ill. Wells decided that friendship demanded he should go. He packed a bag, took a boat from Folkestone and then a train south. He reached the Gissing household on the afternoon of Christmas Day.

An English doctor from Biarritz arrived at the same time and said at once that there was no hope for the patient, who had double pneumonia – this was before the age of antibiotics. Gissing was incoherent but conveyed to Wells some sort of entreaty that he should take him back to England. Wells took over the sickroom, found a nurse, and – believing Gissing was being starved by Gabrielle, and wanting to sustain and comfort him – offered him hot broth, wine and coffee. At the same time he tried to cool Gissing's fevered body by applying wet handkerchiefs. He also sent off a letter to Edmund Gosse about getting a pension for the support of Gissing's two sons, and cabled Roberts again, asking him to come.

Wells accused Gabrielle of starving Gissing to death, while she counter-accused Wells of killing him with unsuitable food that drove up his temperature. They were now on extremely bad terms. Believing Roberts must be on the way, Wells decided to return to England.

He departed, Roberts was delayed, and Gabrielle was left alone with her husband. By her later account he lay gazing at her fixedly all through 28 December, sometimes making inarticulate sounds but unable to speak any words – although she also said he had 'cried aloud for death' in his agony. By the time Roberts arrived he was, mercifully, dead.

Gissing's funeral – a Christian one, which he would have forbidden had he been consulted – was attended by many of the English residents of Saint-Jean-de-Luz. There was an obituary in *The Times*. His sister wrote a memorial piece in which she said that depression was the most strongly marked of Gissing's characteristics. Wells's subsequent behaviour is not easy to understand – on the one hand, he worked very hard indeed to make sure that Gissing's sons, whom he had never met, were given financial support – and on the other, he disparaged his friend's work in the preface he was asked to write to Gissing's last novel, mixing his praise with words suggesting that he had been 'ill-advised' to become a novelist. It was an extraordinary remark to make in the circumstances, and the family rejected the preface. Wells then chose to print it elsewhere, insisting on having his say – a stubborn, ill-judged action. Years later, in his own memoir published in 1934, he wrote affectionately of Gissing, saying how as good friends they had laughed together, and how Gissing had considered Wells to be 'absolutely illiterate'. He also suggested that 'a poison had crept into his blood to distress, depress and undermine his vitality and at last to destroy him.'[1] This had also been the view of Gosse, who considered Gissing's books 'were ground out of him by the contemplation of his own misery'.[2]

Wells never explained his bad behaviour, but managed to concede later of Gissing that 'Some of his books will be read for many generations but because of the warping of his mind they will find fewer lovers than readers.'[3] What actually happened of course was that, after many years of neglect, Gissing's reputation as an original and powerful novelist began to grow in the 1960s and is now firmly established.

No one could have saved his life in 1903, but Wells did what he could, remembering what good friends they had been. The situation in which he had found Gissing in France had made any thought of recovery preposterous: he could only do his best to comfort a dying man. Wells recalled later that 'preposterous' had been one of Gissing's favourite words – and that, despite all his sorrows and difficulties, they had often shared 'abundant fits of laughter' in the past. Jane had fed him well in England, Wells had taught him how to ride a bicycle – with difficulty and more laughter – and they had shared many tastes, beliefs and disbeliefs. They had walked Rome together, Gissing happy and absorbed in the past, where he felt at home as a classical scholar. But Gissing, for all his brilliance, had allowed himself to be humiliated and defeated – by women and by life – while Wells knew how to work for success, how to enjoy women and the world, and how to fight and – usually – to win.

Wells was now thirty-eight. He was still worried about money. In truth he worried more than he had in earlier, leaner times, and became preoccupied with finding ways of making more. Although Pinker had increased his sales steadily, Wells blamed him for failing to do better for him. 'In the last three or four years you have not relieved me of anxiety or saved me from several losses,' he told Pinker in 1904, and from then on he deputed Jane to deal with him.[4] Believing the theatre might help him to make money quickly, he set about trying to write plays, and sought advice from Shaw, who informed him otherwise, telling him that for one play that succeeds there are many that make nothing at all. In any case, Wells got nowhere with his efforts.

He felt he was always under pressure. Writing to a fellow writer, Vernon Lee, an essayist and short-story writer living in Italy with whom he had recently begun a correspondence, he gave this sense of pressure as a reason for inadequacies in his work: 'It's only in quite recent years I've had any leisure to think, and I still can't afford time to read & the idea of any sort of travel – except to recuperate for fresh work – is beyond dreaming. Consequently you will always miss in me certain qualities that you particularly admire.'[5] It did not lead him to make up his mind to write less and revise more – rather, he seems to have speeded up. In the eight years from 1903 to 1910 he produced thirteen books, plus a great deal of journalism, many lectures and a bestselling political tract.

In December 1903 *Strand Magazine* published 'The Land Ironclads', a short story that predicted armoured vehicles or tanks, and, in April 1904, one of Wells's most powerful and memorable stories, 'The Country of the Blind'. It follows an explorer into a lost valley where he finds himself living among a community of sightless people – and slowly finds his sight is not regarded as an advantage. But even a great short story did not bring in much quick income.

Hoping to improve his financial situation, he decided to find another publisher, and in July 1903, bypassing Pinker, he arranged a meeting with the head of the most highly respected publishing company in England, Macmillan: they had Tennyson, Matthew Arnold and George Eliot on their list, and, more recently, Thomas Hardy and Rudyard Kipling. Frederick Macmillan, now in his early fifties, had taken over the management of the firm on the death of his uncle Alexander in 1896. Wells proposed to him that Macmillan should acquire his previous titles, offering all his future fiction as an encouragement: he explained that it would be easier to keep them all before the booksellers – and more economical to advertise them, since the presence of so many titles on sale would be a permanent advertisement. Macmillan was ready to set about attempting this, and Wells did indeed become his most productive author for almost a decade, writing with an energy and inventiveness unmatched by any of his contemporaries – at the same time offering some of his books to other publishers.

During these years he offered Macmillan a volume of short stories – *Twelve Stories and a Dream* in 1903 – and five remarkable novels – *The Food of the Gods* in 1904, *Kipps* in 1905, *In the Days of the Comet* in 1906, *Tono-Bungay* in 1908 – for which Macmillan agreed to advance fifteen hundred pounds – and *Ann Veronica*, also in 1908, which Macmillan refused to publish, on the grounds that it would be distasteful to readers of the kind who bought books published by his firm, since its heroine is shown pursuing a divorced man.[6] Author and publisher failed to become friends. They were never at ease with one another, and they neither dined together nor even visited one another's homes. Macmillan did not appreciate Wells's suggestions for publicizing his books, which included men carrying sandwich boards and posters in Portsmouth railway station announcing 'Kipps worked here'. And when Wells offered him his novel *The New Machiavelli* in 1910, Macmillan, having accepted it sight unseen, was so shocked as he read the proofs and saw that it was about sex again, that he refused to proceed.

All these books were widely read and reviewed in England. Abroad, none did as well as his early science fiction stories. In 1903 the *Revue des deux mondes* devoted ten pages to Wells, with a review of *Love and Mr Lewisham*, but there was much less enthusiasm for the later novels – *Kipps* was not published in French until 1922, *Tono-Bungay* until 1929. In Russia, however, two *Collected Works* were published, one in 1908–9 and another in 1910 – but, since Russia was not then a signatory to the Berne Convention, Wells got no royalties. As to America – although Wells complained in 1902 that 'no decent criticism . . . has ever appeared about me in America' – his reputation was established there by the end of the decade.[7]

Wells believed – when he had time to think about it – that he would write better if he were not always under pressure, forced to work on several books simultaneously. And in 1904 he had another idea for improving his financial position. It came to him after his second meeting with Balfour, at Mrs Webb's dinner table, after which Balfour sent him a copy of a talk he had given on science, to which Wells responded politely by sending a paper of his own. Then, in May 1905, Wells wrote to Balfour again, this time with a bold suggestion: that he should endow him financially, or set up an academic position that would pay him – possibly a chair in sociology – in order to free him from 'the pressure of the market place', of having to write more than he wanted to or should, simply to keep solvent. He explained that he was not 'needy', but that he was at present forced to write too much:

had he only some free time, 'I believe I could do better and more significant work than under existing conditions.'[8] This was almost certainly true – it was, all the same, a surprising request – and he said nothing about it to either of the Webbs.

Balfour did not reply personally – he was about to resign as Prime Minister – but he handed Wells's letter to a private secretary, Ramsay, asking him to look into the matter. Ramsay reported to Balfour on 12 June, saying Wells had made a good case, but that he was not sure Wells was a true genius, and, further, he did not consider sociology to be an exact science. More simply, he believed that since Wells earned over a thousand pounds a year already, an appointment of the kind he had suggested would raise an outcry. Balfour told Ramsay to reply to Wells, and he doubtless wrote with proper tact. Wells acknowledged his letter, saying his suggestion had been 'quite casually made' and that he would have been 'amazed' had it produced any result. He added a sentence saying 'the problem of unremunerated or not immediately remunerative work' was too little regarded – and there the matter ended.[9] Balfour resigned on 5 December 1905 without alluding to Wells's request, the two men met again from time to time without embarrassment, and Wells always spoke respectfully of Balfour.

Wells's mother died on 12 June 1905, a Whit Monday. She had fallen down the stairs at Easter, and been largely cared for by her son Frank. Wells went over and found a nurse to help out, but he was too busy to stay and was not there when she died. He arrived soon afterwards and cleared up her affairs. Then back to work. In October 1905 *Kipps* was published and sold twelve thousand copies before Christmas – good news for Wells's finances.

After Balfour's resignation an election was called for January 1906. Also in December 1905 a magazine called the *Independent Review*, edited by George Trevelyan with assistance from his distinguished Cambridge and Bloomsbury friends, published a political tract by Wells.[10] It was called *This Misery of Boots*, and it is a piece of virtuoso writing that catches you with its first sentence, as Wells starts with his own experience as a child of watching people walking in boots – looking up at them from a basement room – and of having to wear uncomfortable boots himself. He goes on to list all the different sorts of misery boots can give: chafing, rucking up inside, splitting, leaking, letting nails through, forcing wearers to walk askew, preventing them from even trying to go for country walks and causing them to be ashamed of their feet, made ugly and misshapen, with corns and twisted toes.

He writes about girls, who ought to be beautiful, so that 'to see their poor feet askew, the grace of their walk gone, a sort of spinal curvature induced, makes me wretched, and angry with a world that treats them so'. He writes about nails working through the sole, making you limp manfully in the hope of a quiet moment and a quiet corner in which to hammer the thing down again. And of the flapping sole. 'My boots always came to that stage at last; I wore the toes out first, and then the sole split from before backwards. As one walks it begins catching the ground. One made fantastic paces to prevent it happening; one was dreadfully ashamed. At last one was forced to sit by the wayside frankly, and cut the flap away.'

He was of course writing at a time when most people had to put up with uncomfortable and ill-made shoes. And yet, he insisted,

> . . . this misery of boots is not an unavoidable curse upon mankind. If one man can evade it, others can. By good management it may be altogether escaped . . . There is enough good leather in the world to make good sightly boots and shoes for all who need them, enough men at leisure and enough power and machinery to do all the work required, enough unemployed intelligence to organise the shoemaking and shoe distribution for everybody. What stands in the way?

When a friend tells him it is useless to try to change things like boots, he protests:

> . . . don't submit, don't be humbugged for a moment into believing that this is the dingy lot of all mankind . . . Don't say for a moment: 'Such is life.' Don't think their miseries are part of some primordial

curse there is no escaping. The disproof of that is for anyone to see. There are people, people no more deserving than others, who suffer from none of these things. You may feel you merit no better than to live so poorly and badly that your boots are always hurting you; but do the little children, the girls, the mass of decent hard-up people, deserve no better fate?[11]

Further on he writes:

. . . when I . . . look at poor people's boots in the street, and see them cracked and misshapen and altogether nasty, I seem to see also a lot of little phantom land-owners, cattle-owners, house-owners, owners of all sorts, swarming over their pinched and weary feet like leeches, taking much and giving nothing, and being the real cause of all such miseries . . . Is there no other way of managing things than to let these property-owners exact their claims, and squeeze comfort, pride, happiness, out of the lives of the common run of people? Because, of course, it is not only the boots they squeeze into meanness and bad- ness . . . [they] make our houses so ugly, shabby, and dear . . . make our roadways and railways so crowded and inconvenient . . . sweat our schools, our clothing, our food . . . boots we took merely by way of one example of a universal trouble . . . It is this idea of extracting profit they hold which is the very root of the evil.[12]

He declares that: 'there are a number of people who say there is a bet- ter way . . . [who] propose that the State should take away the land, and the railways, and shipping, and many great organised enterprises from their owners, who use them simply to squeeze the means for a wasteful private expenditure out of the common mass of men, and should administer all these things, generously and boldly, not for profit, but for service.' These people, Wells explains, are the socialists:

And as for taking such property from the owners; why shouldn't we? The world has not only in the past taken slaves from their owners, with no compensation or with a meagre compensation; but in the history of mankind, dark as it is, there are innumerable cases of

slave-owners resigning their inhuman rights . . . a change as profound
as the abolition of private property in slaves would have been in
ancient Rome or Athens.[13]

'Socialism means revolution' – a change in the everyday texture of
life, a break with history, the vanishing of whole classes. Socialism
aims to change not only the boots but the clothes people wear, the
houses they live in, the work they do, the education they get, their
places, their honours and all their possessions.[14] 'Until Socialists can
be counted, and counted upon by the million, little will be done.
When they are – a new world will be ours.'[15]

This was Wells's message in *This Misery of Boots*. It remains a brilliant piece of polemical writing. His image of bad boots is of course
not quite so telling today – although feet are still being punished by
ill-fitting footwear – and we must keep in mind that he was writing
before socialism had arrived anywhere. Socialist reforms in England
began in 1908, when Lloyd George introduced the first old-age pen-
sions of five shillings a week for the over-seventies – against strong
resistance from the House of Lords. In 1911 came the first National
Insurance – then a long wait until 1946, when Family Allowances
were started, 1947 when coal mining was nationalized, railways in
1948, and the National Health Service set up in 1948 – too late for
Wells.

But he had laid out a witty, imaginative and beautifully written
call for a socialist revolution. It found many enthusiastic readers, but
hardly fitted with the current political situation, in which the Labour
Party was establishing itself peacefully and the only violence was
coming – not very dangerously – from women demanding the vote.
So it was widely read and appreciated and then forgotten – although
some of its recommendations were taken up in the 1940s. Curiously,
it is rarely listed among Wells's writings or in accounts of his life, and
he himself failed even to mention it in his own autobiography,
though it was published as a Fabian pamphlet in 1907. A shame,
because he is fully alive in the language, writing with such power to
make us see and feel, such polemical energy, that it cries out to be

read today, if not now as a call for revolution, yet still as an argument for change, for justice, for the more equal society that is so badly needed.

For a serious author to manage to produce so many books at such speed was almost unprecedented – and all the more so in that he was writing as much non-fiction as fiction during the same period. The non-fiction proved to be at least as successful as the fiction, giving Wells a double reputation: as a political thinker to be taken seriously and as a novelist and short-story writer. *Anticipations*, published in 1901, was a bestseller, reprinted many times and translated into Dutch, French, German, Polish, Russian and Spanish – more languages than any of the novels of this period. *Mankind in the Making* followed in 1903. *A Modern Utopia* (1905) presented itself as fiction but was effectively offering a programme for the good society: it was, again, very popular in England and was translated into French, Czech, Spanish and Russian. *The Future in America* came in 1906 – and helped to make his name known there. After this came a short treatise called *Socialism and the Family* (1906) – Wells was keen on an idea already current that state payment to mothers, 'the endowment of motherhood', would be a sensible way to improve society, as women Fabians were asking for; it came much later in the form of Family Allowances.

In 1908 came *First and Last Things*, in which he declared his disbelief in personal immortality or a divine mediator, and affirmed his resolve to work for socialism. A copy of this went off to Churchill with a letter, as did *New Worlds for Old*, published in the same year: in it Wells advocated the nationalization of land, mines, railways, housing, and the establishment of a public health service, which he believed every doctor under forty would support. Whether Churchill read all these books or not – he claimed to have read everything Wells wrote – he kept them in his library all his life, and may have glanced into *New Worlds for Old* with some surprise forty years later, when the National Health Service was set up. Wells laid out a great many features of the programme of the post-war Labour government in these books.

1. H. G. Wells, known as 'Bertie' to the family, as a boy, *c.* 1876, already smart and enjoying a book. He wrote his first full-length story, which he illustrated, at the age of eleven.

2. Wells's father, Joseph, cricketer, gardener and reluctant shopkeeper, encouraged his youngest son to become a reader.

3. Sarah, Wells's mother, was forty-four when he was born, her fourth child. She was religious, genteel and a poor housekeeper.

4. Uppark, where Wells's mother became housekeeper – and he educated himself from the books, pictures and telescope he found in the attic.

5. Midhurst, the attractive Sussex town Wells was always fond of. From its grammar school, where he became a pupil-teacher, he won a scholarship to study science in London.

6. Posing with a skeleton at the Normal School of Science in Kensington, *c.* 1884–5. Here he formed lifelong friendships with several of his fellow students.

7. Wells's first cousin Isabel: he married her in 1891 and left her in January 1894.

8. With his second wife, Amy Catherine Robbins, whom he called Jane. They married in 1895 and had two sons, George – 'Gip' – and Frank.

9. Jane at her typewriter, *c.* 1899.

10. Taking tea. Wells in the 1890s.

11. William Henley, poet and editor, ran *The Time Machine* as a serial in his magazine the *New Review*, in 1895.

12. Wells's 'picshua' (*sic*) (self-portrait sketch) of himself and Jane, here reading the manuscript of *Love and Mr Lewisham*, 1900. He has inscribed 'Waiting for the verdik' (*sic*).

13. The novelist Arnold Bennett met Wells in 1900, and became a lifelong friend and correspondent.

14. Bernard Shaw, playwright and social reformer, leading member of the Fabian Society – he and his wife, Charlotte, became close friends of Wells and Jane.

15. George Gissing, brilliant and unhappy novelist – a close friend who showed Wells Rome in 1898. Wells travelled to his deathbed in France in 1903.

16. Henry James, a near neighbour in Rye, befriended and admired Wells for many years – but in 1915 they fell out and Wells published a cruel attack on James shortly before James's death in 1916.

17 & 18. Sidney Webb (*left*) and his wife, Beatrice (*right*), leading Fabians. The most intelligent and effective political woman of her time, Beatrice introduced Wells to politicians and high society.

19. Arthur Balfour, first Earl of Balfour, was Prime Minister from 1902 to 1905.

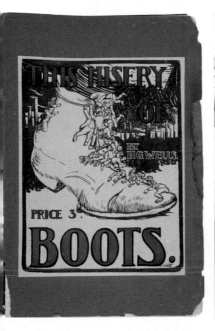

20. The jacket of *This Misery of Boots*, Wells's great essay first published in 1905 and reprinted as a pamphlet by the Fabians in 1907.

21. Amber Reeves, ardent young Fabian, seduced Wells in her room at Newnham College, Cambridge, and bore him a daughter in 1909.

22. Wells in his study at Spade House, built on a clifftop in Sandgate, Sussex, where he and Jane lived from 1901 to 1909. They entertained friends regularly while Wells increased his fame with novels such as *Tono-Bungay* and *Ann Veronica*.

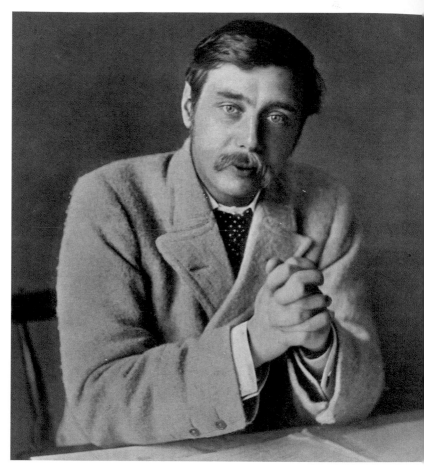

23. A formal portrait of Wells in his Jaeger suit. In December 1901 he announced, 'I am going to write, talk and preach revolution for the next five years.'

All these books aroused interest in English politicians, planners and intellectual readers young and old, Fabian Society members and many others. Wells presented himself in them as a serious – a 'grave' – socialist dedicated to changing society fundamentally and believing the good of the group to be more important than personal gratification. He also said the world needed to move away from nationalism to international government. He made it clear that he did not believe in God or any religion, and that the development of a sense of community and common general purpose was the essential thing. *A Modern Utopia* was particularly popular for its depiction of a future world state, vegetarian, republican and peaceful, ruled by gentle intellectuals who abjure usury, alcohol and sex, take cold baths, read new books regularly, and discipline and revitalize themselves by solitary weeks in the wilderness. They are known as Samurai, a name Wells took over from the Japanese noble military cast. Readers responded so enthusiastically to Wells's concept that groups of self-styled Samurai were formed.

How did the novels fit in with his political ideas? *The Food of the Gods* (1904) – a brilliantly entertaining piece of science fiction – brought congratulations from William James. He told Wells, 'for human perception you beat Kipling and for hitting off a thing with the right words you are unique . . . You are now an eccentric; perhaps 50 years hence you will figure as a classic.'[16] Both the Webbs also enjoyed the 'wit and wisdom' of *The Food of the Gods* as an allegory. Its subject is a newly discovered substance – Herakleophorbia – that hugely enlarges plants and animals, including wasps, rats and humans, who are fed it. It brings terrors – colourfully depicted, entertaining and alarming – and complex moral questions once the human population is divided between the normally sized majority and the giants. G. K. Chesterton called it a delightful romance, while taking exception to what he saw as its message about supermen: it remains a very good read.

Next, in October 1905, the same year as *A Modern Utopia*, came *Kipps*. Kipps is the poor drapers' apprentice who inherits a fortune and finds upper-middle-class life confusing and corrupt. It was welcomed as 'the best story he has yet given us' by the politician and writer Charles Masterman, and by Henry James as 'vivid and sharp and *raw*. Kipps himself is a diamond of the first water . . . exquisite and radiant.'[17] It was popular for coming down strongly in favour of working-class virtues as Wells laid them out – modesty, fidelity and simple tastes – and still more for the fun of the scenes in which Kipps struggles in vain to adapt himself to grand manners and pleasures. Kipps asking an architect to design a simple house for him, and being persuaded he must have a Moorish gallery, one roughcast gable and one half-timbered, a Tudor stained-glass window, crenellated battlements, two-coloured bricks and eleven bedrooms, will always make readers laugh – even if the whole book does not now pack quite the punch it did.

After that came *In the Days of the Comet* (1906), a fantasy with a message, predicting a changed world in which sexual jealousy has disappeared and both men and women feel free to make love with anyone they find desirable – something Macmillan had not taken in before publication. Unusually it was the reviewer for *The Times Literary Supplement* who first raised objections to the book, saying that Wells, as a socialist, was proposing that wives as well as property were to be held in common: 'Free love . . . is to be the essence of the new social contract.' Popular papers seized on this and Wells found himself widely credited with linking socialism and free love. Among the Fabians, Shaw wrote to him suggesting that 'Shaws and Wellses should set up a *ménage à quatre* like characters in *Days of the Comet*' – a Shavian joke of course. It must have occurred to Wells – as he wrote letter after letter to the newspapers defending himself from the accusation that he was advocating free love – that he was lying, since he not only believed in it but also practised it, having obtained his wife's permission. But when Bertrand Russell suggested he was being disingenuous in denying in public the beliefs he advocated in private, he lied again, telling him he did not intend to take up free love until he could afford to do so. It was a surprisingly practical response – multiple sexual partners can make life expensive, as he was to find.

★

As though he needed something more to do in 1906, with *Kipps* selling well, *In the Days of the Comet* more or less ready for publication and his plans for the Fabians in hand, Wells decided to go to America for two months and write a quick account of his impressions. It was partly to please himself by taking a look at the great country across the ocean, partly to make money, partly to introduce himself in person to transatlantic readers. The book was to be called *The Future in America*.

Before he set off, he was determined to launch a preliminary attack on the current running of the Fabian Society, and in February he delivered a manifesto called 'The Faults of the Fabian' to the members, in which he complained that the society was too small, unbusinesslike, uninventive and stuck in its ways. He told them they needed a propaganda campaign, more staff, more members and larger offices. He attacked with wit, telling them, 'You have it from Mr Bernard Shaw that poverty is a crime, and if so, then by the evidence of your balance sheet ours is a criminal organization.' And he mocked their methods: 'We don't advertise . . . not quite our style. We cry socialism as the reduced gentlewoman cried "oranges": I do so hope nobody will hear me.' Support came from a good many members, and Shaw, who never doubted Wells's cleverness, told him he welcomed his attack – but then urged him to be clear about his objectives, and to understand the importance of compromise. Mrs Webb decided he had neither the tradition nor the training for co-operation with others. 'It is a case of *Kipps* in matters more important than table manners,' she wrote, suddenly snobbish. But there was nothing to be done until his return, and, having delivered his attack, Wells set off blithely for America at the end of March.

14.   America in 1906

In the two months he had allowed himself for his trip, Wells managed to visit Philadelphia, Chicago, Boston, the Niagara Falls and Washington, D.C.; but it was in New York that he had his most dramatic experience of the American ethos. It came about as he met another socialist writer who was, like him, making a first visit to America, in his case from Russia: Maxim Gorky.

Gorky was already well known for his play *The Lower Depths*, in which he had given a grim picture of the lives of a group of social outcasts in Russia – thief, prostitute, out-of-work actor – crammed together into squalid lodgings, as they fought among themselves, one dying of tuberculosis, another committing suicide – written from his own observation and played in Moscow to great acclaim in 1902. The aim of his visit to America was to raise funds for the Bolshevik Party, which was seeking to overthrow the tyranny of the tsars and to establish democracy in Russia. It was a cause that seemed likely to appeal to Americans. The year before, in 1905, the Tsar's troops had shot down a peaceful demonstration in St Petersburg, and Gorky had been imprisoned. After his release he joined the Bolsheviks, met Lenin, took part in an armed uprising in Moscow and then left the country for Finland. Many Americans were ready to welcome him as a noble figure who embodied the cause of freedom, and prepared to give money to support the Bolshevik cause.

Gorky and Wells arrived almost simultaneously in New York in early April. Wells commented sardonically on the Statue of Liberty as his ship approached her: 'Poor liberating lady of the American ideal! One passes her and forgets' – but he was impressed by the sight of skyscrapers so huge that they dwarfed the liners. He took a day to wander alone, admiring the Fuller (later the Flatiron) Building, the Brooklyn Bridge and the bright electric subways: 'New York is lavish of light, it is lavish of everything, it is full of the sense of spending from an inexhaustible supply,' he decided. The next day he was invited to an event arranged in honour of Gorky.

In this way the two socialist writers, from West and East, met for the first time. Wells observed that Gorky came dressed as a peasant, in a belted blue shirt, shiny black trousers and boots. Wells had already been taken to see the tomb of the great general and liberal President Ulysses S. Grant, and received visits in his hotel from Mark Twain and William Dean Howells, Henry James's friend and already slightly known to Wells from a meeting in England in May 1904. They told him they were planning a literary dinner to honour Gorky.

Since Gorky spoke no English, he had brought his own interpreter, the actress Maria Andreyeva. She was a good linguist – but as soon as the press understood that she was not his wife, from whom he had been amicably separated for some time, they launched a furious attack on the immoral couple. A sort of hysteria broke out in purit-anical America. Gorky and Andreyeva were summarily turned out of their hotel, their luggage was dumped on the pavement in the dark, and they were unable to find another hotel prepared to take them. 'Infected persons could not have been treated more abominably in a town smitten with a panic of plague,' wrote Wells. It became almost impossible for Gorky to appear in public, and he and Andreyeva had to be sheltered in private houses for the rest of their visit. The head of Columbia was threatened with sacking for giving a reception for him. Mark Twain was put under such pressure that he felt he had to refuse to meet him again. The President, Theodore Roosevelt, was obliged to cancel Gorky's planned visit to the White House. As Wells put it, Gorky was simply obliterated.

Gorky did, however, get to give a talk in Boston in May, and there he met William James, whom he described as 'a wonderful old man' – adding 'but he is also an American.' And he was entertained by a Fabian couple – for there was an American Fabian Society – who invited him to stay in their holiday home in the Adirondacks, upstate New York, and then their house on Staten Island. John Martin was an English Fabian who had gone to lecture in America in 1898, married a rich wife there, Prestonia Mann, and never left. These generous Fabian hosts enabled Gorky to stay in America for several months, and, since he had nothing else to do, he began to write another play – in all other ways the trip was a failure.

Wells did better. He too was greeted by Mark Twain and Howells, who now described his English guest kindly if inaccurately as 'a cockney of brave spirit, who is socialistic in his expectations of the future and boldly owns to have been a dry goods clerk in his own past'.[1]

As a good socialist, Wells insisted that the essential question for America, as for Europe, was 'the rescue of her land, her public service, and the whole of her great economic process from the anarchic and irresponsible control of private owners'.[2] He visited Ellis Island, where more than a million immigrants were due in a single year, and questioned whether such huge numbers could be successfully absorbed into the population – and then was moved to hear the immigrant children singing together and making the Pledge of Allegiance to the flag of the United States. But he still doubted that the Central and Eastern European peasantry would assimilate well, and thought it might become a virtually illiterate industrial proletariat.

He found no aristocracy, no Tories, no Labour Party and no servants – except where there were African-Americans – and he was immediately impressed by them: 'I took a mighty liking to these gentle, human, dark-skinned people,' he wrote. In one of the most striking passages in the book he gave his view that 'Whatever America has to show in heroic living today, I doubt if she can show anything finer than the quality of the resolve, the steadfast efforts hundreds of black and coloured men are making today to live blamelessly, honourably and patiently, getting by themselves what scraps of refinement, beauty and learning they may, keeping their hold on a civilization they are grudged and denied.'

The many child workers he saw – in a Pennsylvanian colliery, in Massachusetts bleaching vats and in the Chicago stockyards – shocked him deeply. He found in Chicago a 'vast, magnificent squalor' and 'a reek that outdoes London' from burning bituminous coal – but he also observed with admiration its 'Field houses', created by the state of Illinois, areas within the slums where there were small parks, playgrounds, paddling pools, reading rooms and decent eating places. 'It is Socialism – let us joyfully admit as much,' he declared. Also in Chicago he was taken to 'a most respectable house of ill fame' – where of course he rejected the girls, he assured Jane. She was missing him and wrote to say she was worried about the 'silly, wasteful muddle of one's life . . . If I set out to make a comfortable home for you to do work in, I merely succeed in contriving a place where you are bored to death . . . well, dear, I don't think I ought to send you such a letter. It's only a mood you know.'[3]

He visited universities, and was well received at Columbia, Harvard and Wellesley – he mocked the last for turning out, at vast expense, young women 'capable of Browning'[4] – taking the view that it would be better for them to be taught to think about the future rather than 'dead poets'.

Reaching Washington, he described it to Jane as 'a pleasant orderly place and very shady and flowery after Chicago and Boston and New York,' and said he was busy writing, and had employed a typist to transcribe what he had already written.[5] He was unimpressed by Congress, which struck him as feeble and inefficient. Then he visited the White House – his fame brought him an invitation – and walked around its grounds with the President, Theodore Roosevelt, talking informally – by agreement he took no notes. He found Roosevelt's mind 'extraordinarily open' and the range of his reading impressive; and, better still, 'he thinks'. He recalled that Roosevelt spoke of the time as being 'one of ample, vigorous, and at times impatient, inquiry, and of intense disillusionment with old assumptions and methods'. Also of the possibility of moving towards 'some constructive scheme which, if not exactly socialism . . . will be closely analogous to socialism'. Wells was charmed by him, and ended his account of their conversation with Roosevelt alluding to *The Time Machine* and its gloomy prophecy of the distant future for humanity: 'Supposing it should all end in your butterflies and morlocks,' he said. Then: '*That doesn't matter now.* The effort's real. It's worth going on with. It's worth it.'

So, although Wells decided that 'America will never declare for socialism', he also wrote in his last chapter, 'my mind tilts steadily to a belief in a continuing and accelerated progress now in human affairs . . . it seems to me that in America, by sheer virtue of its size, its free traditions, and the habit of initiative in its people, the leadership of progress must ultimately rest.'

He did not of course mention that, immediately after leaving Roosevelt, he took a taxi outside the White House and asked the driver to take him to a brothel – 'a gay house', it was called. 'White or Coon?' asked the taxi driver, and Wells chose 'Coon'. The slim, half-naked, brown-skinned young woman he selected in the brothel interested him, telling him she was ambitious to travel to Europe and get some education so that she could change her way of life. He even considered postponing his departure for England, thinking he might take her to New York and spend more time with her. This did not happen, but 'for years I thought of her with tenderness'.[6] If his behaviour was normal behaviour for that time, what was not normal was his leaving a reasonably honest account of it. It was not of course published until long after his death, in 1984, but he had left instructions that his account of his sex life, or love life, should be published in the future, and his son Gip carried out his wishes.

His last evening in the United States was spent with Gorky on Staten Island, hearing of the Russian's disappointment at the attitude of the Americans. Gorky described them as 'base, busy, greedy and childish little men', and he was to leave America in the autumn with hostile feelings, having raised less than ten thousand dollars for the Bolshevik cause.[7] Wells was sympathetic, the two men became good friends and were to meet and talk again over the next years, in London in 1907 at the Fifth Congress of the Russian Social Democratic Labour Party, where Lenin, Trotsky and Stalin were also present; then during Wells's visits to Russia in 1914, in 1920 and in 1934; and they were to love the same woman, the irresistibly alluring Moura Budberg.

The Future in America was serialized in England from July 1906 in the *Tribune* and from July to October in *Harper's Weekly* in America; it was published in book form in November 1906. A readable and wide-ranging account of his visit, it was well received by reviewers both in America and England. Henry James found it 'full and rich and powerful and worthy' – if also 'too *loud*' – while acknowledging that America was 'a yelling country' and the 'the only way to utter many things you are delivered of *is* to yell them.'[8] Beatrice Webb also wrote to Wells, saying she could not 'vie with the reviewers in the extent of their praise – but I *do* think it a most excellent Impressionist picture – full of illumination as to facts and suggestion as to remedies – an excellent piece of work.'[9]

She was determined to keep on good terms with Wells, and the interaction between them remained important to her. 'We are excellent company now for each other's souls,' she wrote to him, inviting him to visit them in the house they had taken near Oxford and saying, 'Do come'; and she added, 'Give my love to Mrs Wells – if you don't come, she must.'[10] He was still set on reforming the Fabian Society, and the next years were to test the friendship between them to its limits.

Aylmer Maude suggested to Wells in 1906 that he should send copies of his books to Tolstoy. Wells agreed and wrote a letter to Tolstoy to go with the books, which Maude translated into Russian. It appears in a volume of Tolstoy's correspondence, along with a note: 'Herbert Wells was an English writer, the author of numerous scientific and social-utopian novels.'[11] Wells's letter reads:

My friend Aylmer Maude told me that you would be interested to look at two or three of my little books. I never sent you my books, because I imagine you submerged in a flood of books presented to you by every whippersnapper writer of Europe and America, Now I am sending you the story *Love and Mr Lewisham*, a collection of short stories, *The Plattner Story*, a novel, *The War of the Worlds*, and a volume of discussions, *A Modern Utopia*, which Mr Maude specially asked me to send to you, because he says that you don't like Utopias. But firstly it's not like other ones, and secondly it's better that you immediately learn everything bad about me. I sincerely hope that this torrent of books will not bore you in the slightest. I think that I have read about eighteen of your works, all the ones that it is possible to obtain in English. *War and Peace* and *Anna Karenina*, in my view, are the most magnificent and comprehensive works of all those that I have had the pleasure of reading.[12]

An acknowledgement arrived from Tolstoy dated 2 December 1906; it would not have reached Wells until mid-January 1907. Tolstoy wrote: 'Dear Sir, I have received your letter and your books thank you for both. I expect great pleasure in reading them.' No further word came from him – he was after all an old man, with only four years more to live. But it must have been a disappointment for Wells. His admiration for Tolstoy's work was qualified by his dislike of his religious views; and when he came to write an introduction to Tolstoy's last great novel, *Resurrection*, he made this plain. This was in 1927, when the Oxford University Press put out new English translations of Tolstoy to celebrate the hundredth anniversary of his birth, in 1828. Wells wrote of Tolstoy's 'stupendous powers of observation', but found his writing lacking in laughter and 'creative fun', accused him of 'copious garrulousness', and of bending stories to fit the situation he is writing about so that 'psychology has snapped in the process'.

Wells published a short story in July 1906 that seems to have gone almost unnoticed at the time, and also when it was then included in a collection of 1911: *The Door in the Wall and Other Stories*. He said he liked his stories to be printed separately, not in collections, so that they could lie around and be picked up by readers, each offering a short release from the limitations of real life. But this never happened.

All his stories surprise and entertain, the range of his imagination being so wide, from ants attacking humans to early man discovering how to get on to the back of a horse. A few carry a powerful charge of feeling that disturbs and even haunts readers. 'The Door in the Wall', written when he was at the height of his powers, is one of these. The image of a simple green-painted wooden door in a long white wall that hides whatever is behind it, stretching along an unfrequented London street, is immediately vivid and of course familiar to many readers. The story begins as two youngish men with successful careers – Lionel Wallace is a politician – are talking together, and Wallace confides to his friend Redmond an odd story of his childhood. We are told in the second paragraph of the story that Wallace is now dead, but it is easy to forget this as one reads on.

Wallace is the son of a well-to-do man who is ambitious for him – his mother has died so early that he hardly remembers her. He tells Redmond of how, aged five, he had seen a door in a wall in a London street and opened it – to find himself in an enchanted garden, where tame panthers came to play with him as he walked on paths among beautiful flowers and trees, then met a woman who spoke warmly to him, held him, mothered him and read to him – until he suddenly awoke and found himself alone and back in the street. He could never find the door again by searching, but, as he grew up, he passed it on a few occasions, each time in a hurry to do something important, which meant he did not attempt to open it. He becomes a politician, set for success.

The story ends with Redmond hearing of Wallace's death – he has been killed by falling into a deep building site off a road in Central London; the door in the fence protecting the site had been left unlocked.

Most urban readers will recognize the building site walled off and the door that arouses a frisson of curiosity. And the idea that there is a hidden paradise to be reached if only one knew how is tantalizingly attractive. It relates of course to the Christian hope of heaven; but Wells was not a Christian, and the concept is presented only to be destroyed by him, or at least questioned. He lets the reader see the magic garden with the boy and then takes it away from the adult. The reader is allowed to remember it – and it is hard to forget. It is one of the best of Wells's stories, plainly told and dazzling in its refusal to explain.

It has lived on, reprinted many times in England and America – and is read all over the world. The 1911 edition was illustrated by

Alvin Langdon Coburn, a young American photographer of great brilliance, with a photogravure showing a solid, panelled wooden door set in a brick wall – beautiful, but nothing like Wells's simple wooden, green-painted door set in a long white wall.

The beautiful garden is a sort of Elysium, with playmates who welcome Lionel Wallace and urge him to return when they see he is leaving. It could represent memories of a prenatal existence – as invoked by Wordsworth ('Our souls have sight of that immortal sea/ Which brought us hither', where 'the Children sport upon the shore', waiting to be born). The critic Bernard Begonzi suggested that the death of Lionel could be Wells's acknowledgment of the loss of his own original talent: that the poetic imagination powering his early romances was lost once he gave himself up to sociology and politics – and that in becoming a propagandist he ceased to be an artist.[13] It is a well-argued case – but readers of the novels that followed – *Love and Mr Lewisham, Kipps, Mr Polly, Tono-Bungay* and *Ann Veronica* – will protest that these are first-rate realist works that can take their place unapologetically beside the poetry of the stories.

After 'The Door in the Wall' he almost gave up writing short stories, producing only nine more in the remaining forty years of his life.

15. Webb and Wells

Although their backgrounds were as different as could be, Beatrice Webb and Wells had a great deal in common. Both were dedicated to bringing socialism to Britain, both were compulsive hard workers, and both gave time and energy to the cause – he through books and articles, lecturing and stirring up the Fabian Society, she also through the books she wrote with Sidney, through their long commitment to the Fabians, the founding of the London School of Economics and then, from December 1905 until 1909, through her work for the Royal Commission on the Poor Laws and the Relief of Distress, to which she was appointed by Balfour in the last days of his prime ministership. During that same period Wells was working on *Tono-Bungay*, which he regarded as his 'finest and most finished novel'.

Their friendship was important to both of them. She regarded him as by far the cleverest of the younger Fabians and, as we have seen, she set about introducing him to eminent politicians and aristocrats who would interest him, and be useful to him. He was impressed and flattered, and pleased by her attentions; and he enjoyed their conversations. She read his books; they argued and exchanged lively letters. Sidney Webb was more cautious about Wells but ready to go along with Beatrice's enthusiasm. When Wells was pressing for an inquiry into the effectiveness of the Fabian Society, and attacking them in the process, she told Sidney 'not to be too hard on him and to remember there was a time when "the Webbs" were thought not too straight and not too courteous in their dealings' – she probably meant over the setting up of the LSE.[1] She never forgot that Wells was primarily a writer, and when they found themselves at odds over Fabian affairs she decided that he, 'with his intelligent sensitiveness will feel he has taken false steps into semi-public affairs and return to his own world of the artist'. She was largely right about this.[2]

From December 1905 Mrs Webb was distracted from Fabian matters, preparing for and attending meetings with her fellow members appointed to the Royal Commission. She took this prestigious appointment extremely seriously and worked hard from the start, briskly registering her disapproval of the way in which things were organized: no agenda, she complained, and some of her fellow commissioners 'too well bred and too feeble in health to be much good'. But, with Sidney's support and the chief researcher she appointed, William Beveridge, she felt confident she could be effective. Churchill had introduced this brilliant young lawyer with an interest in social reform to her; Beveridge was already doing good work in the East End, at Toynbee Hall, addressing poverty. He shared her socialist ideals and proved admirably efficient.[3] Just as well, since even as she started on this demanding work for the commission, she and Sidney were also publishing the first of their eleven volumes on English local government.

But all this hard work did not make her neglect Wells. She gave him lunch on 3 January 1906. On 12 January he delivered his *This Misery of Boots* talk, taken from his 1905 article in the *Independent Review*, to the Fabians – and Shaw told Sidney Webb it was not a mere piece of journalism but had real effect. On 9 February Wells spoke again to the Fabians, 'On the Faults of the Fabian', accusing them of being 'still half a drawing room society' – 'unbusinesslike, unadaptable and uninventive'. He then stayed overnight with the Webbs, and for the first time she found him 'quite unexpectedly unpleasant . . . an odd mixture of underhand manoeuvres and insolent bluster'.[4]

After this Wells left for America, and they did not meet again until July, when the Webbs went to Sandgate to see him. She decided then that he suspected her of worldliness and thought Sidney not strong enough to deal with this – that 'Sidney is weak and I am bad' – whereas she thought Sidney was the one who led. She also prophesied that 'five years will see Wells out of the Society'.[5] But she was set on keeping up their friendship. She continued to invite him and Jane, and she and Sidney were back in Sandgate in

September, finding Wells cast down by the attacks on his novel *In the Days of the Comet* – and possibly by reaching the age of forty on 21 September. She said they tried to smooth him down, and she was determined to remain friends: 'properly managed he will count for righteousness in his own way. So we steadily took position that this little storm in the Fabian Society was nothing compared to his work outside the Society.'[6] And they were right, because he was now busy writing *Tono-Bungay*.

In September Sidney invited Wells to discuss his proposals for the Fabians, which were still that they should take new offices, set up a weekly newspaper, take on paid staff and put out propaganda. Webb pointed out that financing all this would require a large capital sum. 'Have you reckoned it up?' he asked Wells. He did not think the society would accept Wells's proposals – 'But come and talk about them anyhow.'[7] Wells seems to have made no response, but he stayed with the Webbs in Grosvenor Road again in October, after delivering another talk to a large audience of Fabians, 'Socialism and the Middle Classes', in which he asserted that 'the discontent of women is a huge available source for socialism' – and repeated his arguments from *A Modern Utopia* that state-endowed motherhood would strengthen the position of women.

After the talk Emma Brooke complained to Edward Pease, the Secretary of the society, of Wells's ignorance of the feminist activity of the 1880s, when she had published her Fabian tract *The State Endowment of Motherhood*. 'Wells is old porridge rewarmed,' she complained – and it is true that he never referred to her or her ideas – and he may have heard Mrs Webb making disparaging remarks about her intelligence. But other Fabian women were ready to welcome his interest, among them Maud Pember Reeves, who was currently leading the Fabian Women's Group in marches with the Suffragettes. The Reeves and Wells families were now good friends, and both the Webbs were impressed by William Pember Reeves.

Sidney now distrusted Wells and thought him reckless, but Beatrice wrote in her diary that they must stand by him – 'for his own sake and for the good of the cause of collectivism. If he will let us, that is to say.' And, in spite of her workload, she read *In the Days of the Comet*. It made her think about free love, and inspired a surprising passage in her diary, in which she said Wells's 'glowing anticipation of promiscuity in sexual relations' seemed to have some validity in her mind – because

> You do not . . . get to know any man thoroughly except as his beloved and his lover – if you could have been the beloved of the dozen ablest men you have known it would have greatly extended your know-ledge of human nature and human affairs. But there remains the question whether, with all the perturbation caused by such intim-acies, you would have any brain left to think with? I know that I should not . . . Moreover it would mean a great increase in sexual emotion for its own sake . . . And that way madness lies?[8]

She was no doubt thinking back to her past passionate feelings for Joseph Chamberlain, and arguing from her memory of that experience – how she had rejected him because she loved him so much that she feared being swamped by him. These may have been painful thoughts for her, but they were also her justification for choosing a life devoted to intellectual activity rather than passion. Wells later accused her, through his fictional depiction of her in his novel *The New Machiavelli*, of regarding sexual passion as being 'hardly more legitimate than homicidal mania', but he was wrong about this – the diary entry makes it clear that she believed sex, while dangerously distracting, might also extend your understanding.

And, although she did not know what the effect would have been had she succumbed to passionate love, she did know she had found with Sidney a harmonious and outstandingly successful partnership in which they worked as equals. Later she wrote of the unconsum-mated love of Balfour for Lady Elcho as having 'just that touch of romantic regret that it could not be more, that deepens sex feeling and makes such a relation akin to religious renunciation'.[9] Lady Elcho and Balfour were close and lifelong friends, never lovers. To Mrs Webb renunciation was a higher thing than indulgence – an idea that would be anathema to Wells.

The most important change in her thinking now was the question of votes for women, to which she had been formally opposed until then. But on 2 November she wrote to Millicent Fawcett, leader of the suffragists (as opposed to the Pankhursts' militant Suffragettes), telling her she had changed her mind and was now ready to support the admission of women to the franchise. She gave permission for her letter stating her support for the cause to be published in *The Times*, where it duly appeared; and she wrote – not to Jane but to Wells, 'Mrs Wells will rejoice that I have at last thrown in my lot with Women's Suffrage . . . See what you have accomplished with your Propaganda! far more important than converting the whole of the Fabian Society!'[10]

Wells stayed with the Webbs again at the end of November 1906, and had another long talk with her about the last chapters of *In the Days of the Comet*, which described a society in which free love was accepted for married as well as unmarried people. He maintained that what he had written could not be criticized from the standpoint of morality, because it was a work of art – saying that Michelangelo's nudes were not meant to persuade us to take our clothes off – an argument that she rightly brushed aside. He went on to say he did think 'free-er love' would be the future relation of the sexes, and that it was not possible at present because 'No decent person has a chance of experimenting in free-er love today – the relations between men and women are so hemmed in by law and convention. To experiment, you must be base: hence an experiment starts with being damned.'[11] She preferred to believe that mankind might evolve upwards by subordinating physical desires to the intellectual and spiritual side of our natures. And, although there was no meeting of minds here, there was no quarrel either. She calmed and fortified herself with regular visits to St Paul's, where she listened to the Psalms and prayed.

Mrs Webb was prepared to listen to Wells, but Pease, as Secretary of the society, refused to print his recent talk about the endowment of motherhood. Then, in December 1906, two crucial meetings were held to discuss Wells's resolution 'The Reconstruction of the Fabian

Society'. Shaw made a brilliant and witty defence of the status quo, showing the members that Wells's plan meant voting for the ignominious expulsion of the Webbs and himself. Mrs Webb's view was that Wells would have succeeded had he not attacked 'the Old Gang' (as they were known) personally, with preposterous accusations and transparent fibs, which meant that even his followers refused to support him. Wells had also made it easy for Shaw by failing to present a properly thought-out practical programme. But, although he had been defeated, he remained popular with many members, and especially those in the Fabian Nursery, founded that year and made up of young men and women enthused by his ideas.

Beatrice Webb decided Wells would not mind losing his battle to change the Fabians, because, as a writer, it would in due course make excellent 'copy' for him, which would console him. And, although she was heavily overworked and suffering from insomnia, she wrote another friendly letter inviting both the Wellses to stay: 'do not let us drift apart from you – you and we have the same faith tho we hold it somewhat differently – we are all of us too old to change and must take each other as we are – for good or evil.'[12] In May 1907 she wrote again, saying how much she was looking forward to his 'book on Socialism' – *New Worlds for Old* – 'I am longing myself to write down the "Faith I hold" – I wonder how far it would differ from yours – not much I think – merely in perspective and perhaps a little in the way of reaching our ideals. With love to you both.'[13] She was determined to keep their friendship alive. 'With the Shaws our communion becomes ever closer . . . and I hope and believe it will be so with H. G. W.'[14]

She had been working with Shaw and Maud Pember Reeves to add the words 'equal citizenship' for women to the Fabian programme, and on 22 February they did: 'The rise of the suffrage movement had led to an agreement to insert a phrase on equal citizenship.'[15] Mrs Reeves shared Wells's enthusiasm for the state endowment of motherhood, and wrote to Jane Wells, asking her to 'Tell the dear man that it is almost impossible to do anything without him.'[16]

More than a year later, in March 1908, Mrs Reeves founded the

Fabian Women's Group officially. Her daughter Amber, now at Cambridge, was also writing to Wells, asking him to come and speak to her fellow students, and again to advise her on setting up a Samurai Group, which she proposed to bring to London. From then on they exchanged occasional letters, Wells urging Amber to work hard for a good degree. In London, membership of the Fabians was still growing, and the plan to form a Samurai Group was approved in April by Mrs Webb, supported by the socialist thinker Edward Carpenter – he was also an admirer of Wells's *This Misery of Boots* – and by Aylmer Maude, friend and translator of Tolstoy, who had long lived in Moscow and was now settled in England and of course a Fabian.

Meanwhile Wells was still writing *Tono-Bungay*, and still being attacked in the press, month after month, for his alleged approval of free love in *The Days of the Comet*, and obliged to keep sending out explanations and denials.

In spite of his defeat at the Fabian Society, Wells remained active in it, and in March 1907 both he and Jane were elected to the Executive Committee, alongside Mrs Reeves. During this year the membership of the society doubled – 'a little boom', Mrs Webb called it. Wells's next memo suggesting reforms was found incomprehensible by almost all his fellow Fabians, and only twenty-seven messages of support came. Now he was beginning to waver in his commitment to the Fabians. He was still working on *Tono-Bungay*, and told Macmillan he had nothing but a volume of stories and a small book on socialism for him once it was finished. He signed a contract with Amalgamated Press to contribute to a 'History of the World'. He also now chose to become a JP in Folkestone and sat on the bench. And he was soon involved in an attempt to start a new cultural magazine, the *English Review*, with Ford Madox Hueffer, Joseph Conrad and Edward Garnett – *Tono-Bungay* was to be serialized in the first four issues. Wells set about trying to raise money from the wealthy aristocratic families he had met through the Webbs.

Through these years he kept up casual sexual relations with various women writers – the novelist Violet Hunt one, Ella D'Arcy another, whose stories had appeared in the *Yellow Book*. A third was Jane's schoolfriend Dorothy Richardson, a frequent visitor to Spade House. Neither had any compunction about their affair, and he enjoyed her as 'a glowing blonde' while finding her cultural conversation irritating; still, he liked her well enough to dedicate *The Future in America* to her. She may possibly have become pregnant and had a miscarriage in 1907 – at all events, she left London and the affair ended. She went on, of course, to become a writer herself, of Modernist novels which ultimately brought her fame.[17] Jane kept strictly to her agreement with Wells to accept these affairs without complaint. She was now Secretary to the Executive Committee of the Fabian Society, on which Maud Pember Reeves and Charlotte Shaw sat – both were good friends to her.

Beatrice Webb continued to write friendly letters to Wells as she worked on her Royal Commission business. In July 1907 his *New Worlds for Old* began to be serialized, and when he sent Mrs Webb a copy, she responded, 'What I felt most in reading your work was the amount of genuine intellectual and moral sympathy between Wells and Webb.' She thanked him for his flattering references to her, and went on to say how much constructive thought would be needed if they were to produce 'a genuinely collective mind and the machinery to carry this Will into effect'.[18] *New Worlds for Old* was published the following March – 1908 – and reprinted five times over the next six years, with a few revisions: in 1909 twice, in 1912, in 1913 and in September 1914.

For September 1907 he and Jane planned a walking holiday in the Swiss Alps. They were now on such close terms with the Reeves family that they invited Amber to join them. She refused, possibly because she was too busy preparing for her last year at Cambridge. Wells sent her a card from Brig, telling her that Jane had blisters, asking, 'Why didn't you come with us? We did ask you', and sending love to her parents. The Reeves family was flourishing, and the Webbs were about to offer her father the directorship of the London School of Economics.[19] He took up his post in May 1908.

Early in 1908 Wells answered a request from a magazine called the

Labour Leader to describe his lifestyle – because some of their readers were suggesting that a socialist should share his wealth. Wells wrote a fascinating reply, saying he had four servants and a gardener; that he travelled second class on trains so that he could work; that he took his holidays abroad, mixed with people of all sorts and wanted everybody to have 'as much ease, leisure and freedom as I have'. 'But my chief luxury is Socialism. This has cost me in time and energy, in damaged sales for my books, a loss in the last four years of at least £2,000 and that is only the beginning of the damage it will do to the solid world of success I have within my grasp. It is quite worth it.'[20]

It was well argued. But more trouble lay ahead. In April 1908 he gave public support to Churchill, who was standing as a Liberal candidate in the election – against the Labour candidate, who expected support from the Fabians. Sidney defended Wells at the Fabian AGM but then reproved him mildly for not informing the Executive of his support for Churchill. At this, Wells walked off the platform, and wrote the next day saying he was ready to resign. But a month later Beatrice was again asking the Wellses to dinner to meet, among others, a bishop who was 'an ideal type for a novel' – perhaps not as interesting to Wells as she hoped.[21]

Wells finally signed a contract with Macmillan for *Tono-Bungay* on 14 May 1908, after threatening to change publishers, and was paid an advance of fifteen hundred pounds. He had started writing *Ann Veronica* – inspired by the Fabian Nursery girls, some of whom were at a dinner in Cambridge he attended that month. It was given in honour of Sydney Olivier, who was leaving for Jamaica; two of his daughters were with him in Cambridge. Rupert Brooke noticed that Wells and Amber Reeves arrived late together, and perched on a windowsill because they couldn't find a seat – and 'he argued in his little thin voice for a long time, in a very delightful manner.'[22]

Mrs Webb was now finishing the huge task she had set herself: writing the *Minority Report of the Poor Law Commission*, since she could not agree with the official report, which she believed accepted too much of the old Poor Laws. Her report outlined a plan 'to secure a national minimum of civilised life . . . open to all alike, of both sexes

and all classes, by which we meant sufficient nourishment and training when young, a living wage when able-bodied, treatment when
sick, and modest but secure livelihood when disabled or aged.' And
she summarized her intentions with a slogan, saying it was about
'The Break-up of the Poor Law and the Abolition of the Workhouse'.[23] The Fabians printed it, and it sold twenty-five thousand
copies.

Tono-Bungay – which Wells had thought of calling 'Waste' – also
addressed itself to the state of the nation. It was serialized in the new
English Review from December 1908, published in book form in February 1909, and hailed by other writers.

So it happened that Beatrice Webb and H. G. Wells both gave their
chief energies during the years from 1906 to 1908 to producing works
of very great significance and value. In her case she presented social
and political recommendations that would profoundly influence the
future of every man, woman and child in the country through the
introduction of radical reforms and innovations: it would take forty
years for them to be put in place, but she had set them in motion.
Wells offered a novel rich in observation and imaginative power that
displayed and deplored the current condition of England, was taken
seriously and greeted with respect and admiration by his contemporaries, and has been read ever since, often with astonishment and
always with enjoyment. Mrs Webb and Wells were political allies,
socialists intent on changing society. Yet what should have allowed
them to strengthen their friendship and work together for the
changes they both wanted failed to do so. The reason for this was that
his behaviour now overstepped acceptable bounds so outrageously
that she could no longer accept him as a friend.

16. Amberissima

Reading Shelley at Uppark as a young man had led Wells to dream of finding 'free, ambitious, self-reliant women who would mate with me and go their way, as I desired to go my way'.[1] Experience had not fulfilled this dream: his first love, Isabel, would not allow sex before marriage and disliked his love-making on experiencing it. And, although Jane had been ready to break the conventions and become his mistress before any possibility of marriage, and was ever loving and accommodating, she lacked passion – or it might be that he failed to arouse passion in her. Other women were ready to have sexual relations with him on a light-hearted basis, without demanding or giving commitment: Dorothy Richardson, and the older, sophisticated – and feminist – novelist Violet Hunt, who showed him how easy it was to take a private room above a restaurant or rent a room for occasional use in a London lodging house.

Since Wells had persuaded Jane to accept his right to engage in infidelities, their life continued smoothly enough. Both were delighted by their two little sons, Gip, now aged two, and Frank, born at the end of October 1903.

In the spring of 1904 Wells published his vividly inventive and powerful story 'The Country of the Blind', in which a traveller in remote mountains comes on an isolated community of people without sight, stays with them and finds out how dangerous it is to be different. It was not a warning to himself – he was after all set on being different, preaching change through his writing, offering various takes on how men and women might organize their lives, and predicting future possibilities for humanity that startled and sometimes shocked.

And, as we have seen, on joining the Fabian Society in 1903, he had decided it needed to be stirred up and made into something quite different. At a dinner given by Beatrice Webb in April 1904, Wells had been introduced to her friend, Maud Pember Reeves, wife of William Pember Reeves, the current High Commissioner for New Zealand, whom Wells had already met at the Co-efficient dinners. Both were keen Fabians, and she was ready to take political action and especially interested in getting votes for women – something already achieved in New Zealand, where she grew up. The Reeves and Wells families became friendly, and the Wellses naturally met the three Reeves children, Amber, Beryl and Fabian. Amber was to go up to Cambridge in 1905 to read philosophy, then called 'Moral Sciences': she was eighteen, well educated, ambitious and beautiful, with black hair so thick and striking that she was called Medusa in the family, often shortened to Dusa.

Amber started her studies at Newnham College, Cambridge, in October, inhabiting one of the comfortable and airy bedsitting rooms allotted to each student, with the wide green college gardens outside her windows. She worked hard, impressed her tutors and made many friends of both sexes among her fellow students. Soon, as we have seen, she was organizing political clubs: the Utopians – Wells published *A Modern Utopia* in 1905 – then the Samurai. When the Fabian Nursery was set up in 1906, she became a leading member. She asked Wells, as a friend of her parents, for advice about writing the constitution for her group of Cambridge Utopians, and he replied, urging her to work hard for her degree: 'It's of supreme importance to Utopianism that you should do well. Consider how it will further movement if you do.' After this she persuaded him to come and address her fellow students: 'Newnham is agog with expectation!' she told him, adding that she was telling the other girls to wear their prettiest dresses for the occasion.[2] By then the friendship between the Reeves and Wells families meant that Jane sometimes stayed with the Reeves in their Kensington house.

In the autumn of 1906 Wells, now forty, published his novel *In the Days of the Comet*, imagining a future transformation in human behaviour after the world is hit by a passing comet. The effect was to bring not only socialism but the disappearance of sexual jealousy, which meant that men and women are happy to share their wives, husbands or lovers. It was not one of his best books by any means, but, as we have seen, it aroused critics and newspaper writers to rage. They accused him of preaching free love and the end of marriage, adding that this was what socialism was inevitably leading to: 'in future it will not be my wife or your wife, but our wife,' wrote one, and others said he was advocating promiscuous sexual intercourse, the abolition of marriage, polygamy and polyandry. He was kept busy replying, denying, explaining, to little avail: in the pages of the *Daily Express* – and in more august places too – socialism was now linked with free love. Young Fabians did not mind, but senior ones worried that it might set back the cause. When Shaw suggested this to Wells, he replied, 'What an unmitigated moral Victorian ass you are.' Shaw went on teasing Wells and enjoying their disagreements.

At the same time as he was dealing with attacks on his supposed promotion of free love – or 'free-er love', as he called it to Beatrice Webb – Wells was working on his plan to change the Fabian Society. Maud Pember Reeves was one of his allies in this, and in 1908 would set up her Women's Group to press for the vote and equal citizenship – with Jane Wells on its committee. Fabian membership was increasing rapidly and when Wells addressed the Society on 'Socialism and the Middle Classes' in October he drew one of the largest audiences they had ever had. And, although his attempt to change the Fabian Society and make it into what he hoped would be a practically effective political body failed – which was a humiliation – he remained a Fabian for now and continued to serve on committees.

Amber was also fierce in her political enthusiasms, and Wells heard from her father how she had boasted to him that she had 'talked blood and destruction' in a speech in Cambridge, giving her approval to revolutionary Russians who threw bombs and robbed banks. Wells wrote to her joking that he was 'shocked and pained' to hear of such views: in reply she threatened him with getting 'the reputation of a Fickle Shifty and Undecided Person' should he fail to give another promised talk to the Cambridge Fabians, 'and please to remember that we have in our midst several (future) famous historians'; and described going for a supervision with a chaperone, and calling her tutors 'Comrade' while they called her 'Miss'.[3] In January 1907 she suggested he might see her philosophy professor 'and he will tell you – if you are tactful – what my chances of a first (FIRST) are. Please give my love to Mrs Wells: I did, we all did, so awfully enjoy having her to stay.'[4]

Amber was now running a Samurai group that encouraged early rising and other simple virtues.[5] She told Wells that her committee had elected him as a member. And she began to call him 'Master'. She was working hard, and at the end of her second year at Newnham she was awarded a First in Part One of her degree. That autumn of 1907 was when the invitation came from Wells and Jane to join them on their walking holiday in the Alps, which she did not accept.

In February 1908 he agreed to visit Amber in Cambridge, and to take tea with the distinguished college official Blanche Clough, who later became Principal of Newnham – she was the daughter of the poet Arthur Hugh Clough and niece of the first Principal of the college, Anne Clough. Wells was as always rushed off his feet, setting up the *English Review*, publishing *The War in the Air* and working on *Tono-Bungay*. And he was still arguing with his fellow Fabians – and about to publish another political book, *New Worlds for Old*. Being so busy, he asked Amber if she might come to London to collect a book she wanted to borrow from him: 'Or is that an outrage on every Newnham custom? If you could come I'd very much like to walk round with your feminist eye to help me see things.'[6]

In June he went to see Amber again in Cambridge and, since he was now *persona grata* with Miss Clough, he was permitted to visit her alone in her room. It was a week or so before her final exams, and by his own account she declared her love for him – and then flung herself into his arms. Here at last was Shelley's ideal woman – young and beautiful, intelligent, ambitious, independent, and ardently desiring – indeed demanding – a complete and passionate sexual relationship with him. Wells was besotted, and Amber sailed through the Tripos and won another First. With his promised help and advice she agreed

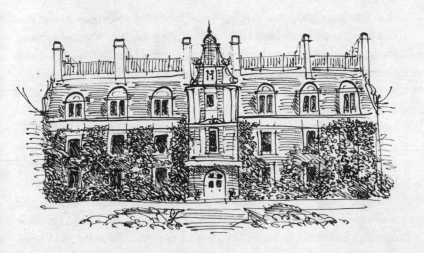

Newnham College, Cambridge

she would now spend the next year writing a thesis at the London School of Economics.

She was twenty-one on 1 July. He took a room near Victoria Station, where they could meet and make love, sometimes overnight, sometimes by day: the classic arrangement for illicit lovers. It was a hot summer and they went for long walks, sometimes in London, sometimes in the country, where they were able to make love in the open air. Years later Wells said the memory of that time still glowed with unregretted exhilaration and happiness – as such experiences of love do.

His energy was such that he was writing *Tono-Bungay* 'at the rate of a thousand a week' and at the same time getting to work on a story for another publisher, Nelson.[7] It was probably *The History of Mr Polly*, one of his most attractive novels of escape from a disliked life into a peaceful rural paradise: 'it promises to be a human sort of lark', wrote Wells. The intense happiness brought by his love affair, far from distracting him from his work, inspired and spurred him on.

But there were problems: one was that Amber lacked discretion. She could not resist boasting of her relationship with him. She told her mother about the affair – and found her privately sympathetic – and also some of the Cambridge dons, and friends among the undergraduates. One of them, Rivers Blanco White, was a very close friend – he was in truth in love with her – and she confided everything to him. Appalled by the thought of her being seduced by a middle-aged married man, he appointed himself her protector. Others became aware that there was something going on: Beatrice Webb observed Amber and Wells together at the Fabian Summer School, and noticed what she called 'a somewhat dangerous friendship'. 'If Amber were my child I should be anxious,' she added.[8] Shaw called her 'an ungovernable young devil'.[9] Jane Wells must have sensed that there was a new and more threatening situation. At this point Jane raised an objection for the first time, when he put up a photograph of Amber in their house. She told him that it would hurt her, and that she would want to smash it when he was away. Wells wept, and Jane decided to engage a governess for the boys. Mathilde

Meyer arrived in October, and saw 'a certain wistful melancholy' in Mrs Wells.[10]

Another problem was that Amber was giving hardly any attention at all to the thesis she was supposed to be engaged on. She had lost the will to work, and she simply gave up any pretence of being interested or wanting to research or study. Wells, on the other hand, kept busy: it becomes increasingly hard to see how he fitted in all his commitments and pleasures. On 15 September 1908 he told Macmillan he was revising *Ann Veronica*, 'the best love story I have ever written', and working on another 'modern political novel' – this was to be *The New Machiavelli*. Now he cleared his decks by resigning from the Fabian Society on 16 September, saying he wanted to concentrate on writing novels, and also complaining that they had disregarded his ideas about the endowment of motherhood to give women freedom.

A crisis came when Macmillan declared himself shocked by what he read of *Ann Veronica* – she pursues and marries a divorced man – and declined to publish it. It was soon solved. Wells at once accepted an offer of fifteen hundred pounds from Fisher Unwin, to whom he had already shown some chapters – and they agreed to publish in October 1909. He was now also busy trying to raise money for the *English Review*, and giving energetic support to Robert Ross in getting an Epstein monument set up on the grave of Oscar Wilde in the Père Lachaise Cemetery in Paris. He had told Ross earlier his feeling that 'in a curious way Wilde and I interweave' – no doubt as outsiders ready to risk public disapproval in following their own desires. And he gave the main toast at the banquet given by the friends of Wilde and Ross. Energy, willpower and ambition drove him on ever harder.

All the while he kept up his letters to Amber between their meetings: 'Wants his Amber. Really wants his Amber.'[11] 'Heart of Life I love you. I love you from the uttermost frizzes of your hair to the nail of your big toe – and all in between . . . I kiss the little button that buttons you up. My story has got well under way. Friday anyhow.'[12] This, like several others, was signed 'Peter' for discretion – Amber could not be trusted to clear out her pockets or to keep letters safe. And he told her to send her letters to him at the Reform Club.

In the middle of his affair with Amber he wrote a description of them as a couple in a letter to her in which he listed each of their bad qualities: he described himself as 'suspicious, angry, cruel, weak, vain, dishonest H. G.' and her as 'slap-dash, vain, garrulous, greedy Amber Reeves'.[13] More often his letters extolled her beauty and proclaimed his need for her. A few of hers survive too, but most are his. They make up a striking collection, with their spontaneity, passion and changing moods, and if reading them one sometimes feels like eavesdropping on the defenceless dead, it must be said that neither was defenceless; rather they were both tough at heart, fighters well able to look after themselves. What the letters offer is a running account of his mood changes – they show how fiercely he was in love with Amber, and also how torn he was in thinking of the future, not wanting to hurt Jane and at the same time bored by her, and tormentedly jealous when he feared losing Amber to anyone else. They were preserved by Amber – she lived until 1981. And who would not be proud to have a love letter reading simply, 'Dear Amber Dearest Amber Amberissima'?[14]

Wells was sometimes tired out, and wrote harshly to her. One long screed accuses her of bad behaviour and complains that she makes it hard for him to work: he writes to her as though describing characters, in the third person:

> . . . he is cross . . . she will get on his nerves . . . yesterday she was such a trial. She was exacting and trying to make him do things he didn't want to do. He didn't want to dine in that damn place, he didn't want to come home in the train. He is cross and tired this morning . . . This morning it is a bother to pick up work again Dusa knocks holes in his work. When she wants a thing, she wants it. Oh Lord! If Dusa does not look out she will get on his nerves. She isn't the only neurotic in this cast. He loves her dearly but he warns her. She hasn't been a rest for him lately or a help. Going to her only seems to stir her up to want him too much. When he feels her tugging him towards something, he says in his heart 'Oh, Goodness what is it now?' He wants to go on with his New Machiavelli. Dusa seems likely to nudge his elbow and spoil all that.

Making them into figures in a novel was perhaps his way of dealing with his annoyance.

Then directly,

> You've just got to shut up Dusa. You've just got to get interests out of things about you. You've lost your nerve with me and my nerves are on edge with you . . . I want people with cuticles on for a bit. It's all right Dusa. I never loved or understood a human being as I do you and you do me. It's simply that my nerves won't stand the strain. If I don't come up on Monday will you be wretched? I don't care . . . I shan't come on Monday because it will not be delightful and I will not do things about you unless they are delightful because I want to keep you all set about with delightful memories in my mind . . . Oh dearest, dearest Dusa! If only you will understand this; it won't hurt you. I kiss your dear shoulders. H. G.[15]

And so back to getting on with *The New Machiavelli* – and *Tono-Bungay*. One of his letters scolded her sharply after she had tried to persuade him to dedicate a book to her: 'I'm going to dedicate Ann Veronica to A. J. and I'm not going to dedicate Tono to anyone. Now don't let me hear any more about dedications ever. I won't be druv'. I hate it like Gip hates being held.'[16]

Another letter reminded her of the force of his will: 'Didn't I have Isabel because I wanted her and chucked her because I wanted to and have Jane? I never gave up anything I wanted (and I ain't going to do so now.)'[17]

He disliked her spending time with Fabian Nursery friends – young men, Rivers among them, who aroused his jealousy.

> These boys will be always draining your time and energy preventing your getting onto the Courses you must make . . . Why the devil Dusa couldn't you stick to our understanding and keep out of it? Vanity and instability. If you and I are to stick together you can't afford to haul along at the pace of that sensation and flutter about with their pottering little intrigues . . . Why couldn't you leave it alone? Oh Dusa, silly Dusa . . . Schoolgirl Dusa who chatters and plunges . . .

There's your scolding (mean every bit of it). Anxiously awaiting you at work on your thesis? You ought to be putting that away. DAMN THE NURSERY![18]

But soon she was again 'Dearest dear Dusa – Dusa my Dusa. Inseparable Congenial' and 'I don't care a rap about Rivers.'[19] On other days the gentlest declarations came from him:

> I love you more than ever I did and every day you possess me more. We may hurt each other, all sorts of things may happen, we will do our utmost to get the good things and avoid the bad ones but deep down eternally you and I lie in one another's arms for ever and ever. These are things of the surface. I may bully you like a church warden bullying a school-girl, you may lie and weep upon the bedroom floor, you may go off with your nose in the air to do a hundred silly extravagances. Mind if you like but don't mind really. Dear one I love you. There is no music in the world like your voice singing; 'Look here, old thing'. I don't want to live unless I can feel your heart beating. Living doesn't matter anything or mean anything apart from you. There is no such thing as 'chucking' nor to be thought of between us. We can't. We will get all the life we can together and if we are sillies & make a mess of that, we will die together. This isn't promises. this is how things are. / Friday about eleven I shall see you.[20]

Thesis abandoned, Amber tried her hand at fiction. She sent Wells a story, to which he responded tactfully: 'Very good stuff indeed – very good. But she is going to write ever so much better . . . I will think it over and tell you what I think shd be done with it. [B]ut N.B. it may be hard to sell. It's awkward long.'[21] Another brought 'Sweet love story has just come – made me feel like laughing and crying . . . dear little Poetess, dear Sister Genius. Not very well written, No!'[22] This was sent from Switzerland, where he was on another skiing holiday with Jane. He reassured Amber that 'Always he wants Dusa. Hasn't had Jane – Doesn't want anyone but Dusa any more . . . Wise Dusa not to hurry him.'

He badly needed time to fulfil all his commitments. A new agent had arranged for *Tono-Bungay* to be published in New York, while Wells had promised it as a serial to start in the first issue of the *English Review* in December 1908 – alongside work by James, Conrad, Hardy, Galsworthy and Hudson.[23] Finishing what had become a long and complex novel required close attention and many hours of uninterrupted writing and revision.

Meanwhile Amber was growing dissatisfied. She wept and told him she wanted to darn his socks as well as being his lover. According to Wells, Rivers Blanco White – now qualified as a barrister – thought he could save her and went to her father, told him about Wells and said he wanted to marry her himself. Reeves raged and threatened to shoot Wells. The scandal became public, discussed among the Fabians. Wells said he and Amber were afflicted with 'jagged masses of inconsistent impulse'. They were driven to decide they must part – although without much conviction. At what was meant to be their last meeting, in March 1909, she asked him to give her a child. She cannot have failed to see that, once she was bearing his child, the strain on his marriage would become very much greater – and if he had possessed even a shred of sense he would have refused her demand. Whether from vanity or weakness, he gave way, and in April she knew she was pregnant. Wells prepared to go abroad with her, driven by conflicting feelings. She had already named the coming child 'Anna Jane' and both of them referred to her by this name from then on, although they could not have known the sex of the baby. Amber was still 'the most maddeningly necessary thing in life' [24] – but at the same time 'Jane's security and pride in our children and my work were the most precious things in life.'

Amber infuriated him by consulting with Blanco White. Before either of them left England Wells told her that he was 'a very nice dear boy but no good for you . . . We'll pull things off. Only now you must go very straight and sober and do exactly what you are told. No scenes in Paris – no complications – no indiscreet letters.'[25] He explained he would slip away after being 'conspicuously present' with Jane at a Society of Authors dinner in London – a very Wellsian touch this – while she must set off alone, pretending to be on a walking tour. His plan was that they should meet in France in April and go on to Belgium. He would arrange the money, he had a ring for her, better than the earlier one he had given her, he told her. Then he returned to the subject of Blanco White, saying he was 'not good enough'.

Now, uncertain and unhappy, he wrote a series of long messages to Amber. One, headed 'Doubts in the Small Hours', talks of her crookedness and lying, her confidence that she can hoodwink and manipulate people, and asks, 'Why should I be exempt?' 'Is this Rivers business straight?' 'Have you lied to me as you have lied to others about the source of rings and suchlike?' – then he ends in a renewed expression of confidence in her love. It is followed by 'Commonsense in the Daylight', which continues to talk about her character: 'I cannot think of you as one person. There you are lover and nearest, and also you are the woman who has failed me. Are you going to fail me again?'

It goes on with a long complaint: 'Our thesis was to be our intellectual child, a fine and noble thing to do, and you have wasted a year in snatched holidays, in vulgar and silly flirtations, you have done hardly anything to build up a social position . . . You preferred trailing about with these rather nasty minded young people . . .' He defends himself: 'I'm restless too but I've held my easier line better than you have done . . . I am much more passionately interested in my work and in my ideas than I care to admit to anyone but you . . . I am better than you and I will not be destroyed or greatly harmed by you.' Finally,

> I believe that together we can work, or if you don't settle down to work and isolation with me clean and Samurai being patient with me and all the inconvenience of our position, then I won't be fussed anymore, I won't stay or be slain, I will cut you off from me though I have to cut off my nose to do it. I shall do this. I shall pack up and come back to England and I shall leave you with your fare to London and a ten pound note, to work out your own salvation – Anna Jane or no Anna Jane. I don't care a damn what people will think of it. That is what I shall do. That is what I ought to do if you fail me.[26]

After this came a further declaration of love, but also asking more questions, an allusion to 'Maud's way' of dealing with their problem – her mother may have suggested an abortion. Yet another letter is headed 'Sic Transit Gloria Mundi' and now assumes she is marrying Rivers. It takes a tone of worldly understanding. 'I didn't think you'd get engaged to Rivers until after you'd been abroad but I suppose you found it difficult to wait . . . You mustn't break faith with old Blanco. It would have been better to have ended things at Christmas perhaps . . . He looks the best of all possible chaps, he's nearly your own age and I don't see why you both shouldn't make a good thing out of fighting the world together. But now it's done it's done.' He reminds her crudely that she is just one of his conquests: 'I'll no more take you back from Blanco-White than I'd take Rosamund back from Clifford Sharp.' Then, 'There's no more sex or sexual consequences or relations to be thought of between us. Close the book.' The tone changes again: 'You've made some magic times for me; it's the saddest thing in the world that we've failed to keep it up. But we have failed.'[27]

Amber was able to calm him and explain away whatever prompted his saying their affair had failed and was closed. But it was not going well: they managed to join each other in a villa in Le Touquet, briefly. She had no domestic skills and he was restless, talking of important engagements in London he wanted to keep. Soon both departed, separately. She let Rivers know she was returning, he met her, and on 7 May 1909, at Kensington Register Office, she married him – something no brave Shelleyan woman would ever have stooped to.

What happened between Wells and Amber Reeves can be described in various ways, depending on where your sympathies lie. One version would be of a headstrong, star-struck, selfish girl pursuing a famous writer, demanding to have a child by him, losing her nerve, behaving badly all round and causing a great deal of trouble. An alternative version would be of a self-indulgent and lecherous middle-aged married man allowing himself to embark on a love affair with the vulnerable daughter of family friends, getting her pregnant, finding it impossible to make up his mind whether to leave his own wife and young children or not, and finally being forced by pressure from her parents and friends to let the girl go. A third account could show two clever and recklessly inconsiderate people embarking on an affair that the man immediately chose to turn into fiction – twice. Wells's first fictional version came in an entertaining novel about the right of women to be free to choose their own path in life – *Ann Veronica* has remained popular ever since it was published in 1909. The second came soon after, in *The New Machiavelli*, which made the man a married MP and the girl a journalist, and has also gone on being read since its 1911 publication. In both these novels the lovers are allowed to remain together, in the first marrying and having a child, in the second leaving England together, he abandoning his promising career as well as his wife. But in life Wells and Amber Reeves separated, she to marry another man and lead a quiet, productive and long life, bearing more children, lecturing and writing – he to remain married to his wife and to embark on another passionate affair in 1913 in which he fathered another illegitimate child – and to enjoy ever growing financial success as writer, and world fame.

17. Heroines

Wells's next move was to invite Jane to bring the boys to Le Touquet: no doubt he reasoned that they might as well enjoy a holiday there, since he had already paid for the villa – and Jane accepted this, as she accepted almost all his behaviour, without recrimination. Once back at Sandgate, they agreed that they both wanted to leave their house there, beautiful as it was, and move to London. It would make life easier for him, and she said she liked the prospect of being closer to friends, and able to go to concerts and other entertainments.

He was still exploring other ideas of how they might change their lives. A letter to Amber sets out one ingenious plan he had devised. It involved asking Jane to take over Amber's baby: 'I've had things out with Jane. Item she is to have a baby. Item Spade House is to be sold. Then you and I will live together, Jane will have a house in London and you will have a little flat for your alleged home (You won't be there much). If that does not work out – divorce, but everybody is to play fair – and no unnecessary confidences or stirring crises too close.'[1] Not surprisingly, nothing came of this proposal.

He had as always a great deal on his mind. He was still putting the finishing touches to *Ann Veronica* – it was not completed until July – and was well into *The New Machiavelli*. He had also made a start on *The History of Mr Polly* – his tale of escape from stress and a bad marriage into tranquil happiness. *Tono-Bungay*, published in book form in England in February, was a critical success, hailed in the highest terms by friends and reviewers. True, his onetime fellow Fabian Hubert Bland found fault, accusing Wells of trying to say too much and producing 'a series of essays bound up in one volume' – but his malice could be ignored.

Spade House was easily sold at the end of May. But Wells was still there on 25 July 1909, and was doing exercises in the garden when the

telephone rang: it was the *Daily Mail*, asking for his comments on the
first crossing of the Channel, from Calais to Dover, in an aeroplane –
made by a Frenchman, Louis Blériot, who flew in a very small and
fragile-looking monoplane, with no instruments – an altogether
extraordinary moment in human history. It took him thirty-seven
minutes. It had a special meaning for Wells, since he had just shown
the hero of *Tono-Bungay* as obsessed with flying and constantly trying, and failing, to achieve flight. The *Mail* had offered a prize of a
thousand pounds for the first cross-Channel flight – its editor Lord
Northcliffe had been a friend of Wells since 1890, when they had met
at Henley House School. Wells wrote his article at once, confessing
that he had underestimated the possible stability of aeroplanes. He
went on to praise French and German education with its respect for
science, and compare it with the neglect of science teaching in England, where 'not one in twenty of the boys of the middle and upper
classes . . . gets more than a misleading smattering of physical science'. He then pointed out that England was no longer an inaccessible
island, and that within a year an aeroplane capable of circling over
London would be able to drop explosives upon the printing machines
of *The Times*. 'I look out upon the windy Channel and think of all
those millions just over there, who seem to get busier every hour. I
could imagine the day of reckoning coming like a swarm of birds,' he
wrote, in an eerily accurate forecast of the Battle of Britain. Blériot's
plane was slightly damaged in landing but quickly repaired and put
on display at Selfridges in London, where thousands queued to see it;
and there was a celebratory lunch at which he received his prize.
Wells did not experience flight himself until 1912, when he was given
a ride in a seaplane at Eastbourne and found it surprisingly smooth
once airborne.

The Wellses were now moving to a tall eighteenth-century house,
No. 17 Church Row, Hampstead. Jane undertook the arrangements.
Nobody liked the house, which was inconvenient and without a garden. And she got few thanks: 'Poor little Jane, poor dear, is such a
bore when I have to spend whole days with her . . . She never starts
anything or says anything I want to hear,' Wells complained to

17 Church Row, Hampstead

Amber.[2] He had set about finding somewhere where she could await the birth of her child – with the help of Elizabeth Robins, a fine American actress, fierce feminist and the first to play Ibsen's *Hedda Gabler* in English; she was friendly with the Reeves family and also ready to help him. Amber was confused and wretched, staying away from home in Hertfordshire, needing support, and refusing to have sexual relations or even to live with Rivers. Wells told Arnold Bennett in confidence that 'the husband, a perfectly admirable man, being married attempted to play a husband's part – (which was asinine of him). Violent emotional storms have ensued and there is a separation.'[3] He went on to say he thought he could free Amber by giving grounds for a divorce between her and Rivers, and added that he was 'extremely happy'. In July he found a cottage at Woldingham in Surrey in which Amber could live, rented and furnished it, hired servants to look after everything and installed her there to await the birth of the baby.

Jane was consistently kind to Amber, and Amber, anxious and unable to see what the future held for her, and uncertain as to whom she could rely on, was ready to accept Jane's kindness. So Jane purchased all the baby clothes for the coming child. She also sent her boys to stay with Amber in Surrey – with their governess, Fräulein Meyer – while she packed up Spade House and supervised the move to Hampstead. Fräulein Meyer is silent about the visit in her account of life in the great writer's household. Amber asked Jane to advise her on housekeeping problems, and invited her to visit too – she does not appear to have gone. The servants showed their curiosity as Wells and Rivers both made regular visits, for the most part separately but occasionally coinciding: on one occasion Amber's father turned up and Wells had to hide behind the curtains – or so Shaw said, making it into a good story.[4]

Wells had pressed Shaw to visit Amber, and assured him that 'we should all be very happy and proud of ourselves if we hadn't the feel of being harried and barked at by dogs.'[5] He accused the Webbs of spreading malicious stories – 'intolerable sneaking nastiness . . . bound to hurt Blanco-White, the Reeves's and my wife', in the same letter saying he and Amber had made 'pretty big sacrifices'.[6] He also now considered Amber's mother Maud as 'not only foolish but treacherous' and warned friends not to talk to her.[7]

In September, as Beatrice Webb heard more details of Amber's story, she decided that it was no longer possible to maintain friendship with Wells. In October, while he was away on a skiing holiday in Switzerland with Jane, Mrs Webb visited Amber in Surrey, and also spoke with Blanco White, who was already known to the Webbs as an intelligent, well-educated and keen young Fabian. She followed this up with a letter to Amber, telling her that she would have to choose either continuing to see Wells and losing Blanco White, or giving up Wells and continuing with her marriage. It was a friendly letter – she had now decided she liked Amber, who appeared subdued by her predicament – and she offered to talk further with her if that would be helpful – or, if she preferred, to leave her to sort out her problems alone. She assured Amber of her friendship and of her respect for Blanco White, and even of 'a quite genuine desire to save H. G. W. from a big smash. But I don't want to interfere, if you prefer that I should not.'[8]

As Amber continued to hesitate, another Wells novel was published, *Ann Veronica*: a 'poisonous and pernicious book' that should be banned for depicting 'the muddy world of Mr Wells's imaginings . . . a community of scuffling stoats and ferrets, unenlightened by a ray of duty and abnegation', according to the *Spectator* (in November). A different view was given in *The Times Literary Supplement* (then appearing as part of *The Times*), whose reviewer found the heroine 'keenly noted and courageously described' and said Wells had put 'the very best of his passion and imagination' into the book. Mrs Webb thought Wells a fool to have published it, 'but I shall not regret if he is permanently "broken up" as a social leader.' And she wrote of her distress at the Reeves parents being 'shrivelled up with the pain' of their daughter's behaviour, and of the publication of *Ann Veronica* adding 'a roar of insult to his injury of the Reeves family'.

Mrs Webb blamed herself for having introduced Wells into aristocratic circles – Lady Elcho, Lady Desborough, Balfour – from whom she thought he had learnt his bad behaviour, expecting to be able to live a double life as a respectable family man on the one hand and a Goethe-like libertine in selected circles. She decided that 'once he sinks in his own estimation and in the estimation of those who count he will be supremely and permanently wretched. I doubt whether he will keep his health – and he may lose his talent. It will be the tragedy of a lost soul.'[9]

In December Wells's friendly correspondent Vernon Lee sent him a plain-speaking letter telling him that a young girl cannot know what she is about in embarking on a love affair, and that 'the unwritten code is right when it considers that an experienced man owes her protection from himself – from herself.'[10] It could not have been put better, but it was of course far too late, and useless advice to Wells. The triumphant experience of sexual and emotional fulfilment he had achieved with Amber, and to which he felt fully entitled, was sacred to him.

Yet he had to give way now. Mrs Webb's advice – and Wells's inability to make up his mind what to do – had made Amber see that it would be best to give him up and live with Rivers – even though she had said she found Rivers physically repellent. And after the birth of the baby – a girl as they had hoped, Anna Jane – on 31 December 1909, this is what she did. Wells told Vernon Lee at the end of December that he and Amber were being forced to separate, and that 'we're doing it chiefly for love of my wife and my boys.' In January he complained that he and Amber had been made to promise 'never to see or write to each other' – but the truth was that Rivers, who was now a barrister, had forced Wells to agree to an undertaking not to see Amber for a period of years. He did this by threatening to bring a court case against Wells for depicting his wife in *Ann Veronica* in a way that friends found recognizable, and showing her as unchaste.[11] And Amber had decided to settle for the marriage to Rivers, who was prepared to bring up Anna Jane as his own child.

Wells made elaborate financial arrangements to leave money to Anna Jane. Almost a year later, in November 1910, he told Elizabeth Robins how much he still wished he could see Amber, and added:

'After this year we shall write – and so far as I'm concerned and I'm pretty sure as far as she is concerned, nothing has altered or can alter between us.'[12] He was already engaged in a new light-hearted love affair, and was never to be without a mistress for long. But he did not forget Amber, and in the long run, after she had borne two more children to Blanco White, in 1912 and 1915, they established openly friendly terms again. In 1939 she wrote to Wells saying that what he had given her had 'stood by' her ever since, and that she had never felt that it was not worth the price. A considerable price was paid by others of course: by Blanco White, and by Jane Wells, 'his patient and all-enduring little wife, who having entered into that position illicitly herself . . . cannot complain', wrote Mrs Webb in her diary.[13] Jane was asked to resign from the Fabian committee on which she sat – which meant losing work she valued, and friends. Jane is the true heroine of this story.

One letter, unpublished and undated, sets out Wells's thoughts of how he and Amber might yet live together – all for love, and the world well lost:

> Now let me see if I can put everything First then dear Heart I love you. Always among beautiful things I want you – and all this morning I have been walking over the hills longing to feel your shoulder touching mine. Always when I am unhappy, I want you. And always when I am proud of success, or thinking out my work I want you. And when I perceive I am a silly fortyish baldish little man, then I want you, to tell me it is so and so. I do want to live with you, to be always in call of you, to sleep near you and eat with you and share our child together . . . that we may live together as man and wife.
>
> But now Dusa here are the difficulties we have to face. You and I are both pampered people. I am accustomed to be waited on, to take no thought of even the brushing of my clothes, to have my work and my moods made the ruling facts in my life. It is clear that this cannot to the same extent be the case if we defy the world. I didn't expect that at Paris-Plage [i.e., Le Touquet]. Now, dear I will gladly carry pails of

water and clean your dear boots if need be, to have you once again. You too will have to pay for me, in hardship, in a narrower life, in bothers. Your fight with the Blythe servants was only a sample of the long persistent bothers you will have as my paramour. We have permanently to give up comfort for the love we bear each other. Do you think we can?

We can't altogether – make no mistake. We shall swear and what is more, we shall shirk (I know us). We shall quarrel over petty things of that sort sometimes quite wickedly. I am ready to trust our love to carry all that off like a flood carries away slums. Are you?

And we must give up many little affections & some that are not little . . . I've got to tear something of Gip and Frank from my heart. We've got to bind up these bleeding places in each other. Can we?

Our life will be a hard fight. I may suffer very heavily in my worldly success, if we do this. I think I can fight that though, but there will be times when we shall feel beaten. Can you stand up to that? And we dare not play with jealousy any more. We must both be utterly faithful to each other . . .

Well, shall we go on with our eyes open? If we do, you must put yourself in my hands, trust me, let me steer out of this tangle. I promise you, you shall be my only wife. I will cohabit with you exclusively and do in the matter of divorces all that seems best for everyone. I will certainly try and get you divorced and if it is possible and not too cruel, I will try to get divorced . . . But I cannot in that matter bind myself with pledges to anyone – and least of all to your people. You have to be my wife, flesh of my flesh, bone of my bone, and to have no helpers, no supports, no people who matter, but the child and me.

What do you think of all this Dusa?

Yours ever, H. G.[14]

He says nothing of this letter in his later account of his affair with Amber: perhaps he forgot that he had written it – or decided it was best forgotten.[15] But I find it the most interesting of all his many surviving letters to her, because he is thinking clearly and setting out to be as honest as he can. Its most surprising – indeed, extraordinary – aspect is his insistence that they must practise a strict monogamy and remain permanently faithful to one another. What has happened to the Wells who believed so strongly in sexual freedom, and insisted on it throughout his life?

Leaving that aside, his readiness to accept the prospect of hardship and discomfort again, after having raised himself out of it, and the possible loss of reputation, make up an impressive offering to set before her – a piece of matchless romantic self-sacrifice. Perhaps Amber did not believe him capable of change, or perhaps she herself could not face what he offered, now that she had a tolerant, affectionate, reliable husband, and could see the prospect of being restored to society, friends, relieved parents, a home of her own – even grand weekends with the welcoming Webbs, who were ready to take up the Blanco Whites seriously. Hard to imagine how their lives might have been had she taken up Wells's offer – but she surely made the most sensible decision for all concerned.

At the same time, she was still writing to him as 'My Darling Master' in 1930.[16]

Tono-Bungay is an ambitious novel, absorbing and – intermittently – brilliantly achieved, in which Wells wrote about the condition of England as he knew it, and about human behaviour, disconcerting and mean, outrageous and passionate. He set out by his own account to write in the tradition of Dickens and Thackeray, and later said the book was planned as a social panorama in the vein of Balzac: and, although *Tono-Bungay* is not perfectly achieved, it can stand comparison with all three of these masters. It drew on his personal history and his observation of the wide social world he had entered and effectively conquered, and on current advances in technology; and it expanded into boldly imagined enterprises and activities. It seems extraordinary that it was written in the two very busy years from 1906 – the year he was forty – to 1908, when his affair with Amber Reeves began and he resigned from the Fabian Society. He gave as part of his reason for resigning that he wanted to concentrate on writing novels – yet concentrating on perfecting his novels was rarely his way, because he was always ready to be distracted by a new idea that presented itself. He did, in fact, publish two short political books during 1908 – *New Worlds for Old* and *First and Last Things* – but, interesting as they are, it might have been better to have put all his energy into perfecting *Tono-Bungay*. As his contemporary Desmond MacCarthy wrote, 'Had patience been added to his cluster of extraordinary gifts he would have been among the world's great novelists.'

His narrator in *Tono-Bungay* is George Ponderevo – like Wells, the son of a housekeeper in a great house, here called Bladesover, and clearly modelled on Uppark. The house educates George through its books and pictures and park – at the same time teaching him that everyone has a fixed position in society. In this opening section of the book Wells used his own experience to great effect, describing how George's mother was housekeeper at Bladesover and consequently he was allowed to sleep in the servant rooms in the attic, and there found piles of discarded books. They had been collected by an earlier lord of the manor – an intelligent and sophisticated man – and banished from the shelves in the great saloon 'during the Victorian revival of good taste and emasculated orthodoxy'. Among them were volumes of Plato, Swift, Tom Paine, Voltaire, Johnson, Shelley – and many more. Young George fell on them and read them greedily, and through reading them he began to think for himself.

At the same time, living in the great house, he learnt the lesson that 'every human being had a "place". It belonged to you from your birth like the colour of your eyes.' He understood that he would have to risk trouble by trying to borrow more books from the shelves in the saloon, which was forbidden territory to him, and he taught himself to dart in unseen, 'like a rat', as he saw it. Outside, however, in the great park, he was free to roam, and took in his earliest impressions of the beauty offered by nature: 'there was mystery, there was matter for the imagination . . . glimpses of unstudied natural splendour.' Wells also introduces him to love when a girl from an aristocratic family visits Bladesover – he names her Beatrice and gives her the 'disorderly wave of the hair from her brow' of Beatrice Webb. She is interested in George, and she flirts with him – only to deny their friendship later and get him into trouble.

George makes his own way from poverty by winning scholarships, as Wells did, and discovers socialism and the Fabian Society. Later he builds and tests gliders he tries to make into powered flying machines. He also finds himself on an expedition sent to steal radioactive material from Africa. In doing so he shoots dead an unknown Black man who observes what he is doing, absolving himself of guilt for this murder with the ruthlessness of a colonial master. Wells was covering a lot of ground, boldly and effectively.

But the great central theme of the book is the selling of Tono-Bungay, a worthless 'tonic' promoted through a tremendous and brilliantly thought-out advertising campaign – 'a game, but an absurdly interesting game', thinks George. It persuades people they are buying health, strength and beauty in a bottle. Tono-Bungay is the invention of George's uncle Edward, whom we first meet running a small chemist's shop in a country town, and it makes him into a multimillionaire, quickly learning how to spend lavishly and live luxuriously, courted by all, and always moving into larger and grander places – until he takes a risk too many. He was partly based on a real figure, Whitaker Wright, a fraudulent businessman who made a colossal fortune, built himself extravagant mansions and ended in ruin and suicide in 1904. But Wells's Edward Ponderevo is an original character – and a great one – revelling in his own success, always ambitious to go further, generous to others and delighted by the new vistas opened up by his business. He is funny too: when he acquires a small black-lead firm,

> . . . it was my uncle's own unaided idea that we should associate that commodity with the Black Prince. He became industriously curious about the past of black-lead. I remember him buttonholing the president of the Pepys Society.
>
> 'I say, is there any black-lead in Pepys? You know – black lead – for grates! OR DOES HE PASS IT OVER AS A MATTER OF COURSE?'
>
> He became in those days the terror of eminent historians.[1]

Wells gives Edward a delightful and witty wife, Aunt Susan, who is half in love with her nephew – and he trusts and appreciates her. She does her best to accept her husband's monstrous success and mistaken pursuits with good grace, and to protect him as far as she can, even when he falls into the clutches of a lady novelist. While he grows ever richer and memorizes the names of the good wines he knows he should drink, she joins the London Library, goes to lectures at Birkbeck (a college that allows part-time students and provides evening lectures) and takes up gardening.

So here is a chronicling of social change, itemizing the habits of the 'fresh invaders of the upper level of the social system' – of which Wells himself was of course one – as they learn new behaviour and convert to gentility, building themselves houses and learning to employ servants. Here is also the matter of sex: George, with no idea of how to make love but desperate to try, marries a nice girl who finds sex a horrid business. It takes time – and a divorce – for him to discover that for true lovers sex is 'tenderness and delight and mutual possession' of a nature difficult to describe in words. Wells makes a good attempt to do so.

Beatrice reappears in his life, grown up and grand – and 'I found scrutiny, applause and expectation in Beatrice's eyes . . . I played to her. I did things for the look of them.' Wells is giving a good account here of how attention and seeing that more is expected of one can stir the senses as well as the will. Beatrice makes her interest in him plain, and there is a truly extraordinary scene – and one that could not have been written before – in which his glider flies low over her as she is out riding and they are both in physical danger for a moment – Wells using his knowledge of new scientific developments to give them a dangerous thrill never before experienced. He lands, safely, she gets off her horse and falls into his arms, murmuring 'those great wings', and passion arises between them: 'neither of us said a word. But it was as though something had been shouted from the sky.' They become lovers – 'Everything we touched, the meanest things, became glorious.' Only she decrees there is to be no future for them together, and the book ends in pain for him – 'It haunts this book, I see; that is what haunts this book, from end to end.' And also in death for his uncle. But Tono-Bungay goes on selling.

So the book is a 'Romance of Commerce'. It is also an attack on the condition of England, where fraudulent businessmen can command great fortunes and power, ignoring 'the gutter waste of competitive civilization', as a procession of unemployed men in London is described. And it is a personal story of doomed love. 'Waste', the title he first thought of, was already taken by Harley Granville-Barker for his new play about a politician whose career is ruined by an affair with a married woman who dies of an abortion – which Wells saw in January 1908: he nevertheless offered 'Waste' as an alternative title in his last chapter. And the peculiarity of his title – *Tono-Bungay* – is one of the book's charms: it has almost certainly cost him readers, but it is always remembered by those who do read the book, and love it and return to it. The vigour of the writing and speed of the narrative is such that it never feels like a gloomy book, even though it is a catalogue of failures: George's marriage fails, he fails to fly effectively, he fails to bring back the valuable radioactive 'quap' from Africa, he fails to save his uncle from disgrace and death, and he fails to win the woman he loves, Beatrice, who, although she returns his love, has not the courage to change her way of life to be with him.

By the last chapter of the book he is alone, and has built a destroyer for the Americans – having failed to get a commission from the British. He has also, during his African trip, speculated on the possibility of 'atomic decay' bringing about the destruction of the world. As he sails his destroyer on a test trip down the Thames, passing the various sights of London – among them, Grosvenor Road, where the Webbs lived – he mocks in his mind Parliament, lords and King under their fine robes, and decides that the realities of English life are 'greedy trade, base profit-seeking, bold advertisement' – and, he might have added, false sexual attitudes, an unjust and outmoded educational system and inefficient politicians. He now faces life alone, probably not in England, and unsure of the world's future. The destroyer he has designed and built seems to predict a war to come – and war did indeed come, five years after *Tono-Bungay* was published.

It was hailed as a masterpiece by many good and fastidious writers – Bennett praised 'the steady shining of the whole' and went on, 'There are passages towards the close of the book which may rightly be compared with the lyrical freedoms of no matter what epic, and which display an unsurpassable dexterity of hand.' D. H. Lawrence, while urging a friend to read it, said, 'But it makes me so sad. If you know what a weight of sadness Wells pours into your heart as you read him – Oh, mon Dieu! He is a terrible pessimist.' Gilbert Murray is said to have told Wells in a letter that his powers of description were as great as Tolstoy's.[2] Not all reviewers were pleased by it, however, and some found the narrative confusing, but the unsigned review in the *Telegraph* described it as 'one of the most significant novels of modern times, one of the sincerest and most unflinching analyses of the dangers and perils of our contemporary life that any writer has had the courage to submit to his own generation' and went on to say it was 'no less than the duty of every thinking citizen to read it, and to give it respectful consideration'. It said the character of Edward Ponderevo would have been impossible to any novelist of fifty years earlier, and suggested that Wells's stage in *Tono-Bungay* was left 'as full of dead bodies of hopes and yearnings as the final platform of Hamlet' – and that the whole had 'the intense conviction of a masterpiece'.[3] And, while *Tono-Bungay* has never become a popular classic at the level of Dickens or Hardy, it has been praised steadily over the years as new readers discover it and are amazed to find how good it is.

Wells might have tidied, cut and sharpened his book with good effect – but he was, as always, in a hurry. And when you look at the circumstances in which it was written it is astonishing that it turned out so well. To begin with, he had done nothing to clear his decks when he embarked on what he himself saw as his most ambitious novel yet. In 1906 he was also bent on reforming the Fabian Society, and put much energy into his attempts to bring this about over the next two years. He made his two-month visit to America, taking the first part of the manuscript of *Tono-Bungay* with him to work on, while also writing a book describing the trip. During that autumn of 1906 he was kept busy defending himself against a barrage of press attacks on his novel *In the Days of the Comet*. He produced his short book about socialism, *New Worlds for Old*, which was serialized from July 1907. He spent four months dashing off *The War in the Air* – a brilliantly entertaining and prophetic novel published in October 1908 – for the princely sum of three thousand pounds from the publishers George Bell & Sons, as he boasted to Arnold Bennett. He gave a talk to the Fabian Nursery that autumn, which became the book *First and Last Things*, serialized and then published in November 1908. In the spring of 1908 he began writing *Ann Veronica*, which he offered to Macmillan later in the year. Meanwhile he had become a justice of the peace for Folkestone in 1907 and sat on the bench. He pursued an eventful sex life outside his marriage. He was a reasonably attentive

father to his two small sons, and he took a skiing holiday with his
wife.

How was it possible for him to have fitted in all these things? How
did he manage to work on several books at the same time? Dickens
managed this in the early part of his career, and occasionally later
when writing a Christmas story while engaged on a novel – but this
was nothing to what Wells took on at this time. Wells, like Dickens,
wrote by hand. Wells gave his copy to his wife or an assistant to type,
then revised it. He did a lot of redrafting. Did he work through the
nights? Did he get up before dawn and write in the early hours of
each day? He and Jane had separate bedrooms, which helped. Jane
engaged Fräulein Meyer as a governess for the boys in the autumn of
1908, giving Jane more time to work for him – she typed in the dining room, as the governess noted. But it remains very hard to see how
it was done. And the sad fact is that he never wrote another novel as
good.

Beatrice Webb wrote to Wells about *Tono-Bungay* in February 1909
and told him she found the first part 'quite the best thing H. G. has
done' – rather spoiling the effect by adding that she thought *The War
in the Air* might outlast it.[4] After this crushing piece of rudeness and
his angry response, in which he too was rude – about her *Minority
Report* – she wrote again, 'I am delighted to know from Amber that
you are at work on a novel which is to combine all the great qualities
of TB with a study of the more ideal elements of human character.'[5]
This was before the affair between Wells and Amber had become
widely known – in fact, it was at the time they were supposedly ending it, and Amber had asked Wells to make her pregnant – and it is
interesting that she was boasting about her special knowledge of
Wells's literary plans.

In May Wells put Spade House on the market and in August the
Wells family moved to Hampstead – and this was when Mrs Webb
noted the end of their friendship with Wells. In October *Ann Veronica* was published, adding to the pain of Amber's parents, according
to Webb, not least because Amber had given her consent to the

publication.[6] Mrs Webb continued to talk of the 'moral rottenness' of Wells.[7] At the same time Wells was preparing his revenge by portraying both the Webbs in another political novel, *The New Machiavelli* – which was, ironically, the novel mentioned by Amber to Beatrice Webb in February, and described as one that was to show the 'more ideal elements of human character'.

19. Friends and Enemies

In November 1909, while Wells was still trying to find a way to keep Amber, and she was awaiting the birth of their child, English politics were in turmoil. The House of Lords voted down the 'People's Budget' proposed by Lloyd George and Churchill, supported by Asquith – and described by Balfour in the House of Commons as 'the first instalment of a Socialist Budget' – because it imposed higher taxes on the wealthy. It was indeed a first step towards helping the poorest in society, and Wells might have been expected to be active in expressing support for such a budget – although there is no evidence that he did.

He had many distractions. *Ann Veronica* had just been published, to virulent attacks as well as praise – privately, even his friend Lady Desborough said, 'The love-making of Ann Veronica and Capes is outside the framework of civilized literature.'[1] And he was now busy writing *The New Machiavelli*, in which he presented a version of himself as Remington, a politician and MP, Cambridge educated, who attends political dinners – based on his experience at the Co-efficient Club – and is advancing new policies. Remington is driven to sacrifice his promising career for love, abandoning his supportive and blameless wife for an Oxford girl graduate, a clever and passionate creature who tells him she is going to work with him, declares her love, calls him 'Master' and proves irresistible. The book ends with Remington throwing up his political career and the lovers leaving England together to live abroad permanently. No one who knew Wells could miss the autobiographical elements of the story – and part of it takes revenge on the Webbs by offering unfriendly portraits of them.

The actual political situation in Britain was that in January 1910 the Liberals won the election and in April Asquith became Prime

Minister. In March Mrs Webb noted in her diary that 'The Progressive movement which the Fabian Society started in 1889 has spent itself', as the Lords blocked the Liberal reform.[2] But Asquith advised the King (Edward VII) to create a huge number of new peers, enough to pass the 'People's Budget' of his chancellor, Lloyd George, through the Lords. With this threat before them, the Lords caved in – and so the first instalment of reform was passed through both houses, the Commons on 27 April and the Lords the following day.

Mrs Webb had private matters on her mind as well as public. She gave lunch to Amber and Blanco White in March 1910, finding her 'shy and subdued' while he was full of affectionate concern for her. A shade pompously she wrote in her diary, 'We are prepared to stand by them and let the past be forgotten.' And indeed she invited them a good deal that year, and for Christmas, with Rosamund Bland and Clifford Sharp, also her protégés – they had married the previous September (1909). Had Mrs Webb and Wells been on better terms, they could have agreed about reactions to the death of the King in May, which inspired her to reflect that the 'ludicrous false sentiment being lavished over the somewhat commonplace virtues of our late King would turn the stomachs of the most loyal of Fabians' – but such sharing was out of the question now.[3] She had decided that Wells was too old to live down the scandals and expected the Wellses to be dropped by many people, and quite possibly disappear from view.[4]

But in May *The New Machiavelli* started to be serialized in the *English Review* and at once aroused a great deal of interest. However, when Macmillan, never to be hurried, read it for the first time in June, he told Wells he would not publish it: he disliked the sex and feared accusations of libel. Two other publishers – Heinemann and Chapman & Hall – turned it down on similar grounds. Wells, after taking a long summer holiday with his family in Germany, told Macmillan that unless it was published properly he saw very little use in going on writing – and he refused to make the changes asked for by Macmillan.

In the same month – October – Wells's father died. He was

eighty-two – and, as Wells said, he followed the family way of dying quickly and without any fuss. After reading his newspaper in bed he had a word with his housekeeper about the suet pudding she was preparing for his lunch, she then left the room and he decided it was time to get up, put his legs out of the bed and fell dead. Wells had been fond of his father, and he had been a good son to both his parents, which meant that he could say goodbye to them without any self-reproach. A page had been turned, and he went forward.

In November 1910 he wrote to Elizabeth Robins, defiantly asserting his confidence in himself: 'I've got more friends than I've ever had before . . . and lots of absurd enemies. I am to be cut and insulted and ruined and pulverized, whereas you know that I belong to the race that lives to 85 and doesn't age before seventy.'[5] In the same month a flattering letter reached him, praising 'your wonderful *Machiavelli* . . . never did a man understand things as you do . . . and the poetry of it, and the aching, desolating truth'. It came from Elizabeth von Arnim, a talented Australian (and a cousin of Katherine Mansfield) who had married a German aristocrat, and whose first book *Elizabeth and Her German Garden* had established her as a best-selling writer. She was now widowed, had built herself a house in Switzerland – the Châlet Soleil at Montana – and had enjoyed love affairs with some of her children's tutors – one was Hugh Walpole, another E. M. Forster, who was presumably not a candidate. She was ready for a new affair, with Wells, who told Jane, 'I think she's a nice little friend to have.'[6] And the two started on the affair at once.

There was no passion, it was simply sexual convenience and fun: Wells was probably rather pleased with himself to have a countess as his mistress. They enjoyed themselves, relished their own defiance of conventional virtue, and made many trips together to various attractive European places over the next three years. He described it as a 'gay and innocent liaison', and it was also useful to him in that he could go abroad with his countess while leaving Jane to deal with practicalities like packing up the house in Church Row in the summer of 1913 and setting up a flat for them in St James's Court. But, as time went by, von Arnim began to grumble that he was only half a lover – she accused him of not trembling with passion as he approached her. The affair came to an end when he was struck by passion again – this was the beginning of his ten-year affair with Rebecca West. There were no bad feelings and Countess von Arnim soon captured another titled husband, Earl Russell, elder brother of Bertrand.

In January 1911 *The New Machiavelli* was finally published in book form, by John Lane at the Bodley Head – a publisher Wells did not rate but had to accept, given the reluctance of others. The Webbs had read most of it by then. Mrs Webb admired it – she was struck by 'the extraordinary revelation of H. G.'s life and character – idealized, of course, but written with a certain powerful sincerity. Some of the descriptions of Society and of the political world, some of the criticisms of the existing order, are extraordinarily vivid.' At the same time she also felt he showed 'his total incapacity for decent conduct'. As to his portraits of herself and Sidney – he gave them the names Altiora and Oscar Bailey – she found them 'very clever in a malicious way', and thought they showed that Wells had never really liked them – which was certainly not true of her.[7] But this was Wells's revenge for the failure of the friendship, as he saw it. Sidney, as Oscar, was described as 'almost destitute of initiative, and could do nothing with ideas except remember and discuss them'; while Altiora, allowed to be aggressive and imaginative, was given a 'bony' soul and 'vanity gaunt and greedy'. Their house and dinner parties – poor food, good talk – were there too. The real Beatrice was large-hearted enough to think the book 'a pretty bit of work' that would probably allow its author to return to distinguished society after all – and she was right about this.

All the same, Wells had felt himself to be in danger. He sent out a statement with the review copies of *The New Machiavelli* claiming there was a 'campaign of personal malice' against it, subjecting him to 'personal insults and anonymous letters'. Some libraries would not handle it, a major Edinburgh bookshop refused to stock it, Birmingham City Council banned it, and the *British Weekly* accused Wells of 'purveying indecency'. Not all his friends liked it: Vernon Lee wrote to Jane saying, 'I feel awfully out of sympathy with Mr Wells's present attitude.' Henry James was less effusive than usual: he told Wells that detachment was needed in writing fiction – and found detachment 'terribly wanting in autobiography brought, as the horrible phrase is, up to date'.[8] Wells thanked him for 'the most illuminating of comments. So far as it is loving chastisement I think I wholly agree and kiss the rod.'[9] But he was storing up resentment against those who criticized either his morality or his literary skill.

He spent more time abroad, in Switzerland in February 1911, where the whole family fell ill, and in France, where they stayed for four months, from June to October that same year, on the Seine in Normandy. His brother Frank joined them, and he invited friends including Bennett and Vernon Lee, who came for brief stays. It looks as though he was glad to be away from England at this point. He tried to set up a world tour for himself, to be financed by very large advances from newspapers for the articles he would write; but he was unable to raise enough to make it possible. The Webbs, meanwhile, had departed for their own long-planned world tour in June 1911 and were not back in England until May 1912. So both Webbs and Wells turned their backs on parliamentary politics just as the Liberals – after another election in December 1910, in which they defeated the Conservatives by allying with Irish Nationalists – were finally able to reduce the power of the Lords to block their bills. This was a historic moment – and, although no one knew it, there was not to be another election for seven years – until after the war, in December 1918.

A month before *The New Machiavelli* started its serialization in May 1910, Wells had another novel published by yet another publisher eager to have his work, Thomas Nelson. It was one that could offend nobody, and it has given readers pleasure ever since. He started writing *The History of Mr Polly* in May 1909 – the month in which he decided to sell Spade House, when he was torn between his wife and children on the one hand and pregnant Amber on the other. Mr Polly is escaping from his marriage, from the permanent indigestion produced by his wife's bad cooking, and from the shop he hates running – so he simply burns the shop down, careful to hurt no one – and disappears with half the insurance money, leaving the other half for his abandoned wife. One critic shrewdly credited Wells's success with Mr Polly to his ability to turn himself into a comic character, and there is some truth in this, because he finds happiness in wandering alone through rural England and reaching the Potwell Inn beside the river – and the Potwell Inn is clearly based on Surly Hall, where Wells had found happiness as a boy. Here Mr Polly does odd jobs for the plump landlady, who feeds him well and invites him to stay. At this point he knows 'he had found his place in the world.'

Wells adds some fun by making Mr Polly a man who loves words but has never quite mastered them, so that his speech comes out somewhere between Mrs Malaprop and James Joyce. He explains that he goes for 'exploratious menanderings' with his bicycle. 'I've always been the skeptaceous sort,' he says. He accuses his neighbour Rumbold of an 'Arreary Pensy' – *arrière-pensée* – when he turns his back on him. Then: 'I'm going to absquatulate.' He notices a window dressing in a smart shop that strikes him as distinctly 'Rockcockyo'. He imagines he might become a ghost one day, 'a sort of diapholous feeling – just mellowish and warmish like'. Mr Polly is breaking free from the waste and sadness of life for the poor and uneducated, not only through his actions but also through his language.

20. 'I warmed both hands before the fire of Life'

I set out to write a book about the young Wells, covering his formation, the years in which he worked, thought and developed his skills as a writer. I see I have followed him into his forties – my excuse being that he still seems and behaves like a young man, and that he was still struggling to achieve the status he felt he had earned. I must also confess that I have found him too interesting to leave: ambitious, generous, hard-working, and astonishingly energetic and original in his thinking. He was playful, fun to be with, attractive to women and eager for sex. He had strongly held political views favouring social equality, republicanism and the establishment of world government. He saw himself as a working writer, not an artist in an ivory tower; he was rightly proud of his achievements, and expected to be well paid for his work. And he could be unreliable, selfish and even vengeful.

Friendships with other writers were always important to him. He and Arnold Bennett kept their early sense of kinship into the years when both enjoyed financial success that allowed them to live very well – although their letters grew shorter and less interesting. Both stayed in the best hotels, sought winter sunshine and mixed with the rich and famous – a letter from Bennett to Jane Wells, whom he always liked, shows the sort of thing: 'I went to Berlin with Beaverbrook [for him Bennett wrote a weekly column in the *Daily Express*], Diana Cooper and Venetia Montagu. And here I am, after a mad 4 days . . . Great fun.'[1] Bennett died from typhoid in 1931, aged only sixty-four, and Wells's tribute is full of affection, humour and acute observation. Bennett had refused to show Wells his yacht, Wells said, because he felt Wells might look at it – and at him – with the wrong expression. And he noted how the stammer that Bennett had never been able to conquer was utilized 'for a conversational method of pauses and explosions'. He invented a sort of preliminary noise like the neigh of a penny trumpet . . . He made his entry into a club or restaurant an event . . . He knew just how far to carry his mannerisms so that they never bored.'[2] Wells never found another writer friend so congenial after Bennett's death.

Wells and Conrad fell out and stopped communicating years before Conrad's death in 1924, although Wells was godfather to his second son; no explanation is forthcoming, but it seems that each found the other's books unreadable. With Ford Madox Ford, Wells had what he described as a 'long, fairly friendly but always rather strained acquaintance';[3] Ford's view was that they became enemies. Their differences were artistic: Wells saw Ford as being, like Conrad, obsessed with 'the just word, the perfect expression', while Wells refused to 'play the artist'.[4] But he was sympathetic to Ford, who never made money from his writing, good as it was – his finest novel, *The Good Soldier*, earned him just sixty-seven pounds when it was published in 1915 – and Wells twice supported him with gifts of money.

Of James Joyce, Wells thought highly, and the two exchanged letters in 1916, when Joyce was in Zurich. Wells contributed to a fund for his support set up by Ezra Pound and reviewed *Portrait of the Artist* favourably in 1917. Joyce and Wells met in Paris in 1928 and got on well – after which Wells wrote saying how much he respected Joyce's genius, but also that he could not follow his experimental writing, which he described as 'vast riddles', 'more amusing and exciting to write than they will ever be to read' – and he was surely right about this.[5]

As to D. H. Lawrence, only one letter to him from Wells is known – a request that he should send a copy of *Lady Chatterley's Lover* to Wells's current lover, Odette Keun. But, on 24 February 1930, Wells travelled from his house near Grasse to Vence to visit Lawrence in a nursing home there, and encouraged the American sculptor Jo Davidson, who was staying with him, to go the next day to make a clay model of Lawrence's head, saying it would do him good: 'I am sure he is not as ill as they think he is. You can cheer him up.' Beyond this, Wells's reaction is not recorded. Davidson went and modelled

Lawrence's head.[6] On 1 March, Lawrence moved into a villa, supported by his wife, Frieda, and the Aldous Huxleys, and died on 2 March. Wells returned to London in May, and appears to have left no account of his visit to Lawrence. But Davidson's small painted terracotta head of Lawrence can be seen in the Metropolitan Museum in New York.

Wells admired Thomas Hardy from 1896, when he reviewed *Jude the Obscure*, at once seeing its great literary and political importance. They first met in 1907 at a dinner given by Hagberg Wright, a translator of Tolstoy and Librarian of the London Library, with Shaw, Conrad and Gorky also present; and then again in September 1914, at Wellington House, to which Charles Masterman, then Chancellor of the Duchy of Lancaster, summoned writers to prepare a statement on the British case and principles in the newly declared war – among them were Galsworthy, Bennett, Gilbert Murray and Hardy.[7] Wells did not record these events, but in January 1919 he wrote to Hardy, addressing him as *Cher Maître*, and asked if he might call at Max Gate with Rebecca West. They were invited to tea, during which Hardy told them about the discovery of a Roman burial ground under his garden – which did not interest West. Wells is said to have described Hardy as 'a little grey man' afterwards – yet he had another view, given in the thank you letter he wrote for Hardy's kind words about his writing – which ended, 'Praise from you is praise from the King.' But, although Wells sent Hardy copies of his books after this, and Hardy wrote to thank him, their letters remained disappointingly short and formal.[8]

The friendship between Wells and Edith Nesbit, which had been enthusiastic on both sides, did not survive the row with Bland over Rosamund. But Rosamund always remembered Wells with affection, and he and Shaw gave her financial help when she needed it in 1931.

The most famous name among Wells's friends must be that of Winston Churchill, who from their first contact in 1901 was intrigued by his work and ideas. Churchill read and reread his books and kept them on his shelves; and, while the two men were never intimate and had some serious disagreements – notably about the Soviet Union – the relationship was important to both of them, to the end of Wells's life – Churchill outlived him by nearly twenty years.

He wrote to Wells in 1916 when the first tanks were used, reminding him that he had predicted the possibility of such vehicles in 1903 in his story 'The Land Ironclads'. He urged his wife to read *Ann Veronica* in 1910, and passed on some 'most secret' gossip to her: that Wells had been 'behaving badly with a young Girton girl of the new emancipated school – and that serious consequences have followed. The book apparently is suggested by the intrigue. These literary gents!'[9] In 1920 Churchill told a colleague that he had read all Wells's books and that Wells had foreseen the war wonderfully.[10] In the 1930s he wrote of how Wells had anticipated 'the wholesale bombing of undefended cities and wholesale slaughter of men, women and children' as part of his campaign to arouse English opposition to Hitler.[11] And he quoted 'that vivid modern philosopher, H. G. Wells, for twenty years past heard but unheeded' in warning of dangers to be dealt with.[12]

In 1937 Wells was invited to become a member of the Other Club, the dining club founded by Churchill, F. E. Smith and Lloyd George in 1911 for politicians and 'distinguished outsiders'. Members were elected, although Churchill became the effective arbiter – men only, of course, and they must be men 'with whom it would be agreeable to dine'. The dinners were held fortnightly in a private room in the Savoy, and the company ranged from Jan Smuts, to Lord Beaverbrook, to Sir Edwin Lutyens. Churchill told his doctor – Lord Moran – that he rated Wells as a writer alongside Swift, and that *The Time Machine* was a book he would 'take to Purgatory' with him – which would have delighted Wells had he known.

Wells's friendship with Shaw was a lasting one, in spite of their disagreements over political issues: about communism, and Marx, described by Wells as 'a shallow third-rate Jew', which Shaw described as 'monstrous ingratitude – you shake all confidence in your judgment and temper'.[13] Although there were long periods when they did not meet, they were faithful friends, sending each other their own books and praising and criticizing each other's work freely. Wells went to see a film version of Shaw's *Major Barbara* in 1941 and wrote to tell Shaw how enthusiastic the audience of young people in uniform was, arguing and joking. They sympathized, argued and joked together. And Wells found Charlotte the most lovable of women.

Shaw was equally fond of Jane. When the Shaws heard that she was terminally ill, they both wrote loving and grieving letters – Shaw ending his, 'I cannot express my feelings: the thing is quite beyond that. There it is, blast it.'[14] Years later, in 1943, Wells wrote touchingly to Shaw on the death of Charlotte: 'People who have lived into our lives never die . . . I still think quite often "Jane wouldn't stand for this" or "How shall I tell this to Jane?" It is as if she had just gone into another room.'[15]

In 1941, when Shaw was eighty-five, he wrote, 'the idea must not get about that the Wellsians and the Shavians have any differences. They are in fact the same body' – which was probably true at that time.[16]

Researching for this book, I found an obituary of Wells by Shaw that described him as a spoilt man of genius – and one of Shaw by Wells that said rejection of sex meant that, although he was a man of genius, he was also an 'incalculable, lop-sided *enfant terrible*'.[17] Later I came on a very different obituary of Wells by Shaw that deserves to be quoted:

H. G. was not a gentleman . . . No conventional social station fitted him . . . he found himself a great popular story teller, freed for ever from pecuniary pressure, and with every social circle in the kingdom open to him. Thus he became entirely classless . . . never behaved like a gentleman, nor like a shop assistant, nor like a schoolmaster, nor like anyone on earth but himself. And what a charmer he was! . . .

H. G. had not an enemy on earth. He was so amiable that, though he raged against all of us none of us resented it . . . H. G. was honest, sober, and industrious: qualifications not always associated with genius . . . he was first-rate company without the least air of giving a performance. Nobody was ever sorry to see him . . .

He foresaw the European war, the tank, the plane, and the atomic bomb; and he may be said to have created the ideal home and been the father of the pre-fabricated house . . .

There is no end of the things I might say about him had I space or time. What I have said here is only what perhaps no one else would have said.[18]

Henry James was another close friend of Wells over many years. Wells's first sight of him had been at the premiere of his play *Guy Domville* in 1895, where Wells also met Shaw; Wells's review admitted the play was a failure, but described it as 'finely conceived and beautifully acted'. Whether James had noticed this or not, he took to Wells at once and after the first visit, in August 1898, wrote to him; and Wells sent him copies of his books. In December of that year he answered a letter from Wells about *The Turn of the Screw*, ending modestly, 'the thing is essentially a pot-boiler and a *jeu d'esprit*'. In 1900 James asked Wells to send him a copy of *The Time Machine*, and he told Wells he had now sent for his other works from his London bookseller.

They went on writing to one another, and meeting, over the next fourteen years. Few of Wells's letters have survived, because James burnt almost all the letters he had ever received in the winter of 1909/10, when he was feeling unwell and decided to destroy all personal documents that might be misused in the future. Whereas Wells kept many of James's letters.

Wells sent him *Love and Mr Lewisham* – in which James found 'a great charm and a great deal of the real thing' – also humour and pathos – but – 'I am not quite sure that I see your *idea* – I mean your Subject, so to speak, as determined and constituted: but in short the thing is a bloody little chunk of life, of no small substance, and I wish it a great and continuous fortune.'[19] This effectively set the tone for his responses to Wells's novels: admiration, affection for the writer, encouragement, almost outrageous praise at times – yet with something withheld.

A very surprising letter about Wells's *First Men in the Moon* came next:

> It is, the whole thing, stupendous, but do you know what the main effect of it was on my cheeky consciousness? To make me sigh, on some such occasion, to *collaborate* with you, to intervene in the interest of – well, I scarce know what to call it: I must wait to find the right name when we meet. You can so easily avenge yourself by collaborating with *me*! Our mixture *would*, I think, be effective. I hope you are thinking of doing Mars – in some detail. Let me in *there*, at the right moment . . . [20]

What could Wells have made of this extraordinary response? Was his offer to collaborate friendly, or patronizing, or just meant to make Wells laugh? We don't know how Wells replied. How I wish they had started on a collaborative trip to Mars.

In fact, as he wrote this letter, James was busy writing *The Ambassadors* – the great novel he himself regarded as his best. In October 1903 James thanked Wells for 'your generous and beautiful letter' praising *The Ambassadors*, newly published. James went on to ask Wells for advice about their agent Pinker.[21] He told Wells that *The Ambassadors* had sold only four copies in a month in England, and that it was likely to sell four hundred in America – whereas he knew that Wells had sold four thousand copies of his latest. Wells's reply to this confidence is again lost.

Over the next years Henry James kept working on his long, final masterpieces, *The Wings of the Dove*, and then *The Golden Bowl*. In November 1905 he apologized for not sending a copy of *The Golden Bowl* to Wells – and at the same time described *Kipps* as 'not so much a masterpiece as a mere born gem' and with 'such extraordinary life . . . vivid, sharp and *raw*'. He praised Wells for having done better than Dickens and George Eliot in conveying English 'lower-middle-class' life, and added, 'Bravo, Bravo my dear Wells!' for his *Modern Utopia*, *Anticipations* and *Mankind in the Making* – and commented on the boldness of his thinking, again applauding his cheek: 'Cheeky, cheeky, cheeky is *any* young man at Sandgate's offered Plan for the life of Man – but so far from thinking that a disqualification of your book, I think it is positively what makes the performance heroic.'[22]

When Wells was attacked for his novel *In the Days of the Comet*, James condemned the 'ignobly stupid' reviews and praised its 'wild charm'.[23] In October 1909 he wrote about *Ann Veronica* and *Tono-Bungay* : 'there is so much too much to say, *always*, after everything of yours . . . you stand out intensely vivid and alone, making nobody else signify at all.' And he went on, applauding the 'extraordinary wealth and truth and beauty and *fury* of impressionism . . . you are a very swagger performer indeed and I am yr very gaping and grateful HENRY JAMES.'[24] It may be that Wells suspected this of being more of a performance than a critical response: although it was written to please, the praise remained resolutely general. After this came James's response to *The New Machiavelli*, in which he expressed his doubts about autobiographical fiction.

In 1913 Wells wrote praising James's memoir *A Small Boy and Others* – and, in responding, James explained that he was now suffering from 'chronic pectoral (anginal, though not strictly cardiac) distress'.[25] He was trying to cultivate 'a grand serenity'. He offered criticism of Wells's new novel *The Passionate Friends*, returning to his dislike of the autobiographical form – and Wells replied saying he knew the book was 'gawky' and that he felt a sense of 'unworthiness and rawness' and wanted to 'embrace your feet and bedew your knees with tears – of quite unfruitful penitence'.[26] James told Hugh Walpole that Wells's 'profusely extravagant' letter showed that he was really profoundly indifferent, and that he had 'gone to the dogs' artistically. This harsh judgement on Wells was something quite new: it was in a private letter, but was a warning of what was to come next.

In 1914 James composed two long articles for *The Times Literary Supplement* about 'The Younger Generation' of English novelists.[27] They appeared in April, and proved fatal to his friendship with Wells – because, although James devoted considerable space to his work, there was nothing to please Wells. As James saw it, Wells was simply describing his own experience in his novels, turning out his mind and its contents 'as if from a high window forever open', with great energy, but without any attempt to *use* it or value his raw material. 'The composition . . . is simply . . . "about" Mr Wells's own most general adventure; which is quite enough while it preserves, as we trust it will long continue to do, its present robust pitch.' He picked holes in Wells's recent novels. Worse, he failed even to mention his best and most interesting work – and this was a curious omission, hard to understand – or indeed to forgive. So there was none of the praise Wells must have been hoping for after all the years of their friendship; and Arnold Bennett fared no better.

When the articles appeared, Wells had recently returned from a visit to St Petersburg and Moscow (in January and February 1914). At home he had fresh problems: his new lover, the young writer Rebecca West, had just informed him that she was pregnant. His letters to her assured her, 'You are going to be my wife . . . I love you as I have never loved anyone. I love you like a first love.'[28] Letters to Jane now began 'Dear Mummy'.[29] Their sons were to be sent off to boarding school in September. Britain declared war on Germany on 4 August 1914, and Rebecca's son Anthony was born the next day. Wells bought his first car and set about learning to drive it – without a teacher; he wrote an extremely funny account of the experience in his war novel, *Mr Britling Sees It Through* – which became a bestseller.

So he had plenty of time to brood over James's *TLS* critique – which he described as an act of treachery three years later.[30] He and James were no longer in touch; the war was a nightmare to James, who feared the world was sinking into barbarism. Wells's response to his article came in 1915, when he published a supposedly humorous book called *Boon*, on which he had been working for several years, and into which he now introduced a parody of James's late style – a clever parody that hits the mark. It was a considered attack on his old friend, and intended to humiliate him.

James's final novels are rewarding for a reader prepared to submit to his demands and accept his elaborate narrative style – not always easy reading. They gave Wells his chance, which he seized, accusing James of having almost nothing to express but

> . . . sparing no resources in the telling of his dead inventions . . . Bare verbs he rarely tolerates. He splits his infinitives and fills them up with adverbial stuffing . . . His vast paragraphs sweat and struggle . . . And all for tales of nothingness . . . It is a leviathan retrieving pebbles. It is a magnificent but painful hippopotamus resolved at any cost, even at the cost of its dignity, upon picking up a pea which has got into a corner of its den.

He mocked James's characterization – 'a friend, a woman, yet not so much a woman as a disembodied intelligence in a feminine costume' – and dialogue – 'almost sentenceless conversations'. And he suggested that James was effectively offering the reader 'a church lit, but without a congregation to distract you, and with every light and line focused on the high altar, and on the altar, very reverently placed, intensely there, is a dead kitten, an eggshell, a bit of string'.

Wells delivered a copy of his newly published book to James's London club, without any accompanying letter, relying on the porter to hand it to him. James was now in his seventies, and in failing health. He wrote to Wells the day after receiving it, saying he had read part of it, and that it was difficult for him 'to put himself *fully* in the place of another writer who finds him extraordinarily futile and void, and who is moved to publish that to the world – and I think the case isn't easier when he happens to have enjoyed the other writer enormously, from far back'. He went on at some length about how he has tried to respond to Wells's attack – but 'one *has* to fall back on one's sense of one's good parts'.[31] It was a dignified letter that did not hide the pain he felt. Wells immediately sent a contrite reply, saying, '*Boon* is just a waste-paper basket.'[32] But he had gone too far. James dictated one last letter, beginning 'I am bound to tell you that I don't think your letter makes out any sort of case for the bad manners of *Boon*', and continuing with a dignified, and lengthy, statement of his own view of literature.[33]

This was the end of their friendship. It coincided with James taking British citizenship as an act of loyalty; Asquith, the Prime Minister, was one of his sponsors. Within months – on 2 December – he had a stroke, and two days later another. After this he remained bedbound and confused in his flat in Carlyle Mansions, Cheyne Walk. He insisted on dictating to his secretary long and disjointed passages and letters. He no longer knew where he was, and on some days he spoke of being mad. The widow of his brother William arrived from America to supervise the many servants and helpers gathered about him. Meanwhile Asquith was persuaded to have the Order of Merit awarded to him on New Year's Day – too late for him to understand the honour that was being paid to him. He watched from his window the ships passing on the Thames and sometimes believed he was on board ship himself. He had nights of terror. He asked for his brother William and believed he saw his dead sister Alice. On 25 February he became unconscious, and on 28 February 1916 he died. The funeral was held in Chelsea Old Church, his body was cremated at Golders Green and Mrs William James took the ashes and later smuggled them out to America, to be buried beside his mother and sister.

In 1919 Arnold Bennett wrote to Wells, saying he had been approached by an unnamed person editing James's letters who was eager to print the final exchange between Wells and James. Wells told Bennett he wanted to be approached directly: 'I wrote carelessly in that correspondence, feeling I was dealing with an old man and being only anxious to propitiate him – without too much waste of epistolary effort on my part. The publication of the correspondence therefore as it stands might entirely misrepresent my attitude towards our "art" . . . I have never given the matter ten minutes thought since . . . So just ask whoever it is to deal directly with me.'[34] The request had presumably come from Percy Lubbock, who printed the exchange between Wells and James in his 1920 two-volume edition of *The Letters of Henry James*.

Years later, in June 1943, when an article in the *New Statesman* mentioned Wells's attack on James, Wells protested in a letter, saying it had been 'quite good natured guying of the Master's style in *Boon*'.[35]

And when questioned by Herbert Read, Wells insisted, 'believe me, Henry James asked for it'.[36]

One of Wells's publishers, Lovat Dickson, who first met him in 1931, when his celebrity was immense, became his friend and wrote an account of him in which he said, 'He could be the best company in the world, and he could be mean, spiteful and quarrelsome.'[37] Dickson was also critical of his writing, taking the view that *The New Machiavelli* was the last of his novels to be written with any great care; and he observed that his later novels were no longer making much impression in the 1930s. But Wells was then making his mark in another way, with his ambitious non-fiction enterprises, *The Outline of History* (1920) and *A Short History of the World* (1922), which made him rich, and were followed by the equally successful *The Science of Life* (1930, written with Julian Huxley and Gip Wells) – all impressive and useful educational works that became great bestsellers – I remember as a schoolgirl in the 1940s becoming totally absorbed in the history books. He went on writing political essays, stories and novels, but his finest work during this period was without a doubt his two-volume *Experiment in Autobiography*, published in 1934. Here, he is again irresistible, charting his journey through the decades so entertainingly and with such charm that you forgive him his lapses and forget his omissions.

Wells's friendship with his college mate Richard Gregory was always important to him – he gave him signed copies of just about every book he published, and wrote in 1925, 'If I have done anything in this world it is largely because you and Simmons [their fellow student] did so much in the crucial years to make me believe in myself.'[38] Gregory gave up his academic position in 1893 to become a freelance journalist and lecturer – and that year he and Wells published a textbook they had written together, *Honours Physiography*. Gregory then became editor of *Nature* magazine, made it into a respected journal of science and was honoured with a knighthood in 1919 and Fellowship of the Royal Academy in 1933. The friendship with Wells was close and very personal – Gregory enjoyed Wells's novels for their human interest, and, after reading his *Experiment in Autobiography*, he wrote to him, 'no one analyses women better than you do or expresses more candidly the feeling of normal men towards them. That is why so many women are attracted to you.'[39] Devoted as he was to Wells, he was unable to help him to achieve his greatest ambition, which was to be elected to the Royal Society. Wells craved to be acknowledged as a scientist as well as a writer. To this end he produced in 1943 – when he was seventy-seven years old – a thesis for a D.Sc., 'The Quality of Illusion in the Continuity of the Individual Life'. It was accepted, but Wells looked in vain for a publisher. He had it printed privately, and sent a copy to the USSR Academy of Sciences. But he was never elected to the Royal Society.

Wells was desired by many clever and interesting women – for his energy and charm, for his reputation as a lover – perhaps for that smell of honey – as well as his fame and, for some, his riches. The most notable thing about the women he had serious love affairs with is that they were all exceptionally gifted, each of them well able to make her own way in life. Amber had her First from Cambridge, Rebecca West was brilliant, Elizabeth von Arnim a bestselling novelist. Margaret Sanger was the great and effective preacher of birth control to Americans. Odette Keun was a Dutch socialist writer, well-travelled and hard-working, whose books Wells admired before he met her. Dorothy Richardson became a respected novelist. Moura Budberg's intelligence and strength of character enabled her to survive through every sort of danger.

The woman who suffered most on Wells's account was surely his second wife, Jane: while she always acted with charm and dignity as his hostess when he was at home, served as secretary and assistant when required, and patiently agreed to whatever he asked of her, she found herself abandoned for ever longer periods as the years went by, while he carried on his love affairs in blazes of publicity. In May 1925 she was reduced to explaining his many prolonged absences abroad by telling a friend that there were too many distractions for him at home at Easton Glebe.[40] She sought to comfort herself in her loneliness by taking a London flat, where she went by herself to write sad short stories and poems. Only when Wells was told by their son Frank that she was dying of cancer, in May 1927, did he return from his house in the sun with Odette to be with her for the four last months of her life – and even then he went back to France each month for a few days.

When Jane became too ill to run the house and continue overseeing Wells's business affairs, she brought in a young woman, Marjorie Craig, a friend of her son Gip, to take over her administrative and secretarial work. Marjorie Craig rapidly became part of the family – she and Gip were married before Jane died. Frank also married, on the day after her death: it was as though both sons were determined to fill the emptiness their mother's death would leave. Their father took to Marjorie at once, and they got on so well that she became his secretary and worked for him for the rest of his life. She was efficient and affectionate, and as well as working for him she gave him two grandchildren.

Jane's courage had been such that Charlotte Shaw told Wells she was 'the gayest and pluckiest person I have ever known'. He mourned her passionately and said she had been 'the moral background of half my life'.[41] 'She stabilized my life. She gave me a home and dignity. She preserved its continuity,' he wrote. There is something disquieting about this posthumous tribute, as though he expected it to put right his neglect, and could not see that it came too late.

He was a bad husband and an unreliable lover. He assured Rebecca West in a letter written in January 1914, when she was pregnant with his child that she would be his wife, a commitment she unfortunately believed, leading to years of struggle between them. Wells told her later, 'Jane is a wife, but you could never be a wife. You want a wife yourself – you want sanity and care and courage and patience behind you just as much as I do.'[42] For Odette Keun, with whom he started an affair in 1925, he built a house in Provence where they set up an inscription reading, 'Two lovers built this house'. It had to be taken down each time they quarrelled, replaced when they made up, and so on, ridiculously. After Jane's death his relationship with Keun deteriorated, finishing in rows, and he ended it in 1932, saying she had become 'dishonourable and intolerable': they argued about the ownership of the house, and each attacked the other in print – an unedifying business.[43]

His last mistress, Moura Budberg, refused to marry him or even keep house with him – and she kept his attachment to the end. She had lived a life of spectacular difficulty and danger, and saved herself – and her children – by courage, charm and ruthlessness. He had met her in 1914 through Gorky, with whom she was living as secretary and acknowledged mistress. Whatever Wells knew or worried about in her past – marriages, love affairs, imprisonment and spying in Russia, Berlin, Estonia and Italy – he did not waver in his determination to keep her. In 1930 he settled an annuity on her, in 1933 he decided he wanted to marry her, in 1934 he asked friends to include her in invitations to him and told Elizabeth Healey, 'We live in open sin and you must meet her some day.'[44] It was Moura who insisted on remaining independent. 'I want a woman at my beck and call,' he wrote, but she was never prepared to be that. She went to Russia in 1936 to see Gorky before he died, and took holidays without Wells. She lied to him about her visits to Russia; he suffered and realized he had to accept her lies. In 1939 he wrote to her from Australia, where he was lecturing, urging her to 'Be a good pure Moura – chaste, non-alcoholic, reading one of my books for an hour every night before going to bed at eleven, walking 4 miles every day. Bless you Aigee.'[45] Whether she carried out his instructions we don't know.

He had to accept that they lived 'with different idea systems but a common temperamental quality', and that they were a great comfort to each other and he must be content with that. Yet as he aged he longed to have a wife living with him in the conventional arrangement he had found unacceptable in the past: 'I still dream of living with a wife, my wife in a house and garden of my own . . . I want to . . . look out of the window and see my own dear coming up the garden to me.'[46] It did not happen.

*

The relationship between Wells and Beatrice Webb did not end with their quarrels over the Fabian Society and his affair with Amber. There was a long period when they neither spoke nor wrote – during which Fenner Brockway, editor of the *Labour Leader*, published an 'open letter' to Wells in October 1913, asking if he was a socialist – and Wells replied with a furious attack on the Webbs. Part of it read:

> I left the Fabian Society . . . because I could not induce that body to alter its Basis and confess to the citizenship of women and the endow-ment of motherhood. From first to last in my relationship with the Fabian Society – I was bitterly antagonistic to the furtive methods of the Webbs. I loathe their game. I believe their cunning and contagious vanity has held back the cause of Socialism in England for a quarter of a century . . . I am the prey in Socialist circles of vague and apparently incurable scandals, distorted stories, and stories partially or wholly untrue. While you Socialists prefer scandal to Socialism I am helpless to do any more for your movement . . . the campaign of scandal against me *followed* a series of bitter attacks upon Webb Socialism.[47]

He went on to say he preferred 'the quiet of a country rectory to the atmosphere of feverish curiosities, wrong-headed accusations, and imbecile political ambitions that I breathed in Socialist circles'. His quiet country rectory was the house he was now renting from the socialist Countess of Warwick on her estate near Dunmow in Essex – once a rectory but no longer. Wells used it as his country house, efficiently run by Jane, where he worked, gave parties and entertained troops of friends. He also kept a flat in London.

Almost everything in Wells's letter is false. Shaw, Beatrice Webb and Mrs Reeves were all in favour of equal citizenship for women. The Webbs were not 'furtive' in their methods – and had in no way held back the cause of socialism – rather, Beatrice Webb had advanced it through her *Minority Report*, and continued to work for it. Both Webbs were avowed socialists. Wells's complaint that he was a 'prey' to scandals and untrue stories was also absurd. And he had resigned from the Fabian Society of his own accord in 1908, saying he wanted to devote himself to writing novels.

With time it became clear that Webb and Wells shared too many memories for their friendship not to be revived. In 1920 Wells sent Mrs Webb a copy of his *Outline of History*, to which she responded warmly, saying she saw it as 'a token of "mutuality" in regard for each other's work – a regard that has been constant on my part' – and invited him and Jane to dinner. She and Sidney then felt they must support him when he stood as Labour candidate in the elections of 1922 and 1923, and Sidney wrote him a friendly letter when he failed to be elected, congratulating him on a speech he had made during the campaign. She decided that he was far too conscious of his literary success, 'a sort of "little god" demanding payment in flattery', but she was softening towards him. When Jane died in 1927, she wrote to him, praising her and their 'inspiring partnership so like our own' – which was overdoing it, even if well meant.

In 1932 the Shaws invited Wells to tea with Moura and the Webbs, who were about to leave for Russia. Beatrice noted that Moura joined in a defence of Soviet Russia alongside Shaw and the Webbs – and that 'H. G. did not like being on the right of the Webbs and was perturbed at our going to Russia and endorsing even a modified Communism.'[48] Wells was in the right here of course, and the Webbs' inability to see what was happening in Russia, and their endorsement of Stalin, was a dismaying failure of perception and judgement.

Wells remained prolific in his writings and political engagement. In May 1933 he had the honour of knowing his books were burned by students in Berlin when Hitler and Goebbels organized bonfires of books they disapproved of all over Germany – Proust, Thomas Mann, Trotsky, Heine, Dostoevsky, Zola, Hemingway and Lawrence were some of the other writers whose works were thrown into the flames. As Heine had written, 'Where they burn books, they will in the end burn human beings.'

For Mrs Webb's eightieth birthday he wrote a tribute to her in the *New Statesman* in which he called her 'the greatest lady I have ever met'. In 1939 she visited him at Hanover Terrace, in his grand house overlooking Regent's Park: 'I found him a physical wreck . . . Poor old Wells. I was sorry for him. I doubt whether we shall ever meet again – we are too old and tired.' Then in 1940 she recalled how he had 'preached the gospel of human progress for forty years – since he published *Anticipations* . . . a fine record'.[49]

In 1940 Wells's *The Rights of Man*, subtitled *Or What are We Fighting for?*, was published by Penguin, and would become one of the sources for the 1948 Universal Declaration of Human Rights. Food, medical care, education, freedom of movement were rights, alongside duties: work, both privately done and as part of civic needs such as jury service. He also wrote of the need for some sort of world government: all admirable ideas – many still waiting to be achieved.

As Mrs Webb aged, she wrote, 'GBS and H. G. Wells cannot stop writing; they will die with an unfinished book on their desk. And I shall die with my diary, pen and ink in a drawer by the side of my bed.'[50]

And so it was – she died in April 1943, and Wells told Sidney he was consoled by knowing that all their ancient bickerings had died out and 'my relations with you both was one of the warmest friendship and admiration.'[51] He delivered a last tribute to her in the *Guardian* on 4 May, in which he said she was the kind of person 'who lives for ever'.

Wells stayed in his house on Regent's Park throughout the war, and throughout the air attacks launched by the Germans – nightly bombing, then the V1 flying bombs, or doodlebugs, which were programmed to cut out and explode on impact, then the V2s that came silently – both causing great damage and loss of life between June 1944 and March 1945. Most of his windows were broken and boarded up, but he was fearless – he shrugged and said that bombs never hit him. Moura and he met almost daily, but she did not stay overnight.

In September 1943 he wrote to Shaw on the death of his wife, Charlotte, and a year later thanked him for sending him a copy of his *Everybody's Political What's What*. Bertrand Russell visited him and reported that he was frail and lively, and 'of course, he was writing'.

Wells went out to vote in the election on 5 July 1945, won by the Labour Party, whose manifesto offered a health service for all, nationalization of major industries and comprehensive social security – the programme laid out in 1942 by William Beveridge, who had been Beatrice Webb's researcher and assistant, working with her on her report on the Poor Laws published in 1909.

The end of the war came in August, and after this Wells was not strong enough to leave the house. He received a few visitors and sometimes got up, wrote a letter, worked on a film script and a last very short and gloomy book – *Mind at the End of Its Tether*, published in November 1945. In it he suggested that humanity was pretty well played out and recommended 'mutual comfort and redeeming acts of kindliness'. Yet he also remembered the importance of literature and celebrated it, through words from the poem 'Invictus' by his long-dead friend William Henley, who had first published *The Time Machine*. Wells quotes the two last defiant lines, written by a man who had struggled all his life against illness and disability:

> I am the master of my fate:
> I am the captain of my soul.

After that Wells put Shakespeare, misquoting lines from the song in *Cymbeline* – he makes the girls into 'lasses':

> Golden lads and girls all must
> Like chimney sweepers come to dust.

And he finished with Walter Savage Landor's matchless envoi:

> I warmed both hands before the fire of Life;
> It sinks; and I am ready to depart.

Wells continued to advocate republicanism to the end, writing a faintly absurd letter to the *Socialist Leader* in July 1946 suggesting that the royal family should leave England 'free to reform its old and persistent Republican tradition'. In truth that tradition had effectively disappeared in the great and general admiration for the courageous conduct of George VI and Queen Elizabeth during the war, and the charm of their daughters. Wells had either failed to notice this, or deliberately shut his eyes to it.

In the afternoon of 13 August he died at home in his bed, alone. Moura was not with him, and he had sent away the nurse, saying he wanted to rest. So he kept up the family tradition of dying quickly and without giving any trouble.

A month later Penguin published reissues of ten of his best books, a hundred thousand copies of each, planned as a celebration of his eightieth birthday. All but one had been published in the fifteen years between 1895 and 1910. Of these, five were written in the 1890s – *The Time Machine*, *The War of the Worlds*, *The Island of Dr Moreau*, *The Invisible Man*, *Love and Mr Lewisham* – and four between 1905 and 1910 – *Kipps*, *Tono-Bungay*, *The New Machiavelli*, *The History of Mr Polly*. The one later one was his *Short History of the World*, from 1922; not only had it been a bestseller but a copy of it had been found in the small collection of books hidden by prisoners in Auschwitz.

At the memorial service for Wells held in October 1946 William Beveridge, now the chief architect of the Welfare State being set up in England, spoke about him. He characterized Wells as receptive to ideas, full of constructive and creative powers, honest, sympathetic and humane – he said his *A Modern Utopia* had influenced him most of all his books – and described him as 'a volcano in perpetual eruption of burning thoughts and luminous images'. His tribute was a reminder of Wells's central passion for social equality and government dedicated to making a better life for all its citizens – which Beveridge was now doing his best to bring about. And perhaps he remembered the words Wells had written in 1905 in *This Misery of Boots* – uttered to the friend who says it is useless to try to change things and get everyone into comfortable boots: 'Don't submit,' he cries. 'Don't be humbugged into believing that this must be the dingy lot of all mankind. Don't say for a moment: "Such is life." '

Wells never said, 'Such is Life.' He imagined a great deal more than the life before his eyes. He revelled in its pleasures, in landscape, sunshine, books, friendship, good conversation, sex, food, walking, bicycling, well-designed and well-built houses, children's games, comfortable clothes – including boots. He wanted to reorganize the world so that everyone could enjoy it, and, if he did not succeed in that as well as he had hoped, he gave his superabundant energy to speaking and writing for the cause. The best of his books will go on being read for generations, entertaining, surprising and provoking different readers to different questions – as good books should.

Bibliography

Bergonzi, Bernard, *The Early H. G. Wells: A Study of the Scientific Romances* (1961)

Bland, Rosamund E. Nesbit, *The Man in the Stone House* (1934)

Briggs, Julia, *A Woman of Passion: The Life of E. Nesbit* (1987)

Brome, Vincent, *H. G. Wells* (1951)

Brooke, Emma Francis, *A Superfluous Woman* (1894; 2015 edn)

Carswell, John, *The Exile: A Life of Ivy Litvinov* (1983)

Dickson, Lovat, *H. G. Wells: His Turbulent Life and Times* (1969)

Edel, Leon, and Gordon N. Ray (eds.), *Henry James and H. G. Wells: A Record of Their Friendship, Their Debate on the Art of Fiction, and Their Quarrel* (1958)

Hammond, J. R., *An H. G. Wells Companion* (1979)

—, *Interviews and Recollections* (1980)

—, *An H. G. Wells Chronology* (1999)

Kagarlitsky, July, 'In a Race against Time', Veronica Muskhell (trs.), in Galya Diment (ed.), *H. G. Wells and All Things Russian* (2007 Russian edn.; 2019)

Lynn, Andrea, *Shadow Lovers* (2001)

MacCarthy, Desmond, 'Bennett, Wells and Trollope' (1930) and 'Last Words on Wells' (1946), in *Memories* (1953)

MacKenzie, Norman (ed.), *The Letters of Sidney and Beatrice Webb* (3 vols.; 1978)

MacKenzie, Norman, and Jeanne, *The Life of H. G. Wells: The Time Traveller* (1973; rev. edn 1987)

—, *The First Fabians* (1977)

— (eds.), *The Diary of Beatrice Webb* (4 vols.; 1982–5)

Meade-Fetherstonhaugh, Margaret, and Oliver Warner, *Uppark and Its People* (1964; 1995 edn)

Meyer, Mathilde Marie, *H. G. Wells and His Family, as I Have Known Them* (1956)

Muggeridge, Kitty, and Ruth Adam, *Beatrice Webb: A Life* (1967)

National Trust, *Guide to Uppark* (1995 edn)

Parrinder, Patrick (ed.), *H. G. Wells: The Critical Heritage* (1972)

Ray, Gordon N., *H. G. Wells and Rebecca West* (1974)

Richardson, Dorothy, *Revolving Lights* (1923) (part of Vol. 3 of *Pilgrimage* (4 vols.; 1979); gives picture of life at Spade House)

Sherborne, Michael, *H. G. Wells: Another Kind of Life* (2010)

Smith, David C., *H. G. Wells: Desperately Mortal* (1986)

— (ed.), *The Correspondence of H. G. Wells* (4 vols.; 1998)

Smith, J. Percy (ed.), *Bernard Shaw and H. G. Wells: Selected Correspondence* (1995)

Swinnerton, Frank, *The Georgian Literary Scene* (1938)

Walter, Nicolas (ed.), *Charlotte Wilson: Anarchist Essays* (2000)

Wells, G. P. (ed.), *H. G. Wells in Love: Postscript to 'Experiment in Autobiography'* (1984)

Wells. H. G., *The Book of Catherine Wells* (1928)

—, *Experiment in Autobiography* (2 vols.; 1934)

—, *The Desert Daisy*, with an introduction by Gordon N. Ray (written 1878; facsimile 1957)

West, Anthony, *H. G. Wells: Aspects of a Life* (1984)

West, Geoffrey, *H. G. Wells: A Sketch for a Portrait* (1930)

Wilson, Harris (ed.), *Arnold Bennett and H. G. Wells* (1960)

Books by Wells 1893–1911

1893
Text-book of Biology
Honours Physiography (with R. A. Gregory)

1895
Select Conversations with an Uncle
The Time Machine
The Wonderful Visit
The Stolen Bacillus and Other Incidents

1896
The Island of Doctor Moreau
The Wheels of Chance

1897
The Plattner Story and Others
The Invisible Man
Certain Personal Matters (a collection of short essays)
Thirty Strange Stories

1898
The War of the Worlds

1899
When the Sleeper Wakes (first version, rewritten as *The Sleeper Awakes*, pub-
    lished in 1910)
Tales of Space and Time

1900
Love and Mr Lewisham

1901
The First Men in the Moon
Anticipations

1902
The Discovery of the Future
The Sea Lady

1903
Mankind in the Making
Twelve Stories and a Dream

1904
The Food of the Gods

1905
A Modern Utopia
Kipps

1906
In the Days of the Comet
The Future in America

1907
This Misery of Boots (Fabian pamphlet)

1908
New Worlds for Old
The War in the Air
First and Last Things

1909
Tono-Bungay
Ann Veronica

1910
The History of Mr Polly

1911
The New Machiavelli
The Country of the Blind and Other Stories
The Door in the Wall and Other Stories
Floor Games

In 1920 he published *The Outline of History*; in 1922 *A Short History of the World*; and in 1930 *The Science of Life* (written in collaboration with Julian Huxley and G. P. Wells)

Notes

Preface

1 George Orwell to Cyril Connolly, 14 December 1938, *Collected Essays, Journalism and Letters of George Orwell. Vol. 4: In Front of Your Nose 1945–1950* (1968), p. 422. See also *Such, Such Were the Joys* (1952), an account of Orwell's unhappy years at his prep school, in which he says, 'Ian Hay, Thackeray, Kipling and H. G. Wells were the favourite authors of my boyhood.'

2 'Wells, Hitler, and the World State', *Horizon*, August 1941.

3 BBC broadcast, 10 March 1942, reproduced in the *Listener*, 12 March 1942.

4 *Tribune*, 6 December 1946.

5 ibid., 7 February 1947.

2. 'What else can you do?'

1 *Experiment in Autobiography* (2 vols.; 1934; 1969 edn), p. 140.

3. Uppark

1 The house was half destroyed by fire in 1989, when it was owned by the National Trust. They decided that enough was left unscathed for them to restore it, treating it as a damaged work of art and bringing in experts able to revive old skills. It took five years and the result is breathtaking – and magnificent.

2 Margaret Meade-Fetherstonhaugh and Oliver Warner, *Uppark and Its People* (1995 edn), p. 57.

3 ibid., p. 55.

4 *Experiment in Autobiography* (2 vols.; 1934; 1969 edn), p. 137.

5 ibid., p. 183.

6 ibid., p. 185.

7 Published in 1879, it was a bestselling, six-penny paperback in England. The book was hugely influential, praised by F. D. Roosevelt, Tolstoy, Shaw and Lloyd George.

4. 'A bright run of luck'

1 H. G. W. to Fred Wells, 23 June 1899, David C. Smith (ed.), *The Correspondence of H. G. Wells. Vol. 1: 1880–1903* (4 vols.; 1998), p. 344.

2 Published in 1910.

3 *Experiment in Autobiography* (2 vols.; 1934; 1969 edn), p. 204.

4 Letter from H. G. W. to Tommy Simmons, 9 September 1886, *Correspondence*, Vol. 1, p. 49.

5. *Blood*

1 Anthony West, *H. G. Wells: Aspects of a Life* (1984), pp. 67–8.

2 Wells had observed of her death, in a letter of 'July 21' to his brother Fred, that tuberculosis proceeded with 'no haste, no pause, no pity', H. G. Wells Papers 1845–1946, Rare Book and Manuscript Library, University of Illinois at Urbana-Champaign.

3 *Experiment in Autobiography* (2 vols.; 1934; 1969 edn), p. 302.

4 H. G. W. to Arthur Davies, autumn 1887, David C. Smith (ed.), *The Correspondence of H. G. Wells. Vol. 1: 1880–1903* (4 vols.; 1998), p. 87.

5 H. G. W. to Tommy Simmons, [n.d. December 1887?], ibid., p. 73.

6 H. G. W. to Tommy Simmons, 13 December 1887, ibid., p. 74.

7 H. G. W. to Tommy Simmons, autumn 1887, ibid., p. 66.

8 H. G. W. to Elizabeth Healey, 11 March 1888, ibid., p. 93.

9 H. G. W. to Elizabeth Healey, 23 February 1888, ibid., p. 82.

10 See *Experiment in Autobiography*, pp. 307–8, where Wells gives his letter.

11 E. A. Hamilton-Gordon gave the paper, and said the fourth dimension had been given some impossible descriptions, among them 'Time', 'Life', 'Heaven' and 'Velocity'.

12 First published in 1895.

13 H. G. W. to Arthur Davies, May 1888, *Correspondence*, Vol. 1, p. 103.

14 H. G. W. to Elizabeth Healey, 19 June 1888, ibid., p. 108.

15 *Experiment in Autobiography*, p. 310.

6. *'For a young man to marry . . .'*

1 *Experiment in Autobiography* (2 vols.; 1934; 1969 edn), p. 422.

2 H. G. W. to Elizabeth Healey, 2 March 1888, David C. Smith (ed.), *The Correspondence of H. G. Wells. Vol. 1: 1880–1903* (4 vols.; 1998), p. 86.

3 See Wells's 'The Pains of Marriage' (*Pall Mall Gazette*, 25 July 1894, reprinted in *Select Conversations with an Uncle*, 1895). In his novel *Tono-Bungay* (1909) he wrote a devastating account of a formal London wedding.

4 Ann Thwaite, *A. A. Milne: His Life* (2006). A. A. was of course the future creator of Pooh Bear and Piglet.

5 H. G. W. to Fred Wells, 28 May 1889, *Correspondence*, Vol. 1, pp. 120–21.

6 ibid.

7 Founded 1846 it was the first professional body for teachers, aiming to raise standards. Fröbel (1782–1852) was a German educationalist who transformed teaching by pointing out that children learn through play.

8 Letter from T. Ormerod, *Manchester Guardian*, 11 August 1946, cited in Norman and Jeanne MacKenzie, *The Life of H. G. Wells: The Time Traveller* (1973; 1987 rev. edn), p. 83.

9 H. G. W. to Fred Wells, [n.d. but mid-December?], P.S. to invitation to come to Haldon Rd, *Correspondence*, Vol. 1, p. 179.

10 H. G. W. to Arthur Davies, autumn, 1887, ibid., p. 66.

11 H. G. W. to Tommy Simmons, 6 July 1891, ibid., p. 168.

12 ibid.

13 H. G. W. to Fred Wells, 18 November 1936, *Correspondence*, Vol. 4, p. 111.

14 *Experiment in Autobiography*, p. 136.

15 No. 28 Haldon Road.

16 *Experiment in Autobiography*, p. 424.

7. More Blood

1 H. G. W. to Arthur Davies, 27 December 1893, David C. Smith (ed.), *The Correspondence of H. G. Wells. Vol. 1: 1880–1903,* (4 vols., 1998), p. 209.

2 Bjørnstjerne Martinius Björnson, *Arne and the Fisher Lassie* (2 vols.; 1890).

3 Chapter 6, 'Struggle for a Living', *Experiment in Autobiography* (2 vols.; 1934; 1969 edn), pp. 367–8.

4 ibid., p. 374.

5 H. G. W. to Amy Catherine Robbins, 'Tuesday' [late autumn 1887], *Correspondence*, Vol. 1, p. 204.

6 H. G. W. to J. V. Milne, November 1893, quoted in Geoffrey West, *H. G. Wells: A Sketch for a Portrait* (1930; 1933 edn).

8. The Time Machine

1 H. G. W. to Sarah Wells, 8 February 1894, David C. Smith (ed.), *The Correspondence of H. G. Wells. Vol. 1: 1880–1903* (4 vols.; 1998), p. 212.

2 H. G. W. to Elizabeth Healey, 11 June 1894, *Correspondence*, Vol. 1, p. 216.

3 H. G. W. to Elizabeth Healey, 25 December 1894, ibid., p. 227.

4 H. G. W. to Elizabeth Healey, 22 December 1894, ibid., p. 226.

5 H. G. W. to Tommy Simmons [n.d. but March 1895?], ibid., p. 236.

6 R. H. Hutton [unsigned], *Spectator*, vol. 75 (13 July 1895), pp. 41–3.

7 *Experiment in Autobiography* (2 vols.; 1934; 1969 edn), p. 534.

8 First published in *New Budget*, 15 August 1895.

9 *Saturday Review*, 16 May 1896.

10 H. G. W. to Elizabeth Healey, 26 February 1895, *Correspondence*, Vol. 1, p. 233.

11 Ivy Low grew up in Hampstead, married Maxim Litvinov, a Russian exile who became a Soviet diplomat serving Stalin as the Ambassador to the United States during the Second World War and managed to survive against the odds. Ivy, strong-minded and independent, learnt Russian, brought up two children in Moscow, wrote stories and had many love affairs. Litvinov died in 1951; she stayed until 1960, when she

got Khrushchev's permission to return to England. There she took up old friendships, sold her stories to the *New Yorker*, lived a full life and died in 1977. For this and more, see John Carswell's *The Exile: A Life of Ivy Litvinov* (1983).

12 H. G. W. to Tommy Simmons [n.d. but spring 1895?], *Correspondence*, Vol. 1, p. 233.

13 Letter to the Editor, *Pearson's Magazine*, March 1897, cited in *Correspondence*, Vol. 1, p. 284.

14 H. G. W. to Sidney Low, 26 October 1895, *Correspondence*, Vol. 1, p. 255.

15 Arnold Bennett, 'H. G. Wells and His Work', *Cosmopolitan*, vol. 33, no. 4 (August 1902), pp. 465–71.

9. *'Uncommonly cheerful and hopeful'*

1 H. G. W. to Elizabeth Healey, April 1896, David C. Smith (ed.), *The Correspondence of H. G. Wells. Vol. 1: 1880–1903* (4 vols.; 1998), p. 261.

2 John St Loe Strachey [unsigned], *Spectator*, vol. 80 (29 January 1898), pp. 168–9.

3 H. G. W. to J. M. Dent, 12 September 1896, *Correspondence*, Vol. 1, p. 268.

4 H. G. W. to Arnold Bennett, 25 September 1899 and 9 September 1902, Harris Wilson (ed.), *Arnold Bennett and H. G. Wells* (1960), pp. 44, 84.

5 H. G. W. to Fred Wells, New Year's Eve 1896, *Correspondence*, Vol. 1, p. 281.

6 H. G. W. to J. B. Pinker, 4 January 1899, quoted in J. R. Hammond, *An H. G. Wells Chronology* (1999), p. 35.

7 H. G. W. to Edward Garnett, 26 June 1900, *Correspondence*, Vol. 1, p. 358.

8 H. G. W. to Edmund Gosse, 10 June 1900, ibid.

9 H. G. W. to Elizabeth Healey, 22 June 1900, ibid., p. 356.

10 H. G. W. to Arnold Bennett, 5 July 1900, *Arnold Bennett and H. G. Wells*, p. 47.

11 Arnold Bennett to H. G. W., 8 October 1903, ibid., p. 101.

12 H. G. W. to Arnold Bennett, 25 September 1905, ibid., p. 121.

13 *Experiment in Autobiography* (2 vols.; 1934; 1969 edn), p. 627.

14 H. G. W. to Arnold Bennett, November 1908, *Arnold Bennett and H. G. Wells*, p. 154; *Experiment in Autobiography*, p. 628.

15 John Halperin, *Gissing: A Life in Books* (1982), p. 238.

16 First published in 1891.

17 *Experiment in Autobiography*, p. 431.

18 H. G. W. to Harry Quilter, late March 1898, *Correspondence*, Vol. 1, p. 308.

19 Copy seen for sale online August 2019.

20 *Experiment in Autobiography*, p. 582.

10. *A House by the Sea*

1 She kept it carefully and was able to sell it when she needed money later.

2 The house is now No. 20 Castle Road.

3 H. G. W. to Fred Wells, 23 June 1899, David C. Smith (ed.), *The Correspondence of H. G. Wells. Vol. 1: 1880–1903* (4 vols.; 1998), p. 344.

4 Henley had printed it in the *New Review*. It was published in America under the name *Children of the Sea: A Tale of the Forecastle*, with the name changed not to avoid giving offence, as it would be today, but because it was thought a novel about a Black man wouldn't sell.

5 It was enlarged for Wells in 1903, with rooms in the attic; then, after he left, an additional wing was added in the 1920s. It is now a nursing home, where I was kindly allowed to wander at will.

6 Four years later Anton Chekhov also died in Badenweiler.

7 H. G. W. to Elizabeth Healey, December 1899, *Correspondence*, Vol. 1, p. 348.

8 Harris Wilson (ed.), *Arnold Bennett and H. G. Wells* (1960), p. 53.

9 ibid., p. 55.

10 H. G. W. to John Galsworthy, 16 November 1900, *Correspondence*, Vol. 1, p. 366.

11 H. G. W. to Elizabeth Healey, 2 July 1901, *Correspondence*, Vol. 1, p. 379.

12 H. G. W. to Winston Churchill, 19 November 1901, *Correspondence*, Vol. 1, p. 457.

13 See Édouard Launet, 'H. G. Wells, inventeur de l'orgasmotron', 13 March 2018, article online crediting the research of Marilyn Pann. http://delibere.fr/hg-wells-inventeur-orgasmotron/

14 *The Intellectuals and the Masses* (1992), chapters 6 and 7.

15 H. G. W. to Elizabeth Healey, 2 July 1901, *Correspondence*, Vol. 1, p. 379.

16 Norman and Jeanne MacKenzie, *The Life of H. G. Wells: The Time Traveller* (1973; rev. edn 1987), p. 156. 'She begged H. G. to forgive her – apparently for making a fuss about his departure – and imploringly assured him of her affection.' They do not quote the letter, which I have not seen.

17 H. G. W. to Richard Gregory, 21 December 1901, *Correspondence*, Vol. 1, p. 391.

11. Fabian Friends

1 *Experiment in Autobiography* (2 vols.; 1934; 1969 edn), p. 247.

2 H. G. W. to Elizabeth Healey, 21 November 1888, David C. Smith (ed.), *The Correspondence of H. G. Wells. Vol. 1: 1880–1903* (4 vols.; 1998), p. 113.

3 *Freedom* was published until 1928 and occasionally revived until 2014, when there were 225 subscribers – with a promise of occasional online versions to follow.

4 Norman and Jeanne MacKenzie, *The First Fabians* (1977), p. 63.

5 She would go on to become one of the leading British campaigners against the Empire in both Ireland and India, and would join the Indian National Congress.

6 Thomas P. Jenkin, 'The American Fabian Movement', *Western Political Quarterly*, vol. 1, no. 2 (1948). In 2020 there are still nearly fifty Fabian groups in towns in Britain.

7 1 March 1910, Norman and Jeanne MacKenzie (eds.), *The Diary of Beatrice Webb. Vol. 3: The Power to Alter Things 1905–1924* (4 vols.; 1982–5), p. 135.

8 Kitty Muggeridge and Ruth Adam, *Beatrice Webb: A Life* (1967), p. 118.

9 ibid., p. 130.

10 *Diary*, 4 January 1891, quoted in MacKenzie, *The First Fabians*, p. 151.

11 MacKenzie, *The First Fabians*, p. 98; Muggeridge and Adam, *Beatrice Webb: A Life*, p. 136.

12 *Diary*, September 1893. Not all of the *Diary* is in MacKenzie; it can be found online at the LSE's digital library: https://digital.library.lse.ac.uk/objects/lse:bin716wef

13 Quoted in MacKenzie, *The First Fabians*, p. 150, from the Graham Wallas Papers, British Library of Political and Economic Science.

14 Quoted in MacKenzie, *The First Fabians*, p. 154.

15 ibid.

16 ibid., p. 155, source given as the Passfield Papers, British Library of
    Political and Economic Science.

17 According to Amy Strachey, quoted in *St Loe Strachey: His Life and His
    Paper* (1930), quoted in ibid., p. 220.

18 12 March 1894, *Diary*, quoted in ibid., p. 205.

19 H. G. W. to John Galsworthy, 16 November 1900, *Correspondence*, Vol. 1,
    p. 366.

20 H. G. W. to Richard Gregory, 29 December 1901, *Correspondence*, Vol. 1,
    p. 391.

12. *Joining the Club*

1   Quoted in Norman and Jeanne MacKenzie, *The First Fabians* (1977), p. 191.

2   23 January 1918, *The Diary of Hugh Walpole*, quoted in Rupert Hart-
    Davis, *Hugh Walpole: A Biography* (1952), pp. 168–171, 286.

3   Winston Churchill to H. G. W., 9 October 1906, cited in Jonathan Rose,
    The Literary Churchill (1914), p. 85.

4   H. G. W. to Graham Wallas, 19 March 1902, David C. Smith (ed.), *The
    Correspondence of H. G. Wells. Vol. 1: 1880–1903* (4 vols.; 1998), p. 396.

5   *The New Machiavelli* (1911; 2005 edn), pp. 172, 166.

6   ibid., p. 164.

7   *The Autobiography of Bertrand Russell. Vol. 1: 1872–1914* (1967), p. 230.

8   H. G. W. to Beatrice Webb, [?]21 March 1904, David C. Smith (ed.), *The
    Correspondence of H. G. Wells. Vol. 2: 1904–1918* (4 vols.; 1998), p. 20.

9   19 April 1904, Norman and Jeanne MacKenzie (eds.), *The Diary of Bea-
    trice Webb. Vol. 2: All the Good Things of Life 1892–1905* (4 vols.; 1982–5).

10 Beatrice Webb to Mary Playne, [?] 20 April 1904, Norman MacKenzie
    (ed.), *The Letters of Sidney and Beatrice Webb. Vol. 2: Partnership 1892–1912*
    (3 vols.; 1978), p. 202.

11 Beatrice Webb to H. G. W., 29 April 1904, ibid., p. 203.

12 H. G. W. to George Bernard Shaw, [n.d.], J. Percy Smith (ed.), *Bernard
    Shaw and H. G. Wells: Selected Correspondence* (1995), pp. 52–3.

13 Julia Briggs, *A Woman of Passion: The Life of E. Nesbit* (1982), p. 320.
    Rosamund wrote a novel, *The Man in the Stone House*, published in 1934,

about a friendship between an older man and a girl – readable but not illuminating about Wells.

14 Quoted in Michael Holroyd's *Bernard Shaw: The One-volume Definitive Edition* (2012), p. 392.

15 H. G. W. to Jane Wells, 16 December 1903, *Correspondence*, Vol. 1, p. 445.

16 ibid., p. 446.

13. *Pressure*

1 *Experiment in Autobiography* (2 vols.; 1934; 1969 edn), p. 567.

2 Edmund Gosse, *Leaves and Fruit* (1927), p. 277.

3 *Experiment in Autobiography*, p. 572.

4 H. G. W. to J. B. Pinker, 29 September 1904, cited in Norman and Jeanne MacKenzie, *The Life of H. G. Wells: The Time Traveller* (1973; rev. edn 1987), p. 187. He broke finally with Pinker in 1915.

5 H. G. W. to Vernon Lee, 6 August 1904, David C. Smith (ed.), *The Correspondence of H. G. Wells. Vol. 2: 1904–1918* (4 vols.; 1998), p. 40. Vernon Lee was the pseudonym of Violet Paget.

6 *Ann Veronica* was published by T. Fisher Unwin, and *The War in the Air* by George Bell, also in 1908.

7 H. G. W. to Arnold Bennett, 8 February 1902, Harris Wilson (ed.), *Arnold Bennett and H. G. Wells* (1960), p. 73.

8 H. G. W. to Arthur Balfour, 10 May 1905, *Correspondence*, Vol. 2, pp. 71–2.

9 *Correspondence*, Vol. 2, p. 73, gives an account of Ramsay's view; Wells's letter to Ramsay, 6 December 1905.

10 In vol. 7, no. 27.

11 *This Misery of Boots*, Fabian pamphlet (1907; 2018 edn), p. 18.

12 ibid., pp. 26, 28.

13 ibid., pp. 27, 37.

14 ibid., pp. 35, 36.

15 ibid., p. 40.

16 Cited in MacKenzie, *The Life of H. G. Wells*, p. 191.

17 Henry James to H. G. W., 19 November 1905, Philip Horne (ed.), *Henry James: A Life in Letters* (1999), p. 424.

14. America in 1906

1 Cited in Leon Edel and Gordon N. Ray (eds.), *Henry James and H. G. Wells: A Record of Their Friendship, Their Debate on the Art of Fiction, and Their Quarrel* (1958), p. 58.

2 *The Future in America* (1987 edn), Chapter 7.

3 Jane Wells to H. G. W., 26 April 1906, cited in Norman and Jeanne MacKenzie, *The Life of H. G. Wells: The Time Traveller* (1973; rev. edn 1987), pp. 201–2.

4 *The Future in America*, Chapter 8.

5 H. G. W. to Jane Wells, 12 May 1906, David C. Smith (ed.), *The Correspondence of H. G. Wells. Vol. 2: 1904–1918* (4 vols.; 1998), p. 99.

6 See G. P. Wells (ed.), *H. G. Wells in Love: Postscript to 'Experiment in Autobiography'* (1984), p. 66.

7 *The Future in America*, p. 138; J. D. Grossman and Ruth Rischin (eds.), *William James in Russian Culture* (2003), pp. 189–90; *New York Times*, 13 April 1906.

8 Henry James to H. G. W., 8 November 1906, *Henry James and H. G. Wells*, p. 115.

9 Beatrice Webb to H. G. W., mid-November 1906, Norman MacKenzie (ed.), *The Letters of Sidney and Beatrice Webb. Vol. 2: Partnership 1892–1912* (3 vols.; 1978), p. 243.

10 Beatrice Webb to H. G. W., 2 August 1906, ibid., p. 236.

11 It is printed in Copybook No. 7, f. 178. Tolstoy's date is Old Style, which fixes the position of the letter in the copybook.

12 H. G. W. to Leo Tolstoy, 21 November 1906, letter in Russian, translated by Michael Frayn.

13 Bernard Bergonzi, *The Early H. G. Wells: A Study of the Scientific Romances* (1961), pp. 88, 168, 173, *passim*.

15. Webb and Wells

1 1 March 1906, Norman and Jeanne MacKenzie (eds.), *The Diary of Beatrice Webb. Vol. 3: The Power to Alter Things 1905–1924* (4 vols.; 1982–5), p. 31.

2 ibid.

3 William Beveridge (1879–1963) was educated at Charterhouse and Balliol; son of humanist parents; his mother was the founder of the Working Women's College in Queen Square.

4 Norman MacKenzie (ed.), *The Letters of Sidney and Beatrice Webb. Vol. 2: Partnership 1892–1912* (3 vols.; 1978), p. 235, editorial summary.

5 15 July 1906, *The Diary of Beatrice Webb*, Vol. 3, pp. 43–4.

6 1 October 1906, *The Diary of Beatrice Webb*, Vol. 3, p. 55.

7 Sidney Webb to H. G. W., 3 September 1906, *The Letters of Sidney and Beatrice Webb*, Vol. 2, pp. 237–8.

8 18 October 1906, *The Diary of Beatrice Webb*, Vol. 3, p. 56.

9 19 March 1908, ibid., p. 68.

10 Beatrice Webb to H. G. W. [mid-November 1906], *The Letters of Sidney and Beatrice Webb*, Vol. 2, p. 243.

11 30 November 1906, *The Diary of Beatrice Webb*, Vol. 3, p. 61.

12 Beatrice Webb to H. G. W., early 1907, *The Letters of Sidney and Beatrice Webb*, Vol. 2, p. 248.

13 Beatrice Webb to H. G. W., 25 May 1907, ibid., p. 255.

14 3 May 1907, *The Diary of Beatrice Webb*, Vol. 3, p. 72.

15 *The Letters of Sidney and Beatrice Webb*, Vol. 2, p. 262.

16 Maud Pember Reeves to Jane Wells, early 1907, cited in Michael Holroyd, *Bernard Shaw: The One-volume Definitive Edition* (2012), pp. 334–5.

17 In 1937 Wells settled a regular income for life on her.

18 Beatrice Webb to H. G. W., October 1907, *The Letters of Sidney and Beatrice Webb*, Vol. 2, p. 317.

19 ibid., p. 316.

20 *Labour Leader* [early February 1908], David C. Smith (ed.), *The Correspondence of H. G. Wells. Vol. 2: 1904–1918* (4 vols.; 1998), p. 210. There were three classes on trains in 1908.

21 Beatrice Webb to H. G. W., 1 May 1908, *The Letters of Sidney and Beatrice Webb*, Vol. 2, p. 312.

22 Cited in Norman and Jeanne MacKenzie, *The Life of H. G. Wells: The Time Traveller* (1973; rev. edn 1987), quoting from Geoffrey Keynes (ed.), *The Letters of Rupert Brooke* (1968).

23 Beatrice Webb to Mary Playne, 15 September 1908, *The Letters of Sidney and Beatrice Webb*, Vol. 2, p. 315.

16. Amberissima

Note: Acknowledgements and thanks for permission to print extracts from the unpublished letters that appear in this and subsequent chapters to the University of Illinois Library, and to the late David C. Smith, who is responsible for transcribing the letters quoted in chapters 16 and 17 and that form part of his unpublished fifth volume of Wells's *Correspondence*.

1 *Experiment in Autobiography* (2 vols.; 1934; 1969 edn), p. 185.
2 January 1907, unpublished letter.
3 Unpublished letter 2870.
4 Unpublished letter 2876.
5 Unpublished letter 2893.
6 4 February 1908, unpublished letter 2899. Note Wells's use of the word 'feminist'.
7 Unpublished letter 2928.
8 15 September 1908, Norman and Jeanne MacKenzie (eds.), *The Diary of Beatrice Webb. Vol. 3: The Power to Alter Things 1905–1924* (4 vols.; 1982–5), p. 315.
9 Cited in Margaret Drabble's chapter on Amber Reeves in *Breaking Bounds: Six Newnham Lives* (2014).
10 Fräulein Meyer taught the boys French and German, stayed with them until 1913, and wrote her own tactful account of her time with the family.
11 Unpublished letter 2903.
12 Unpublished letter 2913.
13 Spring 1909, unpublished letter.
14 Sent from the Oxford Union, where he was speaking, to her in Cambridge in 1908.
15 Unpublished letter 2946.
16 18 October 1909, unpublished letter 2954. *Ann Veronica* was already published, but the dedication to 'A. J.' appeared in the fourth printing, in November, and was possibly to his college friend Alan Jennings, who had given him crucial help through a difficult time in 1888.

17 Unpublished letter 2942.

18 Unpublished letter 2920.

19 Unpublished letters 2923, 2924.

20 Unpublished letter 2943.

21 14 October 1908, unpublished letter 2914.

22 Unpublished letter 2959.

23 William Henry Hudson (1841–1922), writer and nationalist, best known for *Green Mansions* (1904).

24 G. P. Wells (ed.), *H. G. Wells in Love: Postscript to 'Experiment in Autobiography'* (1984), edited and published by his son from manuscripts left by Wells, p. 80.

25 Unpublished letter 2916.

26 Unpublished letter 2997.

27 Unpublished letter 2917.

17. Heroines

1 Unpublished letter 2963.

2 Unpublished letter 2973.

3 July 1909, cited in Harris Wilson (ed.), *Arnold Bennett and H. G. Wells* (1960), p. 167.

4 Anthony West, *H. G. Wells: Aspects of a Life* (1984), p. 14. West says Shaw acted out the scene to him in 1948.

5 H. G. W. to George Bernard Shaw, 24 August 1909, David C. Smith (ed.), *The Correspondence of H. G. Wells. Vol. 2: 1904–1918* (4 vols.; 1998), p. 250.

6 ibid., p. 257.

7 H. G. W. to Elizabeth Robins [n.d.], ibid., p. 248.

8 Beatrice Webb to Amber Blanco White, 11 September 1909, Norman MacKenzie (ed.), *The Letters of Sidney and Beatrice Webb. Vol. 2. Partnership 1892–1912* (3 vols; 1978), p. 335.

9 22 August 1909, Norman and Jeanne MacKenzie (eds.), *The Diary of Beatrice Webb. Vol. 3: The Power to Alter Things 1905–1924* (4 vols.; 1982–5), pp. 123–4.

10 Vernon Lee [Violet Paget] to H. G. W., cited in Norman and Jeanne MacKenzie, *The Life of H. G. Wells: The Time Traveller* (1973; rev. edn 1987), p. 257.

11 This is Anthony West's explanation for Rivers's success in making Wells agree.

12 H. G. W. to Elizabeth Robins, 21 November 1910, *Correspondence*, Vol. 2, p. 290.

13 August 1909, *The Diary of Beatrice Webb*, Vol. 3, p. 121.

14 [n.d.], unpublished letter 2995 – written from Winchombe, where Wells must have been staying at Stanway, Lady Elcho's house.

15 G. P. Wells (ed.), *H. G. Wells in Love: Postscript to 'Experiment in Autobiography'* (1984), edited and published by his son from manuscripts left by Wells.

16 Amber Blanco White to H. G. W. [1930?], David C. Smith (ed.), *The Correspondence of H. G. Wells. Vol. 3: 1919–1934* (4 vols.; 1998), p. 349.

18. Tono-Bungay

1 Book 3, Chapter 1.

2 Gilbert Murray was a friend and political sympathizer with Wells, but I have not been able to find a copy of this letter.

3 The reviewer may have been Charles Masterman, known to Wells through the Co-efficient Club; he had become an MP in 1906 and was about to publish his own nonfiction study, *The Condition of England*, in November 1909.

4 Beatrice Webb to H. G. W., 10 February 1909, Norman MacKenzie (ed.), *The Letters of Sidney and Beatrice Webb. Vol. 2: Partnership 1892–1912* (3 vols.; 1978), p. 323.

5 Beatrice Webb to H. G. W., 24 February 1909, cited in Norman and Jeanne MacKenzie, *The Life of H. G. Wells: The Time Traveller* (1973; rev. edn 1987), p. 245.

6 4 October 1909, Norman and Jeanne MacKenzie (eds.), *The Diary of Beatrice Webb. Vol. 3: The Power to Alter Things 1905–1924* (4 vols.; 1982–5), p. 128.

7 20 March 1910, ibid., p. 138.

19. *Friends and Enemies*

1 Richard Davenport-Hines, *Ettie: The Intimate Life and Dauntless Spirit of Lady Desborough* (2008), p. 158.

2 1 March 1910, Norman and Jeanne MacKenzie (eds.), *The Diary of Beatrice Webb. Vol. 3: The Power to Alter Things 1905–1924* (4 vols.; 1982–5), p. 135.

3 19 May 1910, ibid., p. 139.

4 20 March 1910, ibid., p. 138.

5 H. G. W. to Elizabeth Robins, 21 November 1910, David C. Smith (ed.), *The Correspondence of H. G. Wells. Vol. 2: 1904–1918* (4 vols.; 1998), p. 290.

6 Cited in Norman and Jeanne MacKenzie, *The Life of H. G. Wells: The Time Traveller* (1973; rev. edn 1987), p. 272.

7 5 November 1910, *The Diary of Beatrice Webb*, Vol. 3, p. 147.

8 Henry James to H. G. W., 3 March 1911, cited in Leon Edel and Gordon N. Ray (eds.), *Henry James and H. G. Wells: A Record of Their Friendship, Their Debate on the Art of Fiction, and Their Quarrel* (1958), pp. 128–9.

9 H. G. W. to Henry James, 25 April 1911, cited in ibid., p. 130.

20. *'I warmed both hands before the fire of Life'*

1 Arnold Bennett to Jane Wells, 14 September 1927, Harris Wilson (ed.), *Arnold Bennett and H. G. Wells* (1960), p. 240.

2 *Experiment in Autobiography* (2 vols.; 1934; 1969 edn), p. 629.

3 ibid., p. 618.

4 ibid., p. 623.

5 H. G. W. to James Joyce, 23 November 1928, David C. Smith (ed.), *The Correspondence of H. G. Wells. Vol. 3: 1919–1934* (4 vols.; 1998), pp. 226–7.

6 As told by Harry T. Moore in his *The Priest of Love: A Life of D. H. Lawrence* (1974; 1982 edn), pp. 624–5.

7 Florence Emily Hardy, *The Life of Thomas Hardy: 1840–1928* (1962), pp. 344, 366.

8 On 6 February 1919 Florence Hardy wrote to their friend Sydney Cockerell, saying Hardy preferred the parties with conservative country neighbours to 'the brilliant young writer who is always popping in and

out of the divorce court' – so perhaps Wells had earned his disapproval (Claire Tomalin, *Thomas Hardy* (2007), p. 344).

9 Randolph S. Churchill (ed.), *The Churchill Documents. Vol. 4: Minister of the Crown 1907–1911* (2007), pp. 32–3.

10 Jonathan Rose, *The Literary Churchill: Author, Reader, Actor* (2014), pp. 86, 87.

11 ibid., p. 244.

12 ibid., p. 319.

13 George Bernard Shaw to H. G. W., 7 December 1939, J. Percy Smith (ed.), *Bernard Shaw and H. G. Wells: Selected Correspondence* (1995), p. 185.

14 30 May 1927, ibid., p. 127.

15 *Bernard Shaw and H. G. Wells: Selected Correspondence*, p. 208.

16 15 April 1941, ibid., p. 190.

17 Michael Holroyd, *Bernard Shaw: The One-volume Definitive Edition* (2012), p. 604.

18 The generous affection and admiration of Shaw's portrait might have surprised Wells had he read it – but of course it did not appear until after his death, when it was printed in the *New York Journal-American* and in England in the *New Statesman*. The *New York Journal-American* was a daily published by William Randolph Hearst from 1937 to 1966.

19 Henry James to H. G. W., 17 June 1900, Leon Edel and Gordon N. Ray (eds.), *Henry James and H. G. Wells: A Record of Their Friendship, Their Debate on the Art of Fiction, and Their Quarrel* (1958), p. 69.

20 Henry James to H. G. W., 23 September 1902, ibid., pp. 80–81.

21 Henry James to H. G. W., 14 October 1903, ibid., p. 87.

22 Henry James to H. G. W., 19 November 1905, ibid., p. 105.

23 Henry James to H. G. W., 10 November 1906, ibid., p. 112.

24 Henry James to H. G. W., ibid., pp. 121–3.

25 Henry James to H. G. W., 11 April 1913, ibid., pp. 171–2.

26 H. G. W. to Henry James, 22 September 1913, ibid., pp. 176–7.

27 Printed in ibid., pp. 178–215.

28 H. G. W. to Rebecca West, late January 1914, David C. Smith (ed.), *The Correspondence of H. G. Wells. Vol. 2: 1904–1918* (4 vols.; 1998), pp. 363–4.

29 H. G. W. to Jane Wells, 24 January 1914, ibid., p. 362.

30 H. G. W. to Hugh Walpole [1917?], cited in Norman and Jeanne MacKenzie, *The Life of H. G. Wells: The Time Traveller* (1973; rev. edn 1987), p. 292.

31 Henry James to H. G. W., 6 July 1915, *Henry James and H. G. Wells*, pp. 261–2.

32 H. G. W. to Henry James, 8 July 1915, ibid., pp. 263–4.

33 Henry James to H. G. W., 10 July 1915, ibid., pp. 265, 268.

34 H. G. W. to Arnold Bennett, 25 February 1919, *Arnold Bennett and H. G. Wells*, p. 204.

35 12 June 1943, David C. Smith (ed.), *The Correspondence of H. G. Wells. Vol. 4: 1935–1946* (4 vols.; 1998), p. 396.

36 H. G. W. to Herbert Read, 30 July 1943, ibid., p. 421.

37 *H. G. Wells: His Turbulent Life and Times* (1969), p. ix.

38 H. G. W. to Richard Gregory, 7 November 1925, *Correspondence*, Vol. 3, p. 203.

39 Cited in MacKenzie, *The Life of H. G. Wells*, p. 384.

40 J. R. Hammond, *An H. G. Wells Chronology* (1999), p. 94.

41 *Experiment in Autobiography*, p. 378.

42 G. P. Wells (ed.), *H. G. Wells in Love: Postscript to 'Experiment in Autobiography'* (1984), p. 99.

43 She in a three-part review of his *Experiment in Autobiography*, 'H. G. Wells – The Player', in *Time and Tide*, vol. 15 (13–27 October 1934), he in a novel, *Apropos of Dolores*, in 1938.

44 H. G. W. to Elizabeth Healey, 29 October 1934, *Correspondence*, Vol. 3, p. 547.

45 H. G. W. to Moura Budberg, 12 January 1939, *Correspondence* Vol. 4, p. 218.

46 *H. G. Wells in Love*, pp. 199, 220.

47 Printed in *Correspondence*, Vol. 2, pp. 350–51.

48 4 May 1932, Norman and Jeanne MacKenzie (eds.), *The Diary of Beatrice Webb. Vol. 4: The Wheel of Life 1924–1943* (4 vols.; 1982–5), p. 286.

49 8 January 1940, ibid., p. 446. He moved to No. 13 in 1935.

50 26 August 1942, ibid., p. 485.

51 30 April 1943, *Correspondence*, Vol. 4, p. 385.

Acknowledgements

Acknowledgements and thanks for permission to print extracts from the unpublished letters to the University of Illinois Library, and to the late David C. Smith, who is responsible for transcribing the letters quoted in chapters 16 and 17 and that form part of his unpublished fifth volume of Wells's *Correspondence*.

My warmest thanks go to Professor Patrick Parrinder, who must know more about H. G. Wells and his work than any other living person and has been a most patient and generous adviser. He also lent me copies of the unpublished correspondence between Wells and Amber Reeves made by David C. Smith. My thanks to Jon Halliday, who, when I mentioned I was thinking of trying to write something about Wells, encouraged me to make the attempt.

I am especially grateful to my American publisher, Ann Godoff, for asking me to write about the Fabian Society in more detail, on the grounds that it is not much known to American readers. I found out much more than I had expected, and the book was the better for it.

My warm thanks to Hannah Chavasse, who so kindly showed me over the whole of Uppark House. Thanks also to Sophie Warre of the National Trust, who has answered my queries about Uppark most helpfully.

I was made welcome to Spade House in Sandgate, now a nursing home, by Paul Burns and Hannah de Mesa – and by the residents – and was able to visit every floor, and to walk in the gardens, for which I am very grateful.

The London Library has been indispensable, as always, and in spite of the current problems. The British Library has also been helpful.

Helena Caletta's shop in Richmond, The Open Book, is one of the most pleasant ever to browse in – and also the most efficient in supplying readers' needs. She has been a true friend through these difficult times, and has helped me more than I can say.

My thanks to Tony Hynes of the University of Illinois for his advice and help.

David Gentleman, who has been a friend for nearly sixty years, responded to my tentative suggestion that he might draw some of the places where Wells lived – which has led to the beautiful illustrations that adorn the book. My warmest thanks also to Cecilia Mackay, who has been a wonderful picture researcher.

My husband Michael Frayn has been – as always – an essential part of the process of my research, driving me, walking with me, taking photographs, asking the right questions and listening patiently to my ramblings. His companionship makes research more like fun than work. He was the first to read my text and I have profited much from his comments and advice.

Tony Lacey, now retired after many years as my editor, very kindly read the text and, among other valued suggestions, corrected an error about cricket.

My copyeditor, Donna Poppy, has been exceptionally helpful as always, especially in dealing with my technical difficulties arising from struggles with my computer – as well, of course, as giving her eagle eye to the text.

I am especially grateful to Mary Mount for coming in at a late stage and making many valuable editorial suggestions. My thanks also to Venetia Butterfield and to Isabel Wall for their editorial advice.

Finally, another word of thanks to my agent, David Godwin, and his wife and partner Heather – both indispensable and brilliantly effective.

Index

Page references in italic indicate illustrations by David Gentleman.

air travel, 171–2
Aitken, Max *see* Beaverbrook, Max
    Aitken, Lord
Aldington, 101
Allen, Grant, 71, 83
Amalgamated Press, 153
Amery, Leo, 119
Andreyeva, Maria, 139
Ann Veronica (H. G. W.): Amber in,
    175–6, *176–7*, 186–7; dedication,
    165; publication, 163; quality,
    146; reception, 170, 175–6, 176–7,
    188, 197, 201; themes and plot,
    128–9, 170; writing of, 155, 171
Arnim, Elizabeth von, 190–91, 206
Arnold, Matthew, 128
Asquith, Herbert, 119, 188–9, 204
Astor, William Waldorf, 70
Australia, 208

Balfour, Arthur: becomes PM, 118;
    H. G. W. meets, 119; H. G. W.
    dines with again, 120; H. G. W.
    asks to be given some sort of
    financial endowment, 129–30;
    appoints Beatrice Webb to Poor
    Laws Commission, 147; affair
    with Lady Elcho, 150; on the
    People's Budget, 188
Balzac, Honoré de, 180

Barrie, J. M., 62–3, 71, 89
Beaverbrook, Max Aitken, Lord, 194,
    197
Begonzi, Bernard, 146
Bellow, Saul, 99
Bennett, Arnold: background, 82; on
    The Wonderful Visit, 74; H. G. W.
    discusses *When the Sleeper Wakes*
    with, 79; becomes friends with
    H. G. W., 82–3; H. G. W. writes
    to about Spade House and Jane's
    pregnancy, 97–8; praises *The Sea
    Lady*, 117–18; H. G. W. writes to
    about Blanco White, 174; on
    Tono-Bungay, 184; H. G. W.
    boasts to about sum paid for *The
    War in the Air*, 185; holidays with
    Wellses, 192; at literary dinner,
    196; James on, 202; writes to
    H. G. W. about publication of his
    correspondence with James, 204;
    later life and death, 194–5
    WORKS: *A Man from the North*, 82;
    The Old Wives' Tale, 83
Besant, Annie, 106, 107, 108–9
Beveridge, William, 148, 212, 213
bicycling, 58, 72–3, 88, 111
Blanco White, Amber (née Reeves):
    appearance and background, 122,
    158; H. G. W. exchanges letters

Blanco White – *cont'd.*
with, 153; declines to join Wellses
on holiday in Switzerland, 154;
H. G. W. and she arrive together
late at a Cambridge dinner, 155;
affair with H. G. W., 158–79,
186–7; becomes pregnant with his
child, 167; marries Rivers, 169;
refuses to live with Rivers and is
installed in Woldingham by
H. G. W., 174; Anna Jane born,
176; finally agrees to live with
husband, 176; Beatrice Webb
supports, 189; intelligence, 206;
later life, 177
Blanco White, Anna Jane, 167, 176
Blanco White, Rivers: closeness to
Amber, 162; H. G. W.'s jealousy
of, 165–6; Amber agrees to marry,
167–9; Amber won't live with,
174; Beatrice Webb takes up, 175,
189; Amber finally agrees to live
with, 176
Bland, Hubert: appearance and
background, 121; H. G. W. hears
him speak, 104; and Fabians, 106,
107–8, 109, 121; becomes friends
with H. G. W., 121; prevents
H. G. W. from taking
Rosamund to Paris, 122–3; on
Tono-Bungay, 171
Bland, Rosamund *see* Sharp,
Rosamund
Blériot, Louis, makes first powered
cross-Channel flight, 172
Bloody Sunday (1887), 108
Bodley Head publishers, 191
Boer War (1899–1902), 113–14
Briggs, William, 53, 58, 59
British Weekly, 191

Brockway, Fenner, 209
Bromley: Morley's Academy, 9, 15
Brooke, Emma, 105, 106–7, 112–13, 149
Brooke, Rupert, 155
Brussels, 86
Budberg, Moura, 142, 206, 208, 210, 213
Bullock, Frances *see* Fetherstonhaugh,
Frances
Burns, John, 119
Burton, William: close friend of
H. G. W., 36; H. G. W. hands
over editorship of *Science Schools
Journal* to, 38; publishes some
H. G. W. stories in it, 39; invites
H. G. W. to visit, 42; sends books
to the convalescent H. G. W., 44;
H. G. W. visits, 46–8; later
career, 36
Byatt, Horace, 18, 27, 30, 31

Cambridge: Newnham College, 158,
160, *161*
Carey, John, on H. G. W., 100
Carpenter, Edward, 105, 106, 153
Chamberlain, Joseph, 150
Champion, Henry, 108
Chapman & Hall publishers, 189
Chekhov, Anton, 226
Chicago, H. G. W. visits 140–41
Churchill, Winston: writes to
H. G. W. about *Anticipations*, 99;
relationship with H. G. W., 116,
196–7; admiration for H. G. W.'s
works, 134; H. G. W. supports in
general election, 155; proposes
the People's Budget, 188
Clough, Anne, 160
Clough, Arthur Hugh, 160
Clough, Blanche, 160
Coburn, Alvin Langdon, 145–6

Cockerell, Sydney, 235–6

Co-efficients dining club, 118–19, 158

College of Preceptors, 53, 59

Collins, Dr William, 20, 43–4, 45–6, 54, 55, 56

Columbia University, 141

Conan Doyle, Sir Arthur, 83, 86

Connolly, Cyril, 1

Conrad, Joseph: H. G. W. reviews his work, 71; literary agent, 78; visits H. G. W., 92–3; *The Nigger of the 'Narcissus'*, 92–3; on Crane, 94; falls out with H. G. W., 115–16; H. G. W. sends money to, 124; helps set up *English Review*, 153; work published in *English Review*, 167; overview of relationship with H. G. W., 195; at literary dinner, 196

Cooper, Lady Diana, 194

Cowap, Mr and Mrs, 17–18

Craig, Marjorie *see* Wells, Marjorie

Crane, Stephen, 71, 94–7

Cust, Harry, 70

Daily Mail, 171–2

D'Arcy, Ella, 153–4

Darwin, Charles, 33, 54

Davidson, Jo, 195–6

Davies, Arthur Morley, 36, 43, 47, 55, 58

Davray, Henri (1873–1944), H. G. W.'s French translator, 83

Democratic Federation, 107

Dent publishers, 79, 80

Desborough, Lady, 188

Dickens, Charles, 180, 186

Dickson, Lovat, 205

Disraeli, Benjamin, 10

Dostoevsky, Fyodor, 210

Dunmow, 209

Eastbourne, 62

Educational Times (weekly), 59

Edward VII, King of Great Britain and Ireland, 117, 189

Elcho, Lady, 119–20, 150

elections, general: 1908, 155; January 1910, 188–9; December 1910, 192; 1945, 212

Eliot, George, 128

Elizabeth II, Queen of Great Britain and Northern Ireland, 212–13

Elizabeth, Queen, the Queen Mother, 212–13

Ellis, Havelock, 105, 106

Ellis Island, 140

English Review, 153, 156, 160, 163, 167

Fabian Nursery, 122, 152, 155, 158, 185

Fabian Society: H. G. W. attends meetings, 38; H. G. W. flirts with, 104–5, 109; history, 105–14; Webbs decide to bring H. G. W. into, 114; H. G. W. joins at last, 117, 123; H. G. W. delivers critique, 137; American branch, 139–40; H. G. W. still set on reforming, 143, 147, 148, 149, 151–2; adds equal citizenship for women to programme, 152; H. G. W. and Jane elected to Executive Committee, 153; H. G. W. reproved for supporting Churchill in general election, 155; members worry H. G. W.'s support for free love may damage their cause, 159; increasing membership, 159; H. G. W. resigns from, 163, 180; Jane asked to resign from committee over Amber affair, 177; H. G. W. attacks, 209

Fabian Women's Group, 113, 149, 153, 159

Fawcett, Millicent, 151

Fetherstonhaugh, Frances (aka Bullock): background, 23; employs Sarah Wells as her maid at Uppark, 6; invites her back as housekeeper, 17; generosity to H. G. W., 20–21, 42, 55; unable to help H. G. W. find a job, 46; gives Sarah Wells notice, 60; death, 73

Fetherstonhaugh, Sir Henry, 21–3

Fetherstonhaugh, Lady (Sir Henry's wife), 22–3

Fetherstonhaugh, Lady (Sir Matthew's wife), 21

Fetherstonhaugh, Sir Matthew, 21

First World War (1914–18), 202

Fisher Unwin publishers, 163

Fleury, Gabrielle, 86–7, 125–6

Florence, 86

Ford, Ford Madox, 92, 153, 195

Forster, E. M., 190

Fortnightly Review, 54–5, 68, 118

France, 125–7, 129, 192, 207–8; *see also* Paris

Freedom: A Journal of Anarchist Socialism, 106

Freethinker (weekly), 19

Fröbel, Friedrich, 53, 223

Galsworthy, John, 78, 98, 167, 196

Garnett, Constance, v

Garnett, Edward, 81, 153

George IV, King of Great Britain and Ireland, 21, 22

George VI, King of Great Britain and Northern Ireland, 212–13

George, Henry, 26, 38

George Bell & Sons publishers, 185

Germany, 210

Gissing, George: background, 84; H. G. W. reviews his work, 71; literary agent, 78; becomes friends with H. G. W., 83–4; *New Grub Street*, 84; H. G. W. and Jane holiday in Rome with, 85–6; illegally marries Gabrielle Fleury, 86–7; writes to Jane about his feelings for H. G. W., 88; death, 125–7

Goebbels, Joseph, 210

Gorky, Maxim, 138–40, 142, 196, 208

Gosse, Edmund, 81, 88–9, 125, 126

Grahame, Kenneth, 83

Granville-Barker, Harley, 183

Gregory, Sir Richard: background, 33–5; college friend of H. G. W., 36; writes *Honours Physiography* with him, 59–60; witnesses H. G. W.'s wedding to Jane, 74; H. G. W. presents with copy of *Love and Mr Lewisham*, 86; H. G. W. writes to about politics, 102–3; overview of friendship with H. G. W., 205–6; later career, 36

Greville, Charles, 21–2

Grey, Edward, 119

Guardian, 211

Haldane, Richard, 119

Hamilton, Lady, 21–2

Hamilton-Gordon, E. A., 222

Hardy, Florence, 235–6

Hardy, Thomas, 71, 128, 167, 196

Harmsworth, Alfred *see* Northcliffe, Alfred Harmsworth, Lord

Harper publishers, 86

Harper's Weekly, 142

Harris (schoolmaster), 30

Harris, Frank, 54–5, 71

Harvard University, 141

Hay, Ian, 221

Healey, Elizabeth: background, 36, relationship with H. G. W., 36, 60–61

H. G. W.'s LETTERS TO: on abandonment of teaching, 62; on Budberg, 208; on 'The Chronic Argonauts', 47–8; on his health, 45; on Isabel, 66–8; on Jane preparing to give birth, 101; on life's problems and home building, 97; on *Love and Mr Lewisham*, 81; on marriage, 50; on revolution, v; on *The Time Machine*, 68–9

Hearst, William Randolph, 236

Heine, Heinrich, 210

Heinemann publishers, 69, 79, 80, 86, 189

Hemingway, Ernest, 210

Henley, William, 65–6, 68, 78, 212, 226

Henry Holt publishers, 69

Hick, Dr Henry, 84, 88–9, 91, 93, 121

Hick, Mrs, 88

Hitler, Adolf, 210

Hoatson, Alice, 121

Holt Academy, 41–2

Howells, William Dean, 139, 140

Hudson, William Henry, 233

Hueffer, Ford Madox *see* Ford, Ford Madox

Hunt, Violet, 122, 153, 157

Hutchinson, Henry, 112

Huxley, Aldous, 79, 196

Huxley, Julian, 3, 205

Huxley, Professor Thomas H., 31, 33, 35

In the Days of the Comet (H. G. W.): publication, 128, 158; reception, 136, 149, 150, 151, 153, 159, 201; themes and plot, 136, 151, 158–9

Independent Review, 130–31

Irving, Henry, 12

James, Henry: H. G. W. reviews works by, 70, 71; literary agent, 78; on *Love and Mr Lewisham*, 81; visits H. G. W., 88–9; financial support for Crane, 96–7; on *Kipps*, 135–6; on *The Future in America*, 143; work published in *English Review*, 167; on *The New Machiavelli*, 192; overview of relationship with H. G. W., 199–205; death, 204

WORKS: *The Ambassadors*, 200; *The Golden Bowl*, 93; *Guy Domville*, 70, 199; *A Small Boy and Others*, 201; *Terminations*, 93; *The Turn of the Screw*, 199; 'The Younger Generation', 201–2

James, William, 114, 115, 135, 139, 204

James, Mrs William, 204

Jennings, A. V., 35, 36, 48, 232

Jerome, Jerome K., 83

John Lane publishers, 73

Johnson, Samuel, 24

Joyce, James, 195

Justice (paper), 107

Keun, Odette, 195, 206, 207–8

King, Sir William, 23–4, 46, 55

Kipling, Rudyard, 128, 221

Kipps (H. G. W.): Penguin reissue, 213; publication, 128, 129, 130; quality, 146; reception, 135–6, 200; themes and plot, 135–6; writing of, 89, 97

Kropotkin, Peter, 106

Labour Leader (paper), 154–5, 209

Labour Party, 111–12, 113, 133, 211

Landor, Walter Savage, 212

Lane, John, 191

Lankester, Sir Edwin Ray, 98–9

Lawrence, D. H., 78, 184, 195–6, 210

Lawrence, Frieda, 196

Le Touquet, 171

Lee, Vernon (Violet Paget), 127, 176, 191–2

Lenin, Vladimir Ilyich, 142

Liberal Party, 111–12, 188–9, 192

Litvinov, Maxim, 224

Lloyd George, David, 133, 188, 189, 197, 222

London: Church Row, Hampstead, 172, *173*, 186; Henley House School, 51–3; Mornington Terrace, 66, *67*; Normal (later Royal) College of Science, 32–9, *34*; in *The War of the Worlds*, 76; Wyldes farmhouse, 105–6

London School of Economics (LSE), 112, 154

Love and Mr Lewisham (H. G. W.): Penguin reissue, 213; publication, 81, 86, 91; quality, 146; reception, 81, 86, 129, 199; themes and plot, 29, 71, 82; writing of, 80–81, 88, 89, 91

Low, Alice, 59

Low, Ivy, 72

Low, Sidney, 74

Low, Walter, friendship with H. G. W., 58–9, 72, 74

Lubbock, Percy, 204

Lutyens, Sir Edwin, 197

MacCarthy, Desmond, v, 180

MacDonald, Ramsay, 105, 113

Macmillan, Alexander, 128

Macmillan, Frederick, 128–9, 153, 163, 189

Macmillan publishers, 128–9, 153, 155, 163, 189

Mailer, Norman, 99

Mann, Prestonia *see* Martin, Prestonia

Mann, Thomas, 210

Margaret, Princess, 212–13

Martin, John, 139–40

Martin, Prestonia (née Mann), 139–40

Marx, Karl, 197–8

Mary (kitchen maid), 25–6

Masterman, Charles, 119, 135–6, 196, 234

matchwomen's strike (1888), 109

Maude, Aylmer, 108, 143, 153

Maude, Louise, 108

Maxse, Leo, 119

Meade Fetherstonhaugh, Admiral Sir Herbert, 56

Meade Fetherstonhaugh, Lady, 56

Meredith, Annie, 41–2

Methuen publishers, 79, 117

Meyer, Mathilde, 162–3, 174, 186

Midhurst, 17–18, 29–30

Midhurst Grammar School, *14*, 18, 27–31

Milne, A. A., 51–2

Milne, John, 51, 53, 63

Milne, Mrs, 52

Milner, Alfred, 119

A Modern Utopia (H. G. W.): reception and influence, 134, 135, 158, 200–201, 213; themes, 100, 116, 134, 135, 149; writing of, 116, 120

Montagu, Mrs, 21

Montagu, Venetia, 194

Moran, Lord, 197

Morley, Thomas, 9, 10

Morris, William, 38, 93, 104, 105, 108

Murray, Gilbert, 184, 196

National Health Service, 133, 134, 212, 213

National Liberal Club, 102

National Observer (paper), 65–6

National Review, 119

Nature (magazine), 205

Nazis, 210

Nelson publishers, 162, 192

Nesbit, Edith, 101, 106, 107–8, 121–3, 196

The New Machiavelli (H. G. W.): Penguin reissue, 213; publication, 129, 189, 191; reception, 190, 191–2, 201, 205; themes, content and plot, 102, 170, 188; Webbs in, 150, 187, 191; writing of, 163, 164, 165, 171, 188

New Review, 69, 226

New Statesman (journal), 204, 210, 236

New York, 138–9

New York Journal-American, 236

Newbolt, Henry, 119

Northcliffe, Alfred Harmsworth, Lord, 172

Olivier, Sydney, 106, 107, 108, 109, 155

Orwell, George, 1–3, 79–80

Other Club, 197

Paget, Violet *see* Lee, Vernon

Pall Mall Budget, 66

Pall Mall Gazette, 62–3, 70

Paris, 117, 122–3

Payne-Townshend, Charlotte *see* Shaw, Charlotte

Pearson's Weekly, 80

Pease, Edward, 104–5, 106, 123, 149, 151

Penguin Books, 211, 213

Pennicott, Clara, 11–12, 17

Pennicott, Kate, 11–12, 17

Pennicott, Thomas, 11, 12, 15, 17

People's Budget, 188, 189

Pinker, James: background, 78; begins to act as agent for H. G. W., 77; relationship with H. G. W., 78–9; H. G. W. writes to about *Love and Mr Lewisham*, 81; further agency work for H. G. W., 86, 92; H. G. W. tells him he is near breaking point, 89–91; encourages friendship between H. G. W. and Conrad, 93; becomes Crane's agent, 94, 96, 97; suggests H. G. W. should write *Anticipations*, 98; relations with H. G. W. worsen, 127; H. G. W. bypasses to make deal with Macmillan, 128; James asks H. G. W. for advice about, 200

Plato, 26, 38

Poor Laws Commission *see* Royal Commission on the Poor Laws and the Relief of Distress

Popham, Arthur, 92

Popham, Florence, 92, 98

Porter, Cole, v

Potter, Beatrice *see* Webb, Beatrice

Pound, Ezra, 195

Proust, Marcel, 210

Ramsay (Balfour's private secretary), 130

Read, Herbert, 205

Reeves, Amber *see* Blanco White, Amber

Reeves, Beryl, 158

Reeves, Fabian, 158

Reeves, Maud Pember: background, 158; H. G. W. meets, 120, 158; becomes friends with Wellses, 149, 154; works within Fabians to promote women's rights, 152–3, 159, 209; reaction to Amber's affair with H. G. W., 162, 186–7; and Amber's pregnancy, 169; H. G. W. turns against, 175

Reeves, William Pember: background, 119, 158; H. G. W. meets, 119; becomes friends with Wellses, 149; becomes director of LSE, 154; discusses Amber with H. G. W., 159; reaction to Amber's affair with H. G. W., 167, 174, 186–7

Reich, Wilhelm, 99

Repton, Humphry, 22

Revue des deux mondes, 129

Richardson, Dorothy, 83, 154, 157, 206

Roberts, Morley, 125–6

Robbins, Amy Catherine *see* Wells, Jane

Robbins, Mrs, 63–4, 68

Robins, Elizabeth, 174, 176, 190

Rome, 84, 85–6

Roosevelt, Franklin Delano, 222

Roosevelt, Theodore, 139, 141

Ross, Robert, 163

Royal Commission on the Poor Laws and the Relief of Distress, 147, 148, 155–6, 209

Royal Institution, 102–3, 115–16

Royal Literary Fund, 88–9

Royal Society, 206

Ruskin, John, 74, 93

Russell, Bertrand, 119, 136, 211

Russell, Earl, 191

Russia, 129, 138, 142, 202, 210

Russian Social Democratic Party: Fifth Congress (London, 1907), 142

Saint-Jean-Pied-de-Port, 125

Salisbury, Lord, 118

Samurai, 135, 153, 160

Sandgate, 89, *90*, 91; Spade House, 93–4, *95*, 97–8, 171–2, 186

Sanger, Margaret, 206

Schreiner, Olive, 105, 106

Science Schools Journal, 38, 39, 46, 47

Seaford, 88

Second World War (1939–45), 211–12

Sevenoaks, 68

Shakespeare, William, 212

Sharp, Clifford, 122–3, 189

Sharp, Rosamund (née Bland), 121–3, 189, 196

Shaw, Charlotte (née Payne-Townshend): marries Shaw, 113; and the Fabians, 113, 154; becomes friends with Wellses, 117, 119, 198; on Jane's death, 207; death, 211

Shaw, George Bernard: H. G. W. hears him speak, 38; on George, 38; becomes friends with H. G. W., 70–71; H. G. W. sends him copy of *Anticipations*, 98; H. G. W.'s admiration for, 104; on Wyldes, 105–6; and Fabians, 107, 108, 109, 110, 113; Beatrice Webb on, 110; and origins of Labour Party, 111–12; first success in the theatre, 112; marries Charlotte, 113; reintroduced to H. G. W., 116–17; dines with H. G. W., 119; H. G. W. writes to about Rosamund Bland, 122–3; discourages H. G. W. from writing plays, 127; and *In the Days*

of the Comet, 136; welcomes
H. G. W. 's critique of Fabian
Society, 137; on *This Misery of
Boots*, 148; opposes H. G. W. 's
plans for reforming Fabian
Society, 151–2; and women's
rights, 152, 209; fears H. G. W. 's
support for free love may damage
Fabian cause, 159; on Amber
Reeves, 162; alleges H. G. W. hid
from Amber's father, 174; at
literary dinner, 196; gives
financial help to Bland, 196;
overview of friendship with
H. G. W., 197–9; invites H. G. W.
to tea, 210; H. G. W. writes to on
Charlotte's death, 211

Shelley, Percy Bysshe, 26

Simmons, Tommy, 36, 44, 65, 72, 205

Smith, F. E., 197

Smuts, Jan, 197

Socialist Leader (paper), 212

Southsea: Hyde's Drapery Emporium,
18–19, 27–8

Spectator (magazine), 175

Stalin, Joseph, 142, 210

Staten Island, 139, 142

Stepniak, Sergei, 108

Stevenson, Robert Louis, 66, 71

Stokes publishers, 86

Strand Magazine, 128

Surly Hall, 11–12, 15, 16, 17, 193

Sutherland, Anne, 22–3, 55

Swift, Jonathan, 24–5

Switzerland, 117, 123, 154, 166, 175, 192

Talleyrand, Charles Maurice de, 22

Taylor, Cora, 94–7

Tennyson, Alfred Lord, 128

Terry, Ellen, 12

Thackeray, William Makepeace, 180,
221

The Time Machine (H. G. W.; formerly
'The Chronic Argonauts'):
Penguin reissue, 213; publication,
3, 68–9, 72; reception, 37, 69–70,
72, 141, 197; themes and plot, 69;
writing of, 46, 47–8, 55, 65–6, 68

The Times Literary Supplement, 136, 175,
201–2

Tit-Bits (magazine), 48

Tolstoy, Leo, 105, 108, 143–4, 222

Tono-Bungay (H. G. W.): Beatrice
Webb in, 117, 181; Penguin
reissue, 213; publication, 128, 129,
153, 155, 156, 166–7, 171; quality,
146; reception, 129, 156, 171, 184,
186, 201; themes, content and
plot, 51, 172, 180–84, 223; writing
of, 147, 149, 153, 160, 162, 165,
166–7, 180, 185

Trevelyan, George, 130

Tribune (journal), 142

Trotsky, Leon, 142, 210

Turnour, Colonel The Hon. Keith, 73

Twain, Mark, 139, 140

University Correspondence College,
53, 60

University Correspondent (journal), 59

Uppark: appearance, 21, 22, 24;
history, 21–4; H. G. W. 's mother
works at before marriage, 6, 23;
H. G. W. 's mother returns to as
housekeeper, 17; H. G. W. visits,
17, 20–21, 24–6, 31, 36–7;
H. G. W. convalesces at, 20, 42–6;
H. G. W. returns to for
Christmas, 49; H. G. W.
convalesces there again for last

Uppark – *cont'd*.
time, 53–4, 55–6; H. G. W.'s final
visit, 56; Sarah Wells given
notice, 60; she leaves, 61; Frances
Fetherstonhaugh dies, 73; model
for Bladesover in *Tono-Bungay*,
180–81
USA, 137–43
Utopians, 158

Victoria, Queen of Great Britain and
Ireland, 98
Voysey, Charles, architect, 93–4

Wallace, Alfred Russel, 54
Wallas, Graham: H. G. W. hears him
speak, 38; political beliefs, 98;
becomes friends with H. G. W.,
98; H. G. W. writes to about
joining National Liberal Club,
102; relationship with Webbs,
104; and Fabians, 104, 106, 107,
108, 109; Beatrice Webb on, 110;
and H. G. W., 114; H. G. W.
writes to about sex, 116;
reintroduces H. G. W. to Shaw,
116–17; walking tour with
H. G. W., 123
Walpole, Hugh, 116, 190, 201
Walton, Mrs, 29
Warwick, Countess of, 209
Washington, 141–2
Watt, A. P., 77, 78, 79
Webb, Beatrice (née Potter):
background, 109; visits H. G. W.,
104–5, 115; reaction to
Anticipations, 98; and Fabians,
108–9, 111; marries Sidney,
109–10; married life, 111; sets up
LSE, 112; travels abroad, 113; tries

to bring H. G. W. into Fabian
Society, 114; H. G. W. on, 117; on
society ladies, 118; social circle,
118; arranges social occasions for
H. G. W., 119–21; H. G. W.
insults in letter to Jane, 124; and
The Food of the Gods, 135; reacts
badly to H. G. W.'s critique of
Fabian Society, 137; on *The Future
in America*, 143; continuing good
relations with H. G. W. and Jane,
143; overview of political work,
147, 156; friendship with
H. G. W., 147–56; work on the
Poor Laws Commission, 147, 148;
attitude to sex, 150; passion for
Chamberlain, 150; writes
Minority Report of the Poor
Laws Commission, 155–6, 209;
disapproves of H. G. W.'s affair
with Amber Reeves, 162;
H. G. W. accuses of spreading
malicious stories about the Amber
affair, 174; breaks with H. G. W.
over Amber affair, 175–6, 186–7;
on Jane's complicity in Amber
affair, 177; literary representations
in H. G. W.'s works, 117, 150,
181, 187, 188, 191; on *Tono-Bungay*,
186; on the People's Budget, 189;
takes up the Blanco Whites, 189;
on *The New Machiavelli*, 191;
world tour, 192; relationship with
H. G. W. eventually revives,
209–11; and women's rights, 209;
attitude to Soviet Russia, 210;
death, 211
Webb, Sidney: background, 107;
reaction to *Anticipations*, 98; visits
H. G. W., 104–5; and Fabians,

106, 107, 108, 109; marries
Beatrice, 109–10; becomes
councillor, 110–11; married life,
111; and origins of Labour Party,
111–12; sets up LSE, 112; travels
abroad, 113; tries to bring
H. G. W. into Fabian Society,
114; social circle, 118; makes
Beatrice cut down on parties, 121;
H. G. W. insults in letter to Jane,
124; and *The Food of the Gods*, 135;
relationship with H. G. W., 147,
148–50; supports Beatrice in her
work for the Poor Laws
Commission, 148; literary
representations in H. G. W. 's
works, 150, 187, 188, 191; reproves
H. G. W. for backing Churchill in
general election, 155; H. G. W.
accuses of spreading malicious
stories about the Amber affair,
174; world tour, 192; relationship
with H. G. W. eventually revives,
209–10; attitude to Soviet Russia,
210; H. G. W. writes to on
Beatrice's death, 211

Welfare State: development overview,
133; NHS set up, 133, 212, 213;
Poor Laws Commission, 147, 148,
155–6, 209; People's Budget, 188

Wellesley College, 141

Wellington, Arthur Wellesley, Duke
of, 22

Wells, Frances (H. G. W. 's sister), 6, 23

Wells, Frank (H. G. W. 's brother):
childhood, 6–7; apprenticeships,
7–8, 15; buys boots for H. G. W.,
10; H. G. W. asks his advice about
escaping his apprenticeship, 19;
decides to take up itinerant life,

31–2; visits Uppark for
Christmas, 45; witness at
H. G. W. 's wedding, 56; spends
Christmas with H. G. W., 61;
inspires *The War of the Worlds*, 76,
78; H. G. W. plans to install in
shop, 78; cares for his declining
mother, 130; holidays with
Wellses, 192

Wells, Frank (H. G. W. 's son): birth,
123; and Rosamund Bland, 122;
parents' delight in, 157; Jane hires
governess for, 162–3; holiday in
Le Touquet, 171; Jane sends to
stay with Amber, 174; H. G. W. 's
love for, 178, 185–6; moves to
Hampstead, 186; holidays abroad,
192; marriage, 207

Wells, Fred (H. G. W. 's brother):
childhood, 6–7; apprenticeships,
7–8, 15; lends H. G. W. evening
clothes, 52; H. G. W. writes to
about Uppark, 55, 56; emigrates
to South Africa, 61, 62; H. G. W.
writes to about house has bought
for their parents, 78; H. G. W.
writes to about his good spirits,
80; and Boer War, 114; holidays in
England, 117

Wells, Gip (H. G. W. 's son): birth, 101;
left with nanny while parents
holiday abroad, 117; and
Rosamund Bland, 122; parents'
delight in, 157; Jane hires
governess for, 162–3; hatred of
being held, 165; holiday in Le
Touquet, 171; Jane sends to stay
with Amber, 174; H. G. W. 's
love for, 178, 185–6; moves to
Hampstead, 186; holidays abroad,

Wells – *cont'd.*

192; at boarding school, 202;
co-writes *The Science of Life* with
H. G. W. and Huxley, 205;
marriage, 207; publishes H. G. W.'s
account of his sex life after his
death, 142

Wells, Hannah (H. G. W.'s aunt), 42

Wells, Herbert George (H. G. W.)
GENERAL: appearance, 11, 36, 39, 53,
87; character, 194, 198–9, 205; and
flowers, 52; lifestyle in middle
age, 154–5; literary influences,
24–5; quality of books, 1–3, 146,
205; and racism, 100, 140, 142;
relationship with agents and
publishers, 78–9, 86; relationship
with parents, 6, 12–13, 31, 32, 50;
and religion, 10, 19, 30–31, 54, 74,
99–100, 134, 135; themes, 1; and
travel, 5; voice, 37, 83; writing
habits, 73, 80, 185–6
LIFE: family background, 5–8;
childhood and education, 8–13;
broken leg, 8–9; book-keeping
prize, 9; produces first book,
10–11; visits to Surly Hall, 11–12;
apprenticeship at draper's
shop in Windsor, 15–16; brief
spell teaching, 16–17; first
visit to Uppark, 17; more
apprenticeships, 18–19; brief
attendance at Midhurst Grammar
School, 18; visits to Uppark,
20–21, 24–6, 31, 36–7; first kiss,
25–6; becomes an assistant
schoolmaster, 27–30; wins
scholarship to Normal (later
Royal) College of Science, 30–39;
spends time in London with
cousin Isabel, 35–6, 38–9; shows
interest in forecasting the future,
37; goes to Fabian Society
meetings, 38; becomes teacher at
Holt Academy, 41–2; rugby
tackle provokes health crisis with
recuperation at Uppark, 42–6;
visits Burtons in Stoke, 46–8;
returns to London where he picks
up pieces of work, 48–9; informal
engagement to Isabel, 50–51;
becomes science teacher at
Henley House School while
studying for a degree and
teaching diploma, 51–3; becomes
officially engaged to Isabel, 52;
continues to work at writing, 52;
works for University
Correspondence College, 53;
resigns from Henley House
School, 53; relapse leads to
further convalescence at Uppark,
53–4; marries Isabel, 56–7;
married life disappoints, 57–8;
publishes two textbooks, 59–60;
serious lung haemorrhage forces
abandonment of teaching, 61–2;
writing career takes off, 62–3;
separates from Isabel and moves
in with Jane, 63–4; life with Jane,
65; first science fiction story
published under his name, 66;
divorce proceeds, 68; publishes
The Time Machine, 68–70; review
work, 70–71; moves to Woking,
72; writing output reaches great
heights, 73; marries Jane, 74;
publishes *The War of the Worlds*,
74–8; moves to Worcester Park,
78; expanding circle of friends,

82–4; visits Isabel and demonstrates lasting feelings for her, 84–5; trip to Italy, 85–6; cared for by Dr Hick during serious kidney illness, 88–9; moves to Sandgate for sake of health, 89–91; publishes *Love and Mr Lewisham*, 80–81, 86, 91–2; builds Spade House, 93–4, 97–8; publishes *Anticipations*, his first 'utopia' book, 98–101; Gip born, 101; persuades Jane to accept him having extramarital affairs, 101–2; popularity of works abroad, 102; gives lecture at Royal Institution, 102–3, 115–16; flirts with Fabian Society, 104–5, 109, 114; joins Fabians at last, 117, 123; joins Co-efficients dining club, 118–19; Beatrice Webb expands his social circle, 119–21; failed plan to travel to Paris with Rosamund Bland, 121–3; Frank born, 123; goes to Gissing's deathbed, 125–7; money worries lead to him speeding up his writing, 127–9; Macmillan becomes his main publisher, 128–9; Balfour declines his request to be given some sort of financial endowment, 129–30; mother's death, 130; more political writings, 130–35; trip to America, 137–43; brief correspondence with Tolstoy, 143–4; publishes 'The Door in the Wall', 144–6; relationship with Beatrice Webb, 147–56; proposals to reform Fabian Society fail, 149, 151–2; elected to Fabian Executive Committee, 153; becomes JP,

153; helps set up *English Review*, 153; casual sexual affairs, 153–4; Fabians reprove for supporting Churchill in general election, 155; affair with Amber Reeves, 158–79, 186–7; remains Fabian member, 159; resigns from Fabians, 163, 180; moves from Sandgate to Hampstead, 171–2, 186; Beatrice Webb breaks with, 175–6, 186–7; publishes *Tono-Bungay*, 180–86; father's death, 189–90; affair with von Arnim, 190–91; affair with West, 191, 202; holidays abroad, 192; overview of friendships and later life, 194–211; Anthony born, 202; unfulfilled ambition to be elected to Royal Society, 206; overview of affairs, 206–8; failed attempt to become MP, 210; semi-abandonment of Jane, 206–7; her death, 207, 210; books burned by Nazis, 210; last days and death, 211–13; author's summation, 213–14

WORKS: *Ann Veronica see main entry*; *Anticipations*, 98–101, 114, 134, 200; *Boon*, 202–3, 204–5; 'The Chronic Argonauts' *see The Time Machine*; 'The Cone', 47; 'The Country of the Blind', 1, 24, 128, 157; *The Desert Daisy*, 10; 'The Discovery of the Future', 115; *The Door in the Wall and Other Stories*, 144–6; *Experiment in Autobiography*, 3, 101–2, 205, 206; 'The Faults of the Fabian', 137, 148; *First and Last Things*, 134, 180, 185; *The First Men in the Moon*, 92, 200; *The Food of the Gods*, 128, 135;

WORKS – *cont'd.*

The Future in America, 134, 137, 142–3, 154; The History of Mr Polly, 32, 146, 162, 171, 192–3, 213; Honours Physiography (with Gregory), 59–60, 205; In the Days of the Comet see main entry; The Invisible Man, 79, 80, 213; The Island of Dr Moreau, 73, 78, 80, 213; Kipps see main entry; 'Lady Frankland's Companion', 41; 'The Land Ironclads', 128, 197; Love and Mr Lewisham see main entry; 'The Man of the Year Million', 37; Mankind in the Making, 82, 116, 118, 134, 200; Mind at the End of Its Tether, 212; A Modern Utopia see main entry; Mr Britling Sees It Through, 202; The New Machiavelli see main entry; New Worlds for Old, 134, 152, 154, 180, 185; 'On the Art of Staying at the Seaside', 62–3; The Outline of History, 205, 210; 'The Pains of Marriage', 223; The Passionate Friends, 201; 'The Quality of Illusion in the Continuity of the Individual Life', 206; 'The Rediscovery of the Unique', 54; The Rights of Man, 211; 'Sad Story of a Dramatic Critic', 71; The Science of Life (with Huxley and Gip), 205; The Sea Lady, 92, 117–18; Select Conversations with an Uncle, 73; A Short History of the World, 205, 213; Socialism and the Family, 134; 'Socialism and the Middle Classes', 149, 159; 'The Star', 80; 'The Stolen Bacillus', 66; 'The Story of Tommy and the Elephant', 88; A Text-book of Biology, 60, 63; This Misery of Boots, 130–34, 148, 153, 213; The Time Machine (formerly 'The Chronic Argonauts') see main entry; Tono-Bungay see main entry; Twelve Stories and a Dream, 128; 'The Universe Rigid', 54–5; The War in the Air, 160, 175, 185; The War of the Worlds, 74–8, 213; The Wheels of Chance, 72, 79, 80; When the Sleeper Wakes, 79, 91; The Wonderful Visit, 73, 74

Wells, Isabel (H. G. W. 's cousin and first wife): H. G. W. spends time with in London, 35–6, 38–9; H. G. W. temporarily forgets, 42; H. G. W. returns to lodge with, 48; informal engagement to H. G. W., 50–51; official engagement to H. G. W., 52; Whitstable holiday, 52–3; marries H. G. W., 56–7; married life, 57–8; H. G. W. takes to meet parents, 61; agrees to divorce, 63; H. G. W. asks Healey to befriend, 66–8; divorce proceeds, 68; H. G. W. visits and demonstrates lasting feelings for, 84–5; H. G. W. inscribes copy of Love and Mr Lewisham for, 86

Wells, Jane (née Amy Catherine Robbins; H. G. W. 's second wife): meets H. G. W., 60–61; H. G. W. writes to ask to visit, 62; moves in with H. G. W., 63–4; nature of their relationship, 64; life with H. G. W., 65, 72–3; moves to Woking, 72; marries H. G. W., 74; moves to Worcester

Park, 78; relationship with Bennett, 82, 194; expanding circle of friends, 82–4; trip to Italy, 85–6; stays with Hick family while H. G. W. is seriously ill, 88–9; moves to Sandgate for sake of H. G. W.'s health, 89–91; begins to type H. G. W.'s work and take care of the household, 92; during building of Spade House, 93–4, 97–8; party at Crane's house, 94–6; becomes pregnant, 97–8; Gip born, 101; H. G. W. persuades to accept him having extramarital affairs, 101–2; Beatrice Webb on, 115; becomes friends with Shaws, 117; holidays in Switzerland, 117; H. G. W. discusses dinner at the Webbs' with, 120; Frank born, 123; H. G. W. writes to about Webbs, 124; H. G. W. deputes to deal with Pinker, 127; correspondence with H. G. W. during his trip to America, 141; relationship with Webbs, 143, 148, 152; on Brooke, 149; and the Reeves, 149, 152, 154, 158, 160; elected to Fabian Executive Committee, 153; becomes Secretary, 154; state of married life, 157; on committee of Fabian Women's Group, 159; saddened by H. G. W.'s affair with Amber Reeves, 162–3; H. G. W.'s mixed feelings for, 164, 166, 167; holiday in Switzerland with H. G. W., 166; holiday in Le Touquet with him, 171; H. G. W. considers her taking over Amber's baby, 171;

arranges move to Hampstead, 172; kindness to Amber, 174; another Swiss holiday with H. G. W., 175; asked to resign from Fabian committee over Amber affair, 177; separate bedroom from H. G. W., 186; move to Hampstead, 186; H. G. W. talks to about von Arnim, 190; holidays abroad, 192; relationship with Shaw, 198; and H. G. W.'s affair with West, 202; runs H. G. W.'s Dunmow house, 209; Webbs invite to dinner, 210; later life and death, 206–7, 210

Wells, Joseph (H. G. W.'s father): background and character, 5–7; supplies H. G. W. with books, 8; breaks leg badly, 10; knowledge of publishing, 11; tries to get job for H. G. W. at Hoare's bank, 16; wife agrees to be housekeeper at Uppark, 17; reluctantly agrees to H. G. W. becoming an assistant schoolmaster, 27–8; H. G. W. spends time with, 31, 37, 43; improved relationship with H. G. W., 32; goes bankrupt, 39; visits Uppark for Christmas, 45; problems with alcohol, 48–9; wife rejoins, 61; meets Isabel, 61; H. G. W. tells about Jane, 68; H. G. W. buys house for, 77–8; death, 189–90

Wells, Lillie (H. G. W.'s cousin), 42

Wells, Marjorie (née Craig; H. G. W.'s daughter-in-law), 207

Wells, Mary (H. G. W.'s aunt and mother-in-law), 35, 48, 52–3, 56, 84, 85

Wells, Sarah (H. G. W.'s mother): background and character, 5, 6–7, 23; finds apprenticeships for Frank and Fred, 7–8; teaches H. G. W. his letters, 8; husband breaks leg, 10; her cousin befriends H. G. W., 11; finds apprenticeship for H. G. W., 15; becomes housekeeper at Uppark, 17; finds another apprenticeship for H. G. W., 17; urges H. G. W. to get confirmed, 19; life at Uppark, 20, 24, 26; H. G. W. visits at Uppark, 20–21, 24–6, 31, 36–7, 53; H. G. W. persuades to enable him to become an assistant schoolmaster, 27–8; delight at H. G. W.'s confirmation, 31; improved relationship with H. G. W., 32; brings H. G. W. to convalesce at Uppark, 42; likely to lose job at Uppark, 55; given notice, 60; leaves Uppark, 61; meets Isabel, 61; H. G. W. tells he has separated from Isabel, 66; H. G. W. tells about Jane, 68; H. G. W. offers to take to the theatre, 72; H. G. W. buys house for, 77–8; attitude to Queen Victoria, 98; death, 130

Wells, William (H. G. W.'s uncle), 7

West, Anthony, 202, 234

West, Rebecca, 191, 196, 202, 206, 207

Whitstable, 52–3

Wilde, Oscar, 46, 54, 70, 78, 163

Williams, Uncle, 16–17

Wilson, Charlotte, 105, 106–7, 108

Windsor: Messrs Rodgers & Denyer, 15–16

Woking, 72, 76

Woldingham, 174

women's rights: birth control, 206; Brooke's novel on marriage, 112–13; Fabian attitude, 106–7, 109, 152, 159, 209; Family Allowances, 133, 134; H. G. W. on, 149; matchwomen's strike (1888), 109; the vote, 119, 133, 151, 158

Worcester Park, 78

Wordsworth, William, 146

World War I *see* First World War

World War II *see* Second World War

Wright, Hagberg, 196

Wright, Whitaker, 182

Zola, Émile, 210